perspectives—exploring the unique experience of woman as a central figure in child rearing, tracing the historical roots and contemporary expressions of territoriality, conflict, and examining the exclusion experienced by minority groups and the poor in their attempt to get a piece of the educational pie. Particular attention is paid to the viewpoints of individual teachers searching for new ways of communicating with the children and parents they serve as they strive to function within the myriad institutional and interpersonal forces they must contend with daily.

With great insight and originality Dr. Lightfoot proposes methods of bridging the chasm between families and schools by building positive alliances between them. Parents and teachers must learn to see children as whole, autonomous human beings in order to be able to focus on the best interests of children. Schools must not confuse their token integration of black history into a still overwhelmingly white curriculum with real social and historical change. And teachers must view parents as the primary educators. Finally, Lightfoot suggests that family-school conflict is not only inevitable but potentially useful, and that we must find ways of discerning and redirecting its positive and negative effects.

SARA LAWRENCE LIGHTFOOT, a sociologist of education, is Associate Professor in the Department of Social Policy at the Harvard Graduate School of Education. She has also studied early childhood development at the Bank Street College and the Albert Einstein School of Medicine. This book is based on a study done as a Fellow of the Radcliffe Institute, Harvard Faculty of Arts and Sciences.

Worlds Apart

WORLDS APART

Relationships Between Families and Schools

SARA LAWRENCE LIGHTFOOT

Basic Books, Inc., Publishers

New York

Permission to reprint material from the following sources is gratefully acknowledged.

Sara Lawrence Lightfoot, "Families and Schools: Creative Conflict or Negative Dissonance," *Journal of Research and Development in Education,* vol. 9, no. 1, August, 1975, pp. 34–44.

S. L. Lightfoot, "Family-School Interactions," *SIGNS* 3:2 (1977), selected segments.

Willard Elsbree, *The American Teacher: Evolution of a Profession in a Democracy* (New York: The American Book Company, 1939).

Library of Congress Cataloging in Publication Data

Lightfoot, Sara Lawrence.
Worlds apart.

Bibliography: p. 235
Includes index.
1. Home and school–United States. 2. Students' socio-economic status–United States. I. Title.
LC225.L53 370.19'31 78-54506
ISBN: 0-465-09244-6

Printed in the United States of America
DESIGNED BY VINCENT TORRE
10 9 8 7 6 5 4 3 2

For Orlando

Contents

Acknowledgments

THE inspiration and ideas that shaped this book began in the learning and love of my family. I will always feel blessed and thankful to Margaret and Charles Lawrence, my wise, strong, and all-giving parents; to Chuck, my brother, and Paula, my sister, who provided the support, trust, and unconditional love that made me feel safe to explore my own individuality.

There were many generous and thoughtful colleagues who offered support and help during the gestation of this book. When the ideas for this project were in their infancy stages, I was helped by the comments and constructive criticism of a faculty seminar group at the Center for Research on Women in Higher Education and the Professions at Wellesley College whose members included Mary Jo Bane, Carolyn Elliot, Roslyn Feldberg, Rosabeth Kanter, Jean Miller, Marcia Millman, Patricia Mittenthal, Carol Mueller, Marnie Mueller, Irene Murphy, Carol Ryser, and Barry Stein. Many of these developing ideas took shape as I talked them over with colleagues in teaching and research. I feel especially indebted to Jean Carew, Joseph Featherstone, David Cohen, Beatrice Whiting, Derrick Bell, and James Comer, who supported the growth of my work through their intelligent and knowledgeable contributions to my thinking. Thomas Cottle and Rosabeth Kanter were pathfinders, hand-holders, and constant sources of encouragement.

I feel thankful for the collaboration and assistance of graduate students Sarah Levine, Marguerite Alejandro-Wright, and Edward Gondolf, who worked on chapters 2, 4, and 5, respectively.

They searched out literary sources and esoteric references, and pursued ideas with me. The work of all three was serious, scholarly, and dedicated, and I gained new insights from our continuous conversations and dialogues.

The voices of teachers and parents are heard throughout this book. I am thankful to these people for generously offering their time, energy, and experience, and for enriching us all with their perspectives and wisdom. Very special appreciation goes to Paula Wehmiller, an experienced and insightful educator and practitioner, who helped me trace connections between the daily lives of parents, teachers, and children and my construction of their realities.

Of course, I would have never been able to carve out a quiet space of time to work if I had not received the support of a fellowship from the Radcliffe Institute, an excellent place to think and write where solitude, privacy, and scholarly exchange are highly valued. The research reported in chapter 3 was done under the auspices of a grant from the Office of Child Development. Chapter 4 was based on research partially sponsored by the Ford Foundation and the DuBois Institute at Harvard University. I thank my colleagues on this project, Marcus Alexis, Derrick Bell, Martin Kilson, Audrey Smedley, James Jones, and Preston Williams, for their reading and comments on this piece.

It is with mixed pain and pleasure that I watched and endured the slow and laborious movement of this piece of work into book form. The process enlisted the skills and guidance of many. Judith Thompson followed this manuscript from beginning fragments to final form and offered technical assistance and secretarial support. I also remember Thea Mosket's enthusiastic secretarial work in the early phases, Donna Moffett's excellent efforts in organizing, photocopying, and corresponding toward the conclusion of the book's preparation, and Martha Metzler's careful search for footnotes and references. Amy Bonoff, Barbara Grossman, and Erwin Glikes, my editors at Basic Books, were sympathetic and knowing listeners and initiated me into the world of editing and publishing. I valued their patience, clear-mindedness, and savvy.

And finally, my heart and appreciation go out to my husband, Orlando Brown Lightfoot, Jr., enduringly supportive and resourceful, who offered his experience, his wisdom, his assurance, his humor, and his love during the entire life of this project.

Worlds Apart

Introduction: Beyond the Walls of the Classroom

Classroom Windows

CLASSROOMS have been my primary research domain for the past several years. I have spent hundreds of hours watching the actions of teachers and children, sitting in small children's chairs, hiding in a back corner, trying to fade into the environment and become the "transparent" observer. Primarily I have been concerned with studying the classroom as a relatively self-sustaining, evolving social system with its own established rituals, norms, and patterns of behavior. My observations of teacher-child interactions have focused on dimensions such as authority and power,[1] equality, and positive and negative forms of discrimination.[2] The quantitative behavioral data have been integrated with qualitative data taken from in-depth teacher interviews and sociometric interviews of children, as well as some descriptive and sociological analyses of the school as a social system.

Although I have focused my energies on describing the complexities of classroom life, I have never envisioned the classroom as a closed environment with impenetrable boundaries. As a matter of fact, one of the central themes of my work has been the recognition of the intimate connections between the classroom and the various social settings in which it is embedded. First, of course, classroom life is shaped and defined by the social structure of the school. As a matter of fact, there are those social scientists who argue that the school is the most critical determining force that defines patterns *within* classrooms. In *Teaching and Learning in City Schools,* Eleanor Burke Leacock raised the important issue of the effects of the school and community environments on the teacher.

> . . . The way the teacher structures both her relations with the children and their relations with each other sets up a behavioral model for them, the implications of which extend far beyond the classroom. To some extent the goals she states for children and those she implies through her management techniques relate to her individual style, but for the most part, they must conform to school patterns which, in turn, relate to general social expectations.[3]

The teacher, although establishing a central and dominant role in the classroom, lives within the constraints and boundaries of the institutional norms of the school and has very minimal autonomy and self-defining power. Her ability to transform her classroom environment and to change deeply established patterns of interaction are always limited by the explicit rules and implicit assumptions of the school's collective life.

Second, the social system and life of the school are shaped by the sociopolitical and economic structure of the community of which it is part. Great disparities exist in the education and schooling offered to children from various communities that are reflective of differences in race, ethnicity, and social class. These glaring disparities not only represent economic inequities but also differences in political realities, cultural idioms, and ethnic histories. These powerful structural and societal forces surround schools and deeply touch the lives of teachers and children. The encompassing force of the external world offers either promise and hope or despair and denial to young children and teachers. So as one studies life within classrooms, one must always be cognizant of the prevailing power of the external realities—the world of streets, families, churches, playgrounds, garbage dumps, and movie houses into which these children will run when they leave the constricting (or safe and secure) boundaries of school each day.

The external realities also invade the classroom in a much more elusive and subtle form. Sociopolitical and ideological visions are brought to the classroom through the values, attitudes, and behavior of teachers. In a previous observational and ethnographic study,[4] I found that the teacher's world view—her perceptions of the sociopolitical and cultural realities of contemporary society—was not only communicated to children in an explicit, didactic fashion when she spoke of civics, political events, or social injustices, but also became incorporated into the social structure that she established and sustained within the classroom. In other words, the teacher's social and political ideologies were woven into the very substance and form of her interactions with children and evolved into a reflective microcosm of her *perceptions* of the wider society.

Much of this process of translation and internalization from the macroscopic sphere of the larger society to the microscopic interactions of the classroom was not consciously recognized by the teacher. The process of translation often became conscious after several in-depth interviews when the teacher was probed for the rationale behind her behavior with children or when she reflected on her own personal and professional history and began to recognize the evolution of her own world view. In-depth retrospective analyses often revealed to the teacher how much she had changed in her sociopolitical orientation and how that might be expressed in her pedagogical style, aspirations for children, and in the curricular substance of her teaching.

Sometimes the recognition of the teacher's changing world view was attached to a dramatic, critical life event. A very insightful young black teacher, whom I had observed and interviewed over several months' time, claimed that the assassination of Martin Luther King inspired in her a new sense of political realism that initiated feelings of urgency and pragmatism in relation to political action and transformed her perceptions of educational processes within the classroom. Instead of nonviolent demonstrations and peaceful pleas, black people had to begin to respond to a violent, oppressive society with militant protest. King's death brought despair—a despair that inspired action, mastery, and unity.

> It opened my eyes. Up until then I had been thinking unrealistically. . . . I had to get myself together in order to help people get themselves together. I could see it in my children at school. Everybody had changed. Everybody was together. It changed me. I knew I had something more to do.[5]

Her words reflected the dynamic interaction between her political transformation, her perceptions of children, and her view of her educational function in their lives.

Recognition of the power of one's history and the force of one's emerging ideological commitments was often articulated by teachers when they were in conflict with one another. In other words, when there was a great disparity between the teacher's early childhood socialization and her contemporary beliefs and values, she could more easily recognize what she believed than if there were comfortable parallels and continuity between her own acculturation as a child and her views of teaching and child rearing today. Somehow the conflicting visions of past and present brought struggles that illuminated and clarified the present values and ideology.

Mrs. Jefferson was brought up in a lower-class black family in an urban slum. She was one of several children raised by a strong and enduring mother with a firm hand. Her mother sent the children to parochial school in an effort to save them from the dangerous realities of the urban jungle. The Catholic nuns were strict disciplinarians; the educational message was an overwhelming mixture of secular and spiritual interminglings, and children always feared punishment and damnation and behaved accordingly. Only in retrospect does Mrs. Jefferson view her early education as repressive and overbearing. As a child, she remembers the feelings of safety that overcame her when she entered the orderly, structured, and clean environment of the schools; how she enjoyed the rules and rituals; and even how she delighted in breaking the rules. But much has happened since her very Catholic childhood. She is now middle class and doesn't need so much the asylum of the church to save her from urban destruction. She has now experienced a "liberal" graduate school education that assaulted her narrow views and "closed mind" and prodded her to look at the world through different-colored glasses. As a young adult she began to hear humanistic labels like "child-centered, progressive, individualistic education" bantered around by her professors and peers, and she began to recognize—even resent at times—the limits of her own traditional upbringing. Gradually, her visions of child rearing, politics, culture, and human relationships began to evolve into something new and different. When she became a teacher, she did not want to imitate the nuns of her childhood memories; she wanted to break new ground as a liberal, humanitarian teacher who encouraged self-expression and individualism in children.

One could observe the conflicts of past and present in Mrs. Jefferson's teaching. Most of the time, Mrs. Jefferson's behavior in the classroom reflected the values and ideologies she had learned as an adult. She was rewarding and encouraging of children's efforts, she supported individualistic growth, and she sustained democratic relationships. But when a crisis suddenly developed, the nun in Mrs. Jefferson (i.e., her identification with her early school history) would rush forward and she became the scary autocrat of her childhood memories. It was at these moments that Mrs. Jefferson was made painfully and vividly conscious of who she was becoming and what she was trying to do—an ideological consciousness that only few of us even rarely, if ever, experience with such force.[6]

The story of Mrs. Jefferson underscores the need for researchers to recognize the walls of the classroom as windows onto the world. No matter how teachers might try to separate and isolate the classroom environment from the surrounding context of community life, the sociocultural and political perspectives of teachers (and children) pervade the atmosphere and shape the course of events. On the other hand, classroom life has its own internal momentum with its own form and rituals that separate it from other experiences. And the unique character of that environment that is daily experienced by children makes it a critical setting for documentation and analysis. It is both deeply connected with the structures in which it is embedded and strangely separate from them. It both mirrors the wider society, copying its prejudices, hierarchies, and categories and opposes society's structure by offering its own set of rules, relationships, and forms.

Perspectives on Family

Not only did my ethnographic work in schools reveal the paradoxical interface of classrooms and surrounding social institutions, but I also began to recognize that in the eyes of the teacher the major external intrigue was the family. I use the word intrigue to convey both a sense of preoccupation and a sense of curiosity. From the teachers' perspectives, the family was the other critical institution beyond the school that shaped the world of the child and defined the primary processes of socialization and acculturation. Whether teachers viewed the child's parents in collaborative or competitive terms, they viewed them as central to the child's development and often critical to the child's successful career in school.

In my observations, teachers' recognition of the family's role in their child's education seems to take a variety of forms. Even those teachers who vehemently deny that a knowledge of family backgrounds and origins makes a difference in their style of interaction and perception of children seem strangely preoccupied with families. They are, however, intent upon *excluding* families from school life. They seem to want to establish an exclusive, isolated environment, free from the intrusions of parents (and perhaps free from the potential bias of stereotyping children into fixed social categories). Although there are a few strong-minded teachers who voice this extreme view of isolationism from parents and community, theirs is a minority perspective that is not supported by the prevailing themes of "modern" educational rhetoric —a rhetoric that underscores the need for communication and cooperation between families and schools.

At the other end of the continuum are teachers whose view of children is totally shaped by their perceptions of parentage. Children become shadows of their parents' social position, miniature versions of doctors, garbage collectors, secretaries, accountants. These teachers cannot look at the child without seeing the parents. Neither can they describe the child and his myriad dimensions as an individual person. Sociological, hierarchial categories prevail and individualistic, psychosocial descriptors go neglected and unnoticed.

Somewhere in between the teacher who effectively excludes families from participating in the schooling of their children and/or sees children as unattached to their own familial history and experience and the teacher who relates to the child only as a reflection and extension of his parents are a vast range of teachers who combine strategies for including and excluding families from school life. Some of these teachers, for instance, believe that family background information will help them communicate more effectively and meaningfully with the child and that there are ways of guarding against using this information prejudicially. They believe that bibliographic histories of children can become part of a process of diagnosis and can support healthy child development rather than become an inhibiting and stereotyped label.

Out of these myriad views of family and school, teachers show a concern and curiosity for where their children come from each day. As children enter the classroom, their families also come with them. In the child's head he brings his familial experiences (his half-eaten breakfast, his fights with his bully brother, his mama's warm hug). In the teacher's perception, he comes as his parents' child (with the bright arrogance of his doctor father, with the embarrassed reticence of his shy, withdrawn mother). And in the mother's heart a piece of her relives her own school history as she sees her child off with both relief and apprehension; or as she tries not to communicate her own tortured memories of school by offering words of fond encouragement. In his classic book, *Sociology of Teaching,* Willard Waller spoke vividly of the parents' negative visions of school as arising out of the crystallization of their childhood memories of oppression and fear in relation to the all-powerful teacher.

> This is an idealized and not a factual portrait [of the teacher], because the memory will not hold all the flesh and blood of human beings for so long a time; the general impression remains, but the details fade. The idealized conception tends to become a caricature, and an unpleasant and belittling caricature, because a real enmity exists between teacher and taught, and the memory transmutes the work of memory into irony. In accordance with this theory, each generation of teachers pays in turn for the sins of the generation that has gone before; it would require some decades of sensible and friendly teaching to remove the stigma from the occupation.[7]

So children enter school not only filled with their own apprehensions but also burdened by the hardened images of their parents' passionate recollections.

Observations of classroom life, therefore, reveal the invisible but pervasive presence of families. In the course of my research, I also found that the more time I spent documenting the various personalities, skills, and interactional styles of children in school, the more curious I became about their lives at home. The more I recognized the teachers' vision of children as family members, the more I became preoccupied as a researcher with understanding how families and schools relate to each other. I found myself peering out of the classroom windows at the end of a school day, watching children streak out of the school doors—some spreading their arms like the wings of an eagle and making joyous noises of release and abandon, others moving slowly, almost sadly away from the school, dragging their books behind and wandering aimlessly away. I also was intrigued by the daily exchanges that would take place between parents and teachers at the door. "How was Willie today? Did he do good?" asked one anxious parent. "He did pretty well, but had a little trouble keeping quiet during the assembly," reported the teacher, half protecting the boy from the punishing parent and half wanting him to receive his fair share of reprimands from home. "If he gives you any more trouble, Miss Green, just give him a good licking and he'll stop. Don't be afraid to punish him. He needs it!"

All of these transitional exchanges seemed very important and highly charged with emotion. Even when the request of the parent seemed perfectly mundane or the teacher's comments purely small talk, there was something about the moment that felt loaded with meaning. Words were carefully chosen on either side; mothers tried hard not to offend but to appreciate, and teachers seemed eager to guard some level of privacy and autonomy. These chance, daily interactions certainly had weightier significance than the vacuous, ritualistic PTA meetings scheduled by the school. They were more highly personalized and direct, and they often evoked strong emotion and passion.

Pessimism and Pathology: The Preoccupations of Social Science

Because I recognized the profound impact of family life on the teacher's perceptions of the child, on the child's chances for successfully coping with school, and on the parents' relationships with school as a competing institution of socialization, I began to search for research literature that would document the dynamic intersection of these two institutions. I found, to my great dismay, that even though the issue of family-school relationships was a dominant theme in the lives and experiences of parents, teachers, and children, it was a topic largely ignored in the social science literature.

Social scientists have created a conceptual dichotomy of the child's existence into socialization and education, the one shaped by the family and the other by the school.* Not only has this conceptual division permitted researchers to neglect the process of socialization within schools and education within families, but researchers have also failed to trace the continuities and discontinuities between school and family and their potential impact on the lives of children. Even those sociologists who have sought to analyze the intersections between the family and other institutions of acculturation and socialization have seemed concerned with how the various social systems are organized and constructed, but not with their *relatedness* to one another. Further, they have not focused on the dynamics of the intersection between families and schools *from the point of view of the various participants*. For instance, one does not hear the story of parents who are in the process of trying to communicate their concerns and cope with the complexities of the school system.

> Parents . . . remain nameless and powerless—always described from the position of the middle-class institution, never in relation to their own cultural style or social idiom.[8]

When one does find mention of the intersection of families and schools in the academic literature, the authors tend to focus on the negative dissonance and pervasive distrust that pervade the

* For instance, in *The Handbook of Social Psychology* (Lindzey and Aronson, eds., 1969), the comprehensive monograph on "socialization" by E. Zigler and I. L. Child gives no mention of education. *The Encyclopedia of Educational Research* (R. L. Ebel, ed., 1969), which includes about 200 articles on topics related to education, contains almost no reference to socialization.

interactions. For the most part, researchers consider the quality of family-school contact only when they are analyzing the origins of pathology and deviance in children (i.e., issues of cognitive deprivation, juvenile delinquency, effects of father-absent families on achievement patterns in children). This preoccupation with pathology in children is most evident in discussions of the intense conflicts that develop between families and schools when there are great discrepancies in power and status between the school and the surrounding community.

There is abundant literature, for instance, on the distance and distrust that divide lower-class black families from white middle-class–oriented schools. Researchers have searched for the source of the black child's low achievement and poor acculturation in schools by focusing on the dissonance between family life style and school environment. One of the dominant themes of this research is the abuse of mothers. They are accused of giving inadequate cognitive stimulation, creating disorderly and chaotic home environments, offering restrictive and punitive demands, and devaluing the education of their children.[9] No attempt is made to understand the origins of their behavior, values, and attitudes or to explore the structural and institutional forces that impinge on their lives and shape their relationships with their children. It seems much easier and less threatening to define the inadequacies of the dyadic and individualistic relationship between mother and child than to question the inequities and injustices of society. Within the literature on family-school dissonance, therefore, we find the sexist tradition of blaming mothers for the perceived inadequacies of their children, for the perpetuation of their own poverty, and for the creation of social deviants and societal chaos.

The pessimistic focus on family-school conflict is magnified by the moral tone that pervades much of the literature. The family has always been an extremely difficult topic of inquiry because it is such a profound and intimate aspect of everyone's experience that it is hard to avoid projecting one's values, beliefs, and attitudes onto the lives and experiences of others. As Marion Levy has pointed out, "Down through the years no organization has been the focus of greater moralizing or musing." [10] For instance, one recognizes the pervasive moral tone in the social science definitions of family. Claude Lévi-Strauss's classical definition of the family still prevails in the hearts and minds of contemporary scholars.

> [The family may be defined as a] group manifesting the following organizational attributes: it finds its origins in marriage; it consists of husband, wife and children born in their wedlock, though other relatives may find their place close to this nuclear group; and the group is united by moral, legal, economic, religious, and social rights and obligations (including sexual rights and prohibitions as well as such socially patterned feelings as love, attraction, piety and awe).[11]

Lévi-Strauss's definition is also mirrored in the popular imagery of family life and structure—one that is conceived in the middle-class mold. Any variations from that narrowly construed norm are considered deviant and disruptive to a smooth social order. As Margaret Mead points out:

> The American family pattern is an urban middle-class pattern although upper-class patterns occur, and lower-class practice deviates sharply from middle-class standards, and rural family life still retains the stamp of a certain historic period. Films, comic strips, radio and magazines presuppose a middle-class family.[12]

But the celluloid and plastic images of family conflict with the rich and varied reality of family patterns. One of the critical challenges for researchers and practitioners, therefore, is to escape the definitional boundaries and recognize the adaptive and responsive structures that have emerged in our society. They must move beyond the moralizing blinders and pessimistic tradition of social science, beyond absent fathers and cognitively inadequate mothers, in search of a more comprehensive analysis of family-school relations. As long as teachers cling to the ideal middle-class images of family, they will not be able to search for constructive alliances with the great majority of families who do not match those images.

The moralistic and distressing tone of the family-school literature, the focus on pathology and deviance, gives us a distorted and pessimistic vision—a vision that negates the elements of family and community life and institutional structures that show adaptation, cohesion, and health. The pessimism not only reflects the tendency of social scientists to focus on dysfunction and deviance (perhaps in search of magic cures or scientific remedies), but it also emerges from our nostalgic perceptions of the past. When we think of our historical roots in America, we are likely to picture the scene of hard-working, moral, rural folk living a life of struggle, survival, and simple happiness. The vision is one of homogeneous, stable, and supportive communities where values and prejudices went unquestioned and unmentioned.

Part of the peaceful agrarian scene pictures a perfect and unspoken consonance between families and schools. Often the spinster teacher, virginal, pure, and caring, lived in the homes of the schoolchildren's families. She was not only part of the community but a member of the family, and her classroom teaching was an extension of the child's parenting. Margaret Mead vividly describes the idealized image of the little red schoolhouse teacher in her classic volume, *The School in American Culture.*

> Here the teacher herself often a mere slip of a girl, a young teacher, wrestles with her slightly younger contemporaries, boards with members of the school board, is chaperoned by the entire community of which she is one, and finally marries a member of that community—or goes on teaching forever happily, with at least one attributed romance to give her dignity and pathos. For the teacher in the little red schoolhouse is not an old maid whom no man wishes to marry; she is a girl who is a little more intelligent, a little better educated, and more alert than the others, who will herself be very selective in marriage and who therefore in the end may remain unmarried.[13]

Although our myths of the American past are based in reality, they are half-truths obscured by years of nostalgia and romanticism. Their dreamlike quality renders the contemporary scene grotesquely inadequate and unsatisfying. David Cohen, in an insightful essay, "Loss as a Theme in Social Policy," describes the general tendency for policy analysts to construct social remedies that reflect deep and intense feelings of loss.

> If social policy has been shaped by contention over the extent of social democracy, it also has been the product of a mad rush to repair the traumas of becoming modern. If conflict over the extent of equality has been one major theme in the evolution of social policy, another has been the recurrent desire to recapture a community which seemed about to disappear. Beginning in the second quarter of the nineteenth century, there developed an acute sense that society was becoming unstrung, that common values and cohesive institutions were corroding. This sense of loss powerfully influenced social policy . . . It evoked the belief that primary institutions—families, churches, and communities—had lost their ability to pass a common culture along and this became a powerful inspiration for the development of public education.[14]

Our contemporary efforts in social policy, therefore, are often displaced and misfocused wishes to rebuild solid and integrative communities and reestablish what we believe existed sometime in the distant past. This search for renewal through recapturing our roots obviously removes us from searching for effective, realistic solutions to contemporary societal dilemmas.

Joseph Featherstone, in his analysis of family-school history in America, tells the story of a far less perfect and pastoral heritage than our sense of loss would seem to reflect. He describes a much more transient scene, a rapidly moving, somewhat fragmented community with shifting values and cultural idioms. American immigrants were forging new frontiers and experiencing rapid social transformation, feelings of dislocation and anomie, and intergenerational distance. In other words, many of the same themes of disintegration and struggle were present in the early history of this country, even though we tend to remember the tranquility and the nurturant environment of milk and honey.[15]

In the same spirit of realism, Featherstone also urges us to recognize the strength and sustaining power of those early Americans who overcame great obstacles and forged new paths. For instance, rather than focus exclusively on the fragmentation of family life and the alienation of communities during urbanization and industrialization, he also wants us to consider the adaptive strategies and resilience of families and communities that were being uprooted at an accelerated pace. Both of Featherstone's admonitions not to get stuck in the "History of Amnesia" (seeing things in simplistic blacks and whites, curiously repressing or forgetting the complexities of history) underscore the need for social scientists to give a balanced and comprehensive picture of the dynamic relationship between the two institutions that have had the primary responsibilities for acculturation and socialization of children in this society. The analysis of families and schools needs to search for a balanced perspective that documents the complexities of human experience, institutional construction, and social and cultural change. This volume begins to record some of the complex dimensions of family-school intersection by recognizing both the consonant and dissonant faces of the relationship and by exploring some of the microscopic, interpersonal dynamics as well as the more macroscopic, structural patterns of interaction.

From these chapters emerges a kaleidoscopic vision of family-school interaction. As the light and lens through which we look shifts and the focus changes, we can view different patterns of a complex and multidimensional reality. This book does not offer a holistic, comprehensive, or summative analysis of the relationship between these two major institutions of socialization; but it does reveal a myriad of images that reflect the subtleties and complexities of the interactive process. This volume is written to convey both the institutional and structural forces that shape the dynamic intersection of families and schools and the interpersonal and intrapersonal dimensions that are central to the substance and form of the interactions. The descriptions and analyses are intentionally layered and eclectic, moving back and forth between the voices of the individual participants and the power and determining force of those institutions that surround them and shape their attitudes, values, and behavior. Presenting the *dynamic* quality of the intersection requires that we look at the movement of people within the enduring environments that surround them and search for the origins of intrapsychic, interpersonal, institutional, and cultural change.

The chapters also move back and forth through time, often combining sociohistorical descriptions of family-school patterns with analyses of contemporary realities. The intention is to show that our modern dilemmas are not newly constructed or isolated events, but that they have roots in the sociopolitical and cultural history of American society. A search for the historical origins of contemporary patterns gives us a sense of evolutionary continuity and may reveal more meaningful and realistic strategies for productive social change. For instance, although the realization of repeated and sustained patterns of discrimination and oppression against minorities and the poor may seem to be a despairing and pessimistic message, historical documentation sometimes reveals subtle value changes and behavioral transformations that may point to more informed and realistic strategies for initiating change in the contemporary world.

The references, throughout this book, to social science interpretations of the structures, functions, and processes of families and schools reflects yet another vision and perspective. Not only has social science described and documented patterns of socialization, learning, and acculturation within families and schools, but it has had a profound impact on the perceptions, interpretations, and goals of clinicians, practitioners, and policymakers. In other words, research has not merely offered an "objective" report of sociocultural realities, it has played a critical role in shaping and transforming those realities.

Not only does social science seem to be a guiding force in modern thought, but at the same time, the analytic categories and theoretical constructions created by researchers often seem to claim a reality that is not the "reality" that individuals encounter every day. The speculative structures, roles, and functions that attempt to outline everyday life and experiences for us sometimes appear to be disruptive and distorting impingements. Various social science conceptions, in fact, might be muddling our understanding of the world rather than clarifying it. R. D. Laing, in his sometimes cryptic manner, articulates this dilemma:

> Much current social science deepens the mystification. Violence cannot be seen through the sights of positivism. . . . Fundamentally, the error is the failure to realize that there is an ontological discontinuity between human beings and it-beings. Human beings relate to each other not simply externally, like two billiard balls, but by the relations of the two worlds of experience that come into play when two people meet. If human beings are not studied as human beings, then this once more is violence and mystification.[16]

Social science, therefore, seems to offer a light and cast a shadow that both shapes and distorts our real-life experiences. More important, we see through these chapters that social science research is often heavily laden with values that reflect a deep cultural bias and moral tone. We see that it has often been used as a rationalization and justification for maintaining inequalities. After all, researchers could not be expected to perform without bias, without cultural blinders. We too are products of our culture, proud (or guilty) recipients of the bounty of our relatively advantageous position; and our own self-interest cannot help but be subtly woven into our descriptions of reality and our proposals for appropriate remedies.

1

Boundaries and Bridges

Structural Discontinuities Between Family and School

THIS CHAPTER expresses a great irony—namely, that families and schools are engaged in a complementary sociocultural task and yet they find themselves in great conflict with one another. One would expect that parents and teachers would be natural allies, but social scientists and our own experience recognize their adversarial relationship—one that emerges out of their roles as they are defined by the social structure of society, not necessarily or primarily the dynamics of interpersonal behaviors. Historically, there has been a potential conflict among the several institutions involved in the rearing of children. The controversy has taken a variety of forms and levels of intensity according to the time, place, and specific participants. This chapter will explore some origins of such tensions and argue that we must learn to distinguish between the positive and negative forms of dissonance.

Throughout this book, most of my analysis will focus on parents and teachers of elementary school children (ages 6–12). Although many of the interactional dimensions between families and schools remain constant across grade levels, different issues emerge as children grow older, become more independent of their families, more identified with the values and perspectives of their peers, and feel less need for parental protection, guidance, and support. It is important to explore the special nature of the interactions between families and schools during the early years of the child's schooling because these beginning stages shape the course of action, the quality of relationships, and the perspectives of the various participants during the years that follow. It is during these early years that parents and teachers are most anxious to create bonds of communication and support or build walls of silence and exclusion. One would expect to see the most vivid and intense signs of friendship or hostility when the *adults* feel the greatest sense of responsibility for protecting and ensuring the child's successful accommodation to school. The child takes the precarious journey from home to school, experiences the contradictions between the two settings, and must incorporate the myriad and often dissonant norms and expectations, while the adults seek to shape the environments and define the path in an attempt to assure the child's educational success.*

Some of the discontinuities between family and school emerge from differences in their structural properties and cultural purpose. In other words, conflicts are endemic to the very nature of the family and the school as institutions, and they are experienced by all children as they traverse the path from home to school. In describing the structural contrast between families and schools, for instance, sociologists have pointed to differences in *the scope of relationships* among the participants in these two spheres of the child's life. In families, the interactions are *functionally diffuse* in the sense that the participants are intimately and deeply connected and their rights and duties are all-encompassing and taken for

* Because the great majority of elementary school teachers are women, throughout this book I will use the feminine pronoun when referring to teachers.

granted. In schools, the interactions are *functionally specific* because the relationships are more circumscribed and defined by the technical competence and individual status of the participants.[1]

The relationships are not only differentiated in terms of scope but also in terms of affectivity, the quality and depth of the personal interactions. There are contrasts between the *primary relationships* of parents and children and the *secondary relationships* of teachers and children. Parents have emotionally charged relationships with their children that rarely reflect interpersonal status or functional considerations. Children in the family are treated as special persons, but pupils in school are necessarily treated as members of categories. From these different perspectives develop the *particularistic* expectations that parents have for their children and the *universalistic* expectations of teachers.[2] In other words, when parents ask the teacher to "be fair" with their child or to give him "a chance," they are usually asking that the teacher give special attention to their child (i.e., consider the individual qualities, the developmental and motivational characteristics). When teachers talk about being "fair" to everyone, they mean giving equal amounts of attention, judging everyone by the same objective standards, using explicit and public criteria for making judgments. With fairness comes rationality, order, and detachment. So Susie gets admonished, "Put away your candy. I won't let you bring it to school unless there is enough to share with everyone in the class."

Even those teachers who believe in the individualistic approach to teaching and endeavor to diagnose the special cognitive and social needs of their children seem to have universalistic standards and generalized goals that they are conscious of working toward. A teacher who believes in responding to the developmental stage of each child might proclaim publicly to her charges, "I am letting Richard have a special treat because he seems to have had a difficult morning trying to find a friend to work with." The candy becomes the replacement for the affection of his classmates from which he has been painfully excluded. It is a public recognition of his temporarily unique position, but not an excuse for a general and fixed behavior pattern on Richard's part. As a matter of fact, the teacher's goal is to get Richard to the stage where he can move easily and comfortably into the various social groupings and act as mature and self-sufficient as his classmates.

In his article "The School Class as a Social System," Talcott Parsons rejects the differentiation made between those "progressive" teachers who stress independence, individuality, child-directed and exploratory learning and "traditional" teachers who are said to emphasize the authoritarian role of the teacher, competition among children, and predetermined ways of approaching a curriculum. Parsons claims that even the progressive philosophy does not constitute a separate pattern but a variation on a basic theme.

> A progressive teacher, like any other, will form opinions about the different merits of her pupils relative to the values and goals of the class and will communicate these evaluations to them, informally if not formally.[3]

Clearly, the universalistic relationship encouraged by teachers is supportive of a more rational, predictable, and stable social system with visible and explicit criteria for achievement and failure. It does not suffer the chaotic fluctuation of emotions, indulgence, and impulsiveness that are found in the intimate association of parents and children. The generalized relationship between teachers and children becomes a protective kind of interaction that makes it possible for teachers and children to disengage from each other at the end of the year. Even those teachers who speak of "loving" their children do not really mean the boundless, all-encompassing love of mothers and fathers but rather a very measured and time-limited love that allows for withdrawal.

> The problem confronting elementary school teachers, then, resembles that of parents with young children; to treat them so that they regard certain symbolic and physical expressions as rewards and punishments. As a prerequisite, the parents' initial job is to develop a relationship of love and nurturance with their children; analo-

gously, the elementary school teacher's first job is to create among pupils a diffuse and positive attachment both to herself and to the school.[4]

The scope and depth of relationships between teachers and children reflect the preparatory, transitional, and sorting function of schools in this society. The roles allocated to children in school are evaluated primarily in terms of their contribution to some *future status* rather than reflecting full membership in the present society. The Parsonian analysis of the unique characteristics of school life traces the relationship between the teacher's evaluation of achievement and the child's later participation in the occupational and political world.

> The school is the first socializing agency in the child's experience which institutionalizes a differentiation of status on nonbiological bases. Moreover, this is not an ascribed but an achieved status; it is the status "earned" by differential performance of tasks set by the teacher.[5]

For Parsons, therefore, the classroom is a relatively impartial and objective social structure that is experienced by the child as being strikingly different from his egocentric, child-centered existence before entering school. The classroom is seen as essentially liberating—a place where children can rid themselves of the shackles of sex, family, culture, and race, and can prove themselves anew as achievers or nonachievers. (This is obviously a theoretical rather than an empirical conception of the socialization function of schools not based on data but on a static, democratic state working smoothly and effectively.)

Following the Parsonian model, Robert Dreeben sees the classroom as a microcosm of the wider society—a reflection of the norms and values of the corporate world beyond school. He suggests that schooling experiences impart to children the norms necessary to sustain "organic solidarity" in society.

> The argument of this volume rests on the assumptions that schools through their structural arrangements and the behavior patterns of teachers, provide pupils with certain experiences largely un-

> available in other social settings, and that these experiences, by virtue of their peculiar characteristics, represent conditions conducive to the acquisition of norms.[6]

Individuals will supposedly achieve a "meaningful" position in the differentiated society that these "democratic" norms ensure. Although the structuralist conceptions of Parsons and Dreeben are useful in describing the natural and inevitable boundaries that are drawn between families and schools and the continuities that exist between the normative order of schools and the social and economic structures of society, the authors give us little insight into the process of socialization and accommodation that children must experience when they move from one environment to the other. Their analyses do not move us toward an understanding of how children begin to internalize and integrate the norms of the school environment, nor do they help us interpret deviance or difference in the response patterns among children. There seems to be an implicit assumption that children will be the passive recipients of the school's normative structure, that their socialization will be complete and irreversible, and that the abrupt shift from home to school will be accomplished smoothly. However, the structuralists' conception of social institutions does point to the fact that part of the dissonance between families and schools appears to be functional to the growth, socialization, and liberation of children and that the conflicts emanate from *real* differences in the sociocultural function of families and schools.

Spheres of Control and Territoriality

Although sociologists have created clear conceptual distinctions between the structures and processes of life in families and learning in schools, children, parents, and teachers who are daily engaged in negotiations between these two spheres do not usually feel that the definitional boundaries are so clearly delineated. As a matter of fact, home and school more often appear as overlapping worlds with fuzzy boundaries, and much of the anxiety between parents and teachers seems to grow out of the ambiguities. The struggles for clarity and boundary setting are waged daily as parents and teachers argue (often silently and resentfully) about who should be in control of the child's life in school. For instance, there are ambiguous areas of control around the child's attendance in school (i.e., do parents have the right to keep children out of school for reasons other than illness?); after school hours (i.e., do teachers have the right to demand that children stay after school for detention or extra work?). Although parents and teachers often seem to disagree about who has the right to govern a certain area of the child's life, usually teachers are forced to accept the parents' definition. The only sphere of influence in which the teacher feels that her authority is ultimate and uncompromising seems to be with what happens *inside* the classroom. Behind the classroom door, teachers experience some measure of autonomy and relief from parental scrutiny, and parents often feel, with shocking recognition, the exclusion and separation from their child's world. If teachers welcome the parents within their classrooms, they usually ask them to observe rather than participate and they view their presence as temporary and peripheral to the classroom experiences of children.

The need for boundary setting and territoriality expressed by teachers does not always symbolize threatened feelings toward parents. In a study done by Lightfoot and Carew in an independent, progressive school, teachers were given several in-depth interviews that included questions about how they perceived the legitimate role of parents in and around the school setting. The children were ages 3 through 6, and one might have anticipated more collaboration and interaction between teachers and parents in these early stages of development than in the later elementary school years. The teachers were unusually reflective, thoughtful, and conscious of their evolving relationships with children and parents. The school encouraged, in fact, depended on, parental participation in fund-raising, class trips, and other extra-classroom affairs. The teachers' responses to this potential involvement of parents, however, showed that they were not merely concerned with establishing ultimate and uncompromising control over the classroom environment; their primary reasons for parental exclusion were embedded in their ideas about establishing an enduring and nurturant relationship with the children that would not be modified or entangled with the burdens and problems of home life. In some sense they saw themselves as child advocates, protectors of the child's new domain, and they stressed the developmental and emotional needs for a clear and early separation between familial patterns and the demands made upon children in school.[7]

The origins and motivations for territorial protection by parents and teachers are often entangled with negative and rigid stereotypes of one another. We also find, however, that the reasoned voices of some teachers offer educational justifications for creating separate school and family environments—the clear delineation of home and school supports the positive socialization of young children. Territoriality, therefore, seems to be motivated by both positive and negative reasoning. Ironically, the need for fence building seems to grow out of the ambiguity of roles and relationships. The ambiguous, gray areas of authority and responsibility between parents and teachers exacerbate the distrust between them. The distrust is further complicated by the fact that it is rarely articulated, but usually remains smoldering and silent. One way of easing the tension would obviously be by clarifying areas of responsibility and competence between parents and teachers and providing effective modes for communicating distrust and relieving anxiety.

One of the reasons why the struggles over territoriality are rarely articulated, clarified, and resolved is because there are very few opportunities for parents and teachers to come together for meaningful, substantive discussion. In fact, schools organize public, ritualistic occasions that do not allow for real contact, negotiation, or criticism between parents and teachers. Rather, they are institutionalized ways of establishing boundaries between insiders (teachers) and interlopers (parents) under the guise of polite conversation and mature cooperation. Parent-Teacher Association meetings and open house rituals at the beginning of the school year are contrived occasions that symbolically reaffirm the idealized parent-school relationship but rarely provide the chance for authentic interaction.[8] Parents and teachers who are frustrated and dissatisfied with their daily transactions do not dare risk public exposure in these large school meetings by raising their private problems. Teachers fear the scrutiny of their colleagues and principal, who expect them to conform to the collective image of smooth control and decorum that they want to project to parents. And parents worry that their outspoken, challenging style might have a negative impact on their child's acceptance by his teacher, or even that other parents will view his public confrontations as a sign of his inadequacies and weaknesses as a parent.

Individualized interactions between parents and teachers are rare and specially requested—usually arising out of dissatisfaction, frustration, or anger on the part of parents and/or teachers.

> When we call parents during the year, it's generally to say that your child is being disruptive or your child seems sad. Is there something the matter at home? Your child has been talking about some problem. Is that really true? [9]

Teachers rarely call in praise of a child. Usually when parents are summoned to the school, the teacher is reporting on some trouble their child is having adjusting to the social milieu and/or learning the appropriate cognitive skills. Most often, criticism by teachers brings defensiveness on the part of parents, who blame the problems on inadequate teaching. Parents, on the other hand, rarely call a teacher to praise her. They ask for a parent conference when they sense that their child is unhappy with the school environment or isn't learning to read. The teacher often interprets the parents' concern as an attack on her teaching skills, and she becomes defensive. Contacts, therefore, are rarely neutral and rarely productive. Whether the contact is initiated by teachers or parents, it becomes a highly charged, defensive interaction.

When interactions between parents and teachers become threatening and unresolvable through interpersonal negotiation, teachers often look to their colleagues and the institution for support and protection against parental intrusions. Howard Becker describes the balance of forces and walls of exclusion that were built between the teachers and the community of parents in Chicago's inner-city schools. Teachers and administrators banded together for mutual protection against parental intrusion. Teachers made an implicit bargain with their superiors that they would support the organization as long as the organization served to protect them from parents and critics. The mutual protection of individual teachers and the structure of the total school insulated both from the forces of change.[10]

Gertrude McPherson's description of a small-town school gives a different picture of the school's response to the perceived intrusions and extreme demands of parents. The teachers felt particularly anxious and threatened by the upper-middle-class and upper-class parents because they experienced no institutional protection and because they felt humiliated and demeaned by these parents' attitudes of superiority. The principal, who owed his job and allegiance to those high in the community power structure, worked hard to respond to parental demands even if it meant being irresponsible and demeaning to his teachers.[11] In both Becker's and McPherson's analyses, teachers think of building alliances with other teachers as a move toward strengthening their position against parental criticism.

The need for teachers to seek institutional protection against the perceived dangers and aggression of parents is related to the origins and characteristics of teacher authority and the feelings of competence and security they feel in their role as teachers. Max Weber's classic distinction between *positional* and *personal* authority reveals the connection between feelings of individual incompetence and the need for institutional protection. Legitimate authority is granted to the teacher either through the structure she represents, the socially recognized position she holds (positional authority), or through the teacher's individual qualities of expertise, charisma, and personality (personal authority). Those teachers who lack expertise, an empathy and caring for students, a stimulating teaching style, will look to the school as a protective institution and to their formal, established role in the institution as a source of legitimate power. The less able teachers need more institutional support and work as system loyalists in support of the bureaucracy that is their only source of legitimacy. When administrators, therefore, encourage system loyalists, they are strongly opposing institutional innovation and openness.[12]

This analysis could be extended to incorporate the power alliances and authority networks between administrators, teachers, and parents. In other words, we would expect to find that those administrators who support, encourage, and reward personal authority will probably be, at the same time, encouraging teachers to engage in relationships with parents that do not depend on the protection of institutional barriers. The teachers who are more confident of their skills, expertise, and abilities to communicate will be less dependent on the protection of an insular wall around the school and more dedicated to the establishment of a good educational relationship with children that is encompassing of parents rather than exclusive of them.

Teachers' Perceptions of Parent Groups: Issues of Asymmetry and Power

The conflict and distrust between families and schools are intensified when they reflect differences in status and power in this society. The antagonistic relationship between parents and teachers in an industrial society can be traced to the historical role of schools as major institutions for social order and social control—an institutional strategy designed to ensure that deviant and threatening strangers would not challenge the status quo. Economist Samuel Bowles described the transition from a precapitalist society where the basic productive unit was the family to capitalist production and the factory system where the authority structure, prescribed types of behavior, and response characteristics of the workplace became increasingly distinct from the family. An ideal preparation for factory work was to be found in the social relations of the school—discipline, punctuality, and the acceptance of authority. There was an illusion of a benevolent government offering an opportunity for all. In actuality, American schooling was (and is) a mechanism of social control and a place to inculcate workers with the motivational schemes for factory work.[13]

In a recent observational study done in middle- and lower-class public schools in New York, anthropologist Eleanor Burke Leacock noted the strong class interests of school bureaucracies and found the same systematic patterns of discrimination and differentiation described by Bowles. The social relations of the educational process mirrored the social relations of the work roles into which students were likely to move. There was a clear difference in rules, expected modes of behavior, and opportunities for choice. Middle-class students were rewarded for individuality, aggressiveness and initiative, while lower-class students were reinforced for passivity, withdrawal, and obedience.[14] There is, therefore, an *illusion* of mobility and assimilation through schooling that creates distance and hostility between middle-class–oriented teachers and lower-class parents, while in reality the educational system serves less to change the results of primary socialization in the home than to reinforce (and denigrate) and render them in adult form. In other words, poor and minority parents expect that schools will support their child's entry into middle-class life; parents are made to feel inadequate in preparing children for an uncharted future; and families relinquish the final remnants of their cultural patterning and familiar social structures.

In *Small Town Teacher*, McPherson documented the differential relationships that teachers sustained with parents from varying socioeconomic backgrounds. Teachers identified with the average people in town, felt vulnerable and powerless in relation to the upper-middle class, and considered only the lower class as really inferior to them. Sometimes teachers tried to form temporary alliances with identifiable subgroups of parents who were perceived as being cooperative. Poor parents were sometimes taken into the teacher's confidence when they adopted an obsequious and humble manner. The teachers were viewed as the gatekeepers for their children's social mobility, and teachers appreciated the parents' nonthreatening appreciation. Middle-class parents often became potential allies for teachers because of their shared convictions about the value of achievement and hard work.[15] But for the most part, teachers felt they could not trust or depend upon coalitions with parents, and they feared that real collaboration might lead to an awkward confusion of roles.

In my own interviews with black teachers in a public ghetto school, I found varying perceptions of the abilities and strengths of poor black parents, ranging from the stereotypic image of parents as shiftless, lazy, uncaring, and lacking ambition for their children to understanding and empathic views of parents as committed and caring but unable to negotiate the complexities and hostilities of the school system. The latter group of teachers viewed poor black parents as potential collaborators in an educational, cultural, and social enterprise. The teachers' perceptions of parents seemed to be related to their own view of parents as *victims* of an unjust and racist society (rather than responsible creators of their own helpless condition) and the teachers' identification of their own place on the social ladder—their own sense of power and influence in the occupational and social world.

> I lived in a real big ghetto, in a housing project. I was not really hungry or anything, but I know what it is to be a welfare recipient . . . and see my mother sneak out to work. . . . I think I can identify

quite easily with people who are lower class. People who are trying. *My family is the working class.*[16] (Emphasis added.)

This teacher was expressing both an ideological and political vision of the world and a personal need to identify with her own roots and culture. Part of her identification with the lives of the working class was reflected in her attitude toward parent involvement and participation in the educational process of their children. Teaching was not considered to be solely within the lofty province of the professional, learning was not reserved for inside classrooms; the concept of teaching was far-reaching and inclusive and involved the active and critical participation of parents.

> No matter what you do as teachers, or what is done as a community, or what is done as a school system, *the parent is the first teacher*. Unless black parents come together, there's not going to be much hope for their children, they've got to be concerned. [Emphasis added.][17]

Another distinction between parent groups made by teachers in a progressive, independent school seemed to combine elements of social class, life style, and attitudes toward child rearing. Upwardly striving middle-class parents (both black and white) were seen as aggressive, overly demanding of their children, and obsessed with the child's achievement. Teachers often felt they had to protect the child and themselves from the unrealistic ambitions of the parents and establish classroom relationships that were consonant with the child's developmental stage. Another group of noncollaborators included a group of parents who were labeled laissez-faire and were seen as possessing a sloppy, overly permissive approach to child rearing. Teachers accused these parents of responding to their children with their heads (i.e., looking for the origins of and motivations for poor behavior) rather than their hearts (i.e., responding spontaneously to children without the benefit of a psychological orientation). In some sense, lower-class parents who demanded order and respect, who didn't overintellectualize their responses to children, were seen by these teachers as potential collaborators. Teachers appreciated their realistic and objective appraisal of their child's abilities and development, and the parents seemed to permit the teachers a large measure of autonomy and held a genuine respect for the difficulties and complexities of their role as teachers. The mutual admiration seemed to be a circular and sustaining relationship that was rarely articulated, but deeply enjoyed.[18]

These teachers' voices reflect a wide range of work experiences, personalities, skills, and ideological views. McPherson's teachers worked in a relatively heterogeneous and stable community in a small town, which exaggerated the distinctions of a hierarchical social order. My own research was done in a poor black ghetto school that was surrounded by decay and the false promise of urban renewal. The Lightfoot and Carew study took place in a relatively progressive, independent school. In these three divergent settings teachers gave different reasons for trusting some subgroups of compatible parents, but they saw the parent-mass as a threatening force. They formed strong bonds among themselves in fear (and disdain) of parents and looked for institutional support to protect their interests. Although the incipient bureaucracy of schools has effectively excluded the powerless strangers of society and teachers' relationships with families often express the prevailing "middle-class efficiency," the asymmetry and dissonance between teachers and parents cannot be reduced to contrasts in race and class. The perspectives of teachers in the three studies citied above reveal the origins of conflict to be far more complex and multidimensional.

Perspectives and Values of Parents

Sociologists have traditionally been concerned with describing the role of parents within families. They have studied the family's structure, interactional modes, developmental patterns, value orientation, and socialization of children. The focus of their concern has been primarily with how the family is created and sustained internally, the structure and function of the family as a comprehensive, self-sustaining social system. Even those sociologists who have documented the intersection of primary and secondary social institutions have seemed mainly concerned with how their different structural arrangements define contrasting social norms, rituals, and interactional patterns, but not with their *relatedness* to one another.[19]

Not only have social scientists largely neglected the dynamic, evolving relationships between families and schools, but they have not given careful attention to the perspectives of parents who are trying to communicate their concerns and negotiate the complexities of the school system. As a matter of fact, part of the overly simplified vision of the unequal power between middle-class schools and lower-class families and communities comes from the social scientists' preoccupation with describing and analyzing the behaviors of the more powerful mainstream groups in society. The school is seen as the forceful and dominant institution that projects middle-class values, stability, and the American way, while families (especially from minority and poor groups) are seen as the reluctant, uncooperative consumers who merely respond to the school as a monolithic force but rarely initiate positive and productive interactions on behalf of their children. If both sides of the transactional process between families and schools were described from the point of view of the various participants, a very different and highly complex story would be told. Instead the literature offers a distorted, oversimplified picture—one that emphasizes the dissonance and inequalities between home and school and justifies the hardened stereotypes about parent groups.

The stereotypic views of parent groups are deeply embedded in public imagery and become part of the defensive posture of educational practitioners. Without actually knowing parents, without actually hearing their point of view, teachers and principals have developed strong negative images of them that justify their exclusion from the schooling process. For instance, one of the predominant myths about black parents and poor parents who live in the depressed areas around inner-city schools is that they do not care about the education of their children, are passive and unresponsive to attempts by teachers and administrators to get them involved, and are ignorant and naive about the intellectual and social needs of their children. However, when the parents of black children are questioned about their attitudes toward schooling and their ambitions for their children, education is not only valued, but formalized schooling is often seen as the panacea. In his study of black communities in Washington, D.C., sociologist Hylan Lewis points out that "the added value placed on education of black children as a means of escaping low and achieving high status is a myth-like cultural theme." [20] As a matter of fact, he suggests that the conflict between the lofty aspirations of black parents for their children and the limited, realistic social and economic opportunities available to them is precisely the pattern that invites deviant behavior in their children.

In an interview I had with a very sensitive and strong black woman teacher in an inner-city school, it was clear that she recognized some of the reasons why black and poor parents are often unable to initiate contact with schools on behalf of their children. Although she had survived several years of public school teaching, she strongly identified with the concerns and struggles of parents and felt that if poor black parents were questioned about their priorities, education would be the most important issue in terms of their children's lives. For most of these parents, however, the educational institution is a threatening monolith, not only in the sense that the power of knowledge makes them feel inadequate because many of them are illiterate and uneducated but because every bit of communication from the school comes as a negative appraisal of their child, a destructive comment about their lives.

> You can't always get them to conferences, but you can understand why. Each time you call them, it's because their child is bad and who wants to hear that, especially if she's got five or six kids.[21]

According to the experience of this teacher, the insensitive, paternalistic policies of the school system encouraged parents to develop an unresponsive, apathetic attitude toward participating in the educational process.

The myths and stereotypes of parent groups will be nurtured and sustained by researchers and practitioners as long as we do not begin to comprehensively describe their attitudes and behaviors in relation to the education of their children and their perspectives on the school as a social and economic institution. In order to understand the complex narrative of family-school relationships we must recognize the *interaction* of forces and consider the voices, perspectives, and actions of the excluded and ignored groups. It is only when we view the asymmetric relationship between families and schools as a dynamic process of negotiation and interaction that we will gain an authentic picture of the nature of conflict and the potentials for resolution.

Positive and Negative Faces of Conflict

In this chapter, we have seen that the tensions and difficulties between parents and teachers have various origins and motivational roots. Teachers tend to be defensive about their professional status, their occupational image, and their special skills and abilities. They are threatened by the possibility of observation and participation by outside people, especially those of higher occupational and educational status. They wish to form coalitions only with parents who are obsequious, appreciative, and uncritical, or accepting of their needs for autonomy. Most parents are viewed as a critical force that, if permitted to interfere, would threaten the teachers' already insecure professional status and self-image. The teachers' behavior reflects economic and psychosocial fears.

Parents are a relatively unknown force. The social science literature gives us a distorted view of them—parents are viewed, judged, even condemned without a hearing. In real life, parents are not helpless, voiceless victims. They are, however, systematically excluded from life inside schools, and the extent of their participation reflects their social class, race, and ethnicity, the teachers' perspective on parents and community, and their individual personalities. The fears of parents grow as they lose control of their child's daily life, as someone else becomes the expert and judge of their child's abilities, and as they are perceived as interlopers, unwelcome intruders by teachers and the administration.

Although my discussion has echoed the themes of threat and distrust that pervade the social scientists' analyses of family-school interaction, it is important that we not perceive family-school dissonance as necessarily dysfunctional to healthy child development or destructive to the social fabric of society. I certainly believe that hostility, distrust, and unequal power between families and schools cause great anxiety in children and threaten a smooth and constructive transition between these two environments.

But differences and dissonance are not only historically determined, but are also functional to child growth and social change. Philip Slater argues that in American society, people have endured a historical pattern of chronic change that has created an "experiential chasm" [22] between parents and children. This generational distance has, to some extent, invalidated parental authority and wisdom because parents have not experienced what is of central importance to the child, nor do they possess the knowledge, attitudes, and skills that are adaptive to the conditions of contemporary society. This child-adult discontinuity is viewed by Slater as a natural lever for social change in society. Schools (and any other nonfamily-based collectivity) have served the important function of regulating and modifying parent-child relationships.

> One segregates children from adult life because one wishes to do something special with them—to effect some kind of social change or to adapt to one. Such segregation insulates the child from social

patterns of the present and makes him more receptive to some envisioned future.[23]

Dissonance between family and school, therefore, is not only inevitable in a changing society; it also helps to make children more malleable and responsive to a changing world. By the same token, one could say that absolute homogeneity between family and school would reflect a static, authoritarian society and discourage creative, adaptive development in children.

It would appear that parents and teachers are most comfortable with one another when they recognize the validity and necessity of both parenting and teaching for the effective socialization of young children in this society. Teachers, for instance, are most at ease with parents who seem to respect the importance and value of the teacher role, who feel the teacher is performing a critical task, and who respond to her needs for autonomy and control. Teachers have the most difficulty with parents who do not seem to value their special competence and skills, who do not differentiate between the demands of the primary relationships within families and the requirements of the secondary relationships within schools.

Themes of possessiveness seem to underlie much of the friction between parents and teachers. Parents often view their relationship to the child as one of ownership, and they attempt to extend the years of parental protectiveness and control. This seems to reflect a view of children as *property*—a commodity to be owned by nuclear families, a competitive resource that will give potential status to their hard-working parents. In that sense, children are viewed as the projection of their parents. When parents defend their child and argue for continuous and ultimate control over his life, they are also (perhaps primarily) concerned with protecting their own status in the economic structure of society and assuming some measure of control over their child's projected future.

Parental feelings of ownership and control are complicated by the fact that middle-class, status-seeking parents in this society also recognize the need for the child's successful and complete separation from them as a prelude to his future achievement in the corporate world beyond family and school.

> When one joins the values of independence, hope in the future and mobility, it is easy to understand why the successful separation of the child from his family of orientation and his own willful launching upon a career are both possible and necessary. But the potential and recognized consequences extend to the very nature of relations within the family itself. Consciously the future is optimistically viewed; and the task of the family is to equip the child as effectively as possible in the present with all available means for his solitary climb to better and more prosperous worlds lying far ahead of him.[24]

Parents, therefore, experience ambivalence in their possessive and protective relationship toward their child and their equally strong recognition that their child's success depends on his autonomy, mobility, and separation from family. These conflicting needs and expectations on the part of parents and children create confusion and anxiety within nuclear families and inevitably lead to difficulties in the family's relationship to schools.

The tensions arising between parents and teachers, therefore, are part of the very fabric of competition and materialism in this society. The school is seen as the major mechanism of standardized competition of human resources: children are viewed as possessions to be developed, protected, and controlled by parents; and parents are their ambivalent sponsors who must find effective strategies for securing their child's status in some future and unknown society.

It is critical, therefore, that we distinguish between creative conflict and negative dissonance between family and school. The former is inevitable in changing society and adaptive to the development and socialization of children. The latter is dysfunctional to child growth and acculturation and degrading to families, communities, and culture. Educational practitioners, who are daily engaged in trying to shape and clarify their relationship with parents and community, must especially learn to discern the positive and negative faces of conflict. Teachers and administrators must recognize that differences and discontinuities between home and school are not necessarily signs of hostility and threat, but rather are potentially constructive for the teaching and learning process. Both teachers and parents, therefore, should be socialized to anticipate and tolerate a level of creative tension, differences, perspectives, and opposing value systems. As early as 1932, Willard Waller noted that the child will experience more freedom of expression and autonomy when different demands are being made by teachers and parents. In *Sociology of Teaching,* he argued persuasively that conflicts between families and schools are not only inevitable, but from the point of view of child growth, it would be unwise for parents and teachers to empathize completely with each other's perspectives.

> Parent-teacher work has usually been directed at securing for the school the support of the parents, that is, at getting parents to see children more or less as teachers see them. But it would be a sad day for childhood if parent-teacher work ever really succeeded in its object. The conflict between parents and teachers is natural and inevitable, and it may be more or less useful. It may be that the child develops better if he is treated impersonally in the schools, provided the parents are there to supply the needed personal attitudes. . . . But it would assuredly be unfortunate if teachers ever succeeded in bringing parents over completely to their point of view, that is, in obtaining for schools the complete and undivided support of every parent of every child.[25]

Discontinuities between families and schools become dysfunctional when they reflect differences in power and status in this society. When we perceive the origins of conflict as being rooted in inequality, ethnocentrism, or racism, then the message being transmitted to the excluded and powerless group (both parents and children) is denigrating and abusive. When schooling serves to accentuate and reinforce the inequalities in society, then it is not providing a viable and productive alternative for children. The message of ethnocentrism is conveyed to parents and children when socialization, acculturation, and learning within schools are defined in the narrow, traditional terms of the dominant culture. The negative and paternalistic messages are also communicated when schools begin to take on the total range of familial functions —not just the responsibilities for intellectual and social learning adaptive to a changing society but also the dimensions of primary socialization usually found within the family domain. Creative conflict can only exist when there is a balance of power and responsibility between family and school, not when the family's role is negated or diminished.

In an effort to initiate and sustain productive interactions with parents, educators must begin by searching for strength (not pathology) in children and their families. Teachers need to communicate praise and support for children so that criticism will not be viewed as a negative assault and so that children and parents will not begin to adapt their behaviors to negative expectations. There must be a profound recognition that parents are the first teachers and that education begins before formal schooling and is deeply rooted in the values, traditions, and norms of family and culture.

Positive relationships with parents are not merely related to a deep appreciation of different cultures, traditions, and histories, but also are interwoven with the teacher's feeling of competence and self-esteem. If a person feels secure in her abilities, skills, and creativity as a teacher, then parents will not be perceived as threatening and intrusive. As teachers express the dimensions of personal authority rather than the constraints of positional authority, they will feel less need to hide behind the ritualistic barriers of institutionalism and professionalism. There is need, therefore, to clarify and articulate areas of teacher competence, to make more explicit the spheres over which teachers have ultimate and uncompromising authority and those areas where collaboration with parents could be an educational and creative venture.

2

The Other Woman: Mothers and Teachers

Cultural Images

MOTHERS and teachers are at the center of the socialization process. Mothers are thought to be the dominant shapers of the child's primary socialization, and teachers are perceived as being the most important force in determining the child's transition into the adult world. Even though fathers, grandparents, siblings, memories of ancestors are important agents of socialization, our society focuses on the attributes and characteristics of mothers and teachers and gives them the ultimate responsibility for the child's life chances.

The cultural roles of mothers and teachers have been given a demeaning and negative caste in this society. This is especially ironic when one considers the contradictory cultural dogma that claims that children are our most precious resource. The negative images attached to mothers and teachers are not merely a reflection of their low socioeconomic status in this society; the images are emotionally charged. Mothers and teachers receive all the blame for this society's failure to produce generations for which we can feel proud. When people tremble at the decaying social institutions, disintegrating life in communities, when values, traditions, and rituals seem to be fading away, mothers and teachers become the focus of abuse, the objects of discontent. This cultural dissatisfaction is expressed in demeaning cultural images and rationalized in social science research. Many child development researchers, for instance, blame (at least implicitly) mothers for the social and intellectual incompetence of their children (i.e., mothers of cognitive "deviants" are said not to provide enough visual stimulation or social and verbal interaction or blamed for not creating a highly structured and orderly home environment) and rarely consider the material, social, and emotional resources that mothers have at their disposal.[1]

Our cultural images reflect the extremes, our stereotypic conceptions. They also often reflect our idealistic wishes to return to the simplicity of life in the past (not the real past, but our idealization of the past) where roles were clear and uncomplicated and where people felt comfortable and happy in their assigned roles. In other words, social and cultural images let us distort present realities, negate the dynamics and complexities of people's lives today. Although they are distortions of reality, they are half-truths. They are incorporated into the way people define the scope of their lives. For example, even though a professional woman might resist the all-encompassing, passive mother image, she still feels pangs of guilt or moments of ambivalence when she leaves her children for full-time work. The stereotypic cultural image causes her anguish, and she spends much of her energy negating, resisting, or coping with its influence upon her. Cultural images, therefore, are important to identify because they have a powerful impact on attitudes, values, and behavior, and because whether our lives correspond to them or not, they must be reckoned with.

Imagery is well-grounded in the economic and social structures of our society. This chapter will explore the historical and structural origins of the cultural imagery surrounding mothers and teachers and analyze the dissonance between the myths and realities of their contemporary lives. We will search for the boundaries that define the womanly spheres of influence, power, and responsibility in schools and families as well as define the bridges of support and potential collaboration between them.

Historical Perspectives: Women and the Evolution of American Education

Our contemporary visions of mothers and teachers in American society are shaped by our collective memories and historical images of women as caretakers and educators of children. A parallel investigation of the history of women and the evolution of education in this country helps us explore the origins of our contradictory images of mothers and teachers and understand the complex, often discordant relationship between them. Our search for the historical roots of their social and cultural roles underscores the intimate connection between changes in the sociocultural and economic realities and the transformations of female imagery and status.

In the colonial era, education was primarily the province of boys and men. Nevertheless, the period sets the stage for later attitudes toward teaching and learning as well as establishes the status of girls and women.

> It was always understood that children were boys only, girls did not count. There were no girls in the schools sustained by towns or by endowment at the period of American settlement. To read her Bible and psalm-book devoutly and to use her needle deftly were the only necessary accomplishments for a woman, and these could be got in a dame school or at home. . . . The education of the most favored girl ceased at thirteen or fourteen, at which age she began to assume

> the responsibilities of a young woman and to blossom into a waiting candidate for wifehood.[2]

Without question, the place of women and of girls was in the home. Even the dame schools set up for girls were established to teach religion and the skills necessary for homemaking. Often, lessons were conducted by a busy housewife or sometimes by a young woman a little better educated than the rest.[3]

That learning, in whatever form it took, was closely linked to religion for both boys in grammar schools and girls in the home helps to explain the high moral standards exacted of teachers and the exalted expectations still tied to education.

> The conduct of American school teachers has always been a matter of public concern. From colonial days to the present time, teachers and ministers have been associated together in the minds of people, and the high character standards which have been imposed upon the latter have quite commonly been required of the former. Emphasis has been placed upon the peculiar nature of the vocation of teaching—the fashioning of human lives—and upon the importance of exemplary conduct on the part of teachers, both within and without the classroom.[4]

Teachers, therefore, were burdened by the combined imagery of the secular and spiritual spheres. They could not enjoy the untouchable safety and the respectful distance afforded the clergy, nor could they perform their duties guided by divine wisdom. On the one hand, teachers were expected to understand the complexities and uncertainties of "real" life and prepare children to negotiate the path toward responsible adulthood, while on the other hand, they were supposed to be removed from the ugly temptations and pleasures of mere mortals. Echoes of their ambiguous identity still survive today—the expectation that teachers will understand better than anyone the complex dimensions of contemporary life and at the same time float above the turmoil and struggle in some ethereal zone.

The emergence of schools and the value given to education varied from one part of the country to another, underscoring the importance of regional differences in patterns of development both now and then. In colonial times, geographical distinctions could be more clearly delineated. The zeal for schools was less pronounced in the middle colonies than in New England.

> Indeed, in none of the middle colonies in the eighteenth century did the schoolmaster occupy an exalted position. The average colonial teacher was considered to be a "cheap commodity," an "unproductive worker," a "tolerated necessity, maintained by free subsistence and little, if any wage." [5]

The somewhat more enthusiastic interest in education farther north was a product of several factors. Communication and organization were facilitated by compact communities with strong social networks; support and regulation were available from active local governments. Finally, the strong religious orientation of the people who settled in New England was a natural impetus to an education that was still inextricably tied to the spiritual side of life.[6]

Even though schools did develop more rapidly and more extensively in some parts of the country, it is important to recognize the generally subordinate role that schooling played in colonial life. Farming was the vital preoccupation. And though males were preferred as teachers, in the summer months, when men were needed to work the land, women were recruited to take their places. This practice both establishes the economic priorities of the times and hints at the subordinate position of women—suitable only as replacements even for this undervalued and peripheral position.

Looking ahead to the strict moral codes applied to the single women who later began to enter teaching, it is interesting to note the wide range of behavior tolerated, if not sanctioned, by communities for these early schoolmasters. Elsbree reports cases of drunkenness, slander, and even immorality.[7] Although he is careful to point out that these indiscretions were not typical, he devotes a large section to their documentation.

> The colonial schoolmaster is unclassifiable. He was a God-fearing clergyman, he was an unmitigated rogue; . . . he was a classical scholar, he was all but illiterate; . . . he was a cultured gentleman, he was a crude-mannered yokel; he ranked with the cream of society, he was regarded as a menial.[8]

Perhaps the latitude of behavior is consistent with the low regard given to teaching during these times. Surely, it connotes a toleration for far greater freedoms and expressiveness for men than are later recorded for women.

With the development of graded schools around 1830, and particularly with the evolution of primary schools, rationales were created to allow more women to enter teaching. The need for discipline in the ungraded schoolrooms of the colonial period was no longer an argument for requiring the superior strength of men. Before this time, moreover, women as a class lacked the required formal education; now opportunities for their education were expanding. Most important, as teachers were needed to care for young children in the primary grades, the very frailties of women were converted to strengths.

> It is the manner and very weakness of the teacher that constitutes her strength and assures her success. For this occupation she is endowed with peculiar faculties. In childhood the intellectual faculties are but partially developed—the affection much more fully. At that early age the affections are the key of the whole being. The female teacher readily possesses herself of that key, and thus having access to the heart, the mind is soon reached and operated upon.[9]

Single women were thus sanctioned to fulfill a need for which they were seen as naturally suited. Their skill and strengths were defined very narrowly, however. Beyond the sphere of young children, their nurturant, affective strengths were perceived as human inadequacies. Women were restricted, therefore, to caring for the very young. Their success at this task was closely allied to their customary inclinations toward motherhood—for which, in fact, teaching was seen as an appropriate training ground. Beyond the realm of the affective, the important intellectual functions of education were left to the men. Women were thus gaining access to the teaching profession, but significantly at low levels. Even with the present preponderance of women in elementary education, the prominence of males in administrative, supervisory positions reveals a persistent trend.

The arguments developed to satisfy the need for primary school teachers perpetuated stereotypes about both the natures and the roles of men and women. In 1841, the Board of Education in Boston recorded:

> That females are incomparably better teachers for young children than males, cannot admit of a doubt. Their manners are more mild and gentle, and hence more in consonance with the tenderness of childhood. They are endowed by nature with stronger parental impulses, and this makes the society of children delightful, and turns duty into pleasure. Their minds are less withdrawn from their employment, by the active scenes of life; and they are less intent and scheming for future honors or emoluments. As a class, they never look forward, as young men almost invariably do, to a period of legal emancipation from parental control, when they are to break away from the domestic circle and go abroad into the world, to build up a fortune for themselves; and hence, the sphere of hope and of effort is narrower, and the whole forces of the mind are more readily concentrated upon present duties. They are also of purer morals . . . on this account, therefore, females are infinitely more fit than males to be the guides and exemplars of young children.[10]

Views of women, on one side, as inwardly directed toward home and family and notions of men, on the other, as outwardly striving toward fame and fortune have resounded throughout literature and in the texts of history, biology, and psychology until they seem uncontestable. Such dichotomous views defy the complexities of individuals and stifle the potential for people to reveal different dimensions of themselves in various settings. While elaborate rationales may serve the economic and social purposes of a particular historical period, they do a disservice to the unique development and spontaneous interaction of men and women. The tendency to classify women as a group, moreover, obliterates vast intragroup distinctions, which are often greater than intergroup differences.

> Despite all the evidence of great intrasex differences . . . we still speak—and think—as though "women" were a homogeneous population.[11]

In the 1840s, the numbers of teachers needed to accommodate the expansion of the common school increased, making women an increasingly valued resource. As men began to expand and diversify their interests into other areas and their service became more economically valuable, women teachers were seen as "cost effective." A community could engage the services of a single woman, now as qualified as a man, for one third to one half the salary.[12] The acceptance of low wages by women teachers did nothing to elevate the status of either the women or the profession.

When the Civil War erupted, woman teachers replaced the men who became soldiers. The 1870 census indicates that 66 percent of the teachers were now women.[13] While they remained unmarried, these women emerged from a variety of social classes and ethnic backgrounds, and came to teaching with different values, motivations, and dreams. Many continued to be poor young girls who taught primarily for money or who were spurred on by deep religious convictions. However, a number of women from upper-class homes saw the easy entry into teaching as a road to adventure, autonomy, and freedom.

> Girls who were not obliged to teach for a living . . . wanted jobs that would give them personal independence and a chance to see the world. To these young women teaching promised adventure outside the narrow confines of their small home towns and emancipation from family supervision.[14]

As the continued expansion of industry at the turn of the century drew these women into higher-paying labor, efforts were made to lure the daughters of recently settled immigrant families into the profession. The hope of gaining social status and rapid assimilation were potent attractions to this segment of the population.

Though little has been written about mother-teacher interactions during this time of rapid industrial growth, one would expect that the variety of women who were teaching must have encountered different experiences and created diverse relationships in the communities they served. Rural and urban teachers certainly had different relationships to families and communities. In small towns and rural villages teachers were kept under careful watch and ritual scrutiny. Boarded around from one family to another, they had little personal or social freedom. Nor were they always welcome visitors.

> The patrons of the school were less hospitable on the whole to females than to males and many homes were not open to the former. In all probability this was due to the feeling that they required more attention and were generally more trouble to the housewives.[15]

In this setting, teachers must have felt frustrated, isolated, and constrained. One might also guess that, although in these simple, homogeneous communities mothers and teachers shared consonant values, within the household they must have experienced subtle competition for the nurturant role. The female teacher was intruding upon sacred territory—a territory that the mother was used to ordering and controlling in her own way, safe from the judgments or watchful eyes of another adult female.

In the cities, teachers certainly enjoyed more anonymity, but frequently separated from the parents of their pupils by superior education, they could be subject to a lonely and isolated existence. Moreover, because women teachers were a transient group, leaving after a few years to be married, there was little opportunity for forming bonds within the profession. Not only would this exacerbate the loneliness of these women, but it would reduce their professional and political effectiveness—retarding educational reforms and slowing efforts to achieve status.[16]

It is interesting to speculate upon the quality of mother-teacher interactions as young single women began to enter teaching in greater numbers during the early part of this century. Mothers, experienced in child raising and deeply attached to their children, were surrendering their young primarily to single women who had no experience in motherhood and minimal formal training. Could these teachers empathize with the particularistic concerns and strong feelings of identification mothers showed for their children? Did mothers spurn the teachers' inexperience or fear their education? Or did they envy their youth, mobility, and relative freedom? Certainly, the transiency of these unmarried ladies made it difficult for parents and teachers to build enduring and meaningful relations and establish the beginnings of trust. The backgrounds of both parents and teachers also varied widely, creating cultural and economic barriers that were difficult to overcome. And differences in individual personalities and temperaments added yet another dimension to the complex mixture.

As formal education grew more important and valuable as a concomitant to industrial expansion, the social and economic position of teachers in the society did not keep stride. As married women and then mothers began to enter the work force with increasing frequency after World War I, notions about their proper place and role came under sharp criticism. When women were encouraged to become teachers, it was expected that they would remain single. In the early 1900s, marriage on the part of women teachers was the most frequent grounds for dismissal. Indeed, "in 1903, the New York Board of Education enacted a bylaw forbidding a woman teacher to marry." [17]

Whether traditional conceptions of marriage and motherhood were more at stake than politics and economics is a significant question. The growth of primary schools had allowed women to expand their "natural" qualities in new directions. Now the rise of teacher-training institutions provided qualified young teachers.

> As soon as teacher-training institutions were able to furnish an adequate supply of technically qualified teachers for public schools,

> there was a movement instituted to oust married women in order to make room for their "more needy" sisters. . . .[18]

The economic hardships of the Depression years supported the argument that two incomes within a single family were inequitable, and married women were frequently prevented from working. The census of 1930 records that 77.3 percent of the total group of women teachers were unmarried—a proportion similarly represented in other occupations.[19]

After World War II ended, however, several factors combined to create work opportunities for married women and mothers. Unmarried females were in short supply at this time, as were childless married women. The low birth rate between 1930 and 1945 reduced the number of men entering employment in the two decades following. After the war, a large number of men who would have been workers chose instead to further their education. War casualties, finally, depleted the young male population.[20] Suddenly, it was no longer unusual for married women and even for women with children to be working outside the home.

The persistent image of mothers as primary caretakers of children in the home, however, did not easily accommodate the combined roles of these working women. When mothers became teachers with this period of post-war expansion, mother-teacher relations were negatively affected. Since a mother's place was at home, these teacher-mothers were looked upon critically for the neglect of their womanly duties. Often, it was rumored that they could neither cook nor clean, and the damage they were causing their families was uncontested.[21] That this criticism came from the women in the community rather than the men underscores the strong and painful tensions between mothers and teachers in family-school relations and suggests conflicts both for the mothers who were compelled to criticize and the teacher-mothers (i.e., those who filled the dual roles of mother and teacher) who could not escape the guilt of the criticism. Rather than assault the social structures and institutions that enforced their constricting roles and subservient status, women challenged each other's small moves out into the work world. The guilt, ambivalence, and conflicts were self-inflicted. Relationships between these mothers and teachers could not have been very productive for either side, and one wonders about the effects on the children who must have experienced the subtle (and not so subtle) warfare.

The intense feelings surrounding the redefinition of motherhood in the 1940s and 1950s created even greater tensions between mothers at home and mothers who were working. Still, the number of working mothers during this period was relatively small. As late as 1940, only one mother out of ten worked outside the home compared with today, when half of all mothers with school-age, but not preschool-age, children are employed.[22]

In this period, the birth rate rose sharply and did not decline again until 1957.[23] Family remained important, but the perceived value of schooling soared to new heights. While the self-worth and identity of most mothers was heavily invested in their families, they began to recognize the need for their children to succeed and to achieve independence in the world beyond the nurturant bonds of the family. They carried their ambivalence and feelings of loss into their interactions with teachers—the most visible symbols of competition. It is not unrealistic to suspect that these full-time mothers resented the takeover of their responsibilities by teachers. As technology conspired to make the housewife's role less consuming and less valued, these resentments became sharper. When children were usurped by school, nonworking mothers often experienced loneliness, emptiness, and frustration. An article entitled "Problems of the Modern Homemaker-Mothers" written in 1952 describes the tedious and unfulfilling aspects of domestic chores for many of these women and the gnawing questions they raised about the usefulness of their work.

> Modern conveniences plus modern high standards, while freeing women from the back-breaking physical labor of the pioneer women, have increased enormously her petty cleaning-up tasks. The number of things which modern women have to wash and polish and starch and iron and sterilize, and the number of times they have to do it,

> have multiplied until many housewives spend most of their time cleaning one thing or another and can't imagine how the pioneer woman found time to do all she did. If the pioneer woman had spent so much time on the luxury and boredom of cleanliness, she wouldn't have been paying her way, and the modern woman knows in her heart that she isn't paying hers, either.[24]

We do not have access to the pioneer woman's heart. Perhaps because the homemaker-mother role has never earned economic credit in a society that equates value with monetary reward, she harbored similar concerns and feelings. A crucial difference between the early American mother and her "nonworking" contemporary counterpart, however, is the secure notion of place held by the first and the uncertain sense of role surrounding the second.

> In the old days, women knew where they stood and their lives were spent in the care of their families. Their world was bounded by the walls of their homes. From there, a resolute minority thrust out into the world of business and public affairs and succeeded in being admitted largely to the extent that they were willing to turn their backs on home and family.[25]

For many mothers, the late fifties and the sixties initiated a time of acute ambivalence as larger numbers of women with children went to work. The guilt and confusion remaining with mothers at home when children went off to school also drained the energies and spirits of the women struggling to integrate the tasks of mothering with the demands of working. Although today, the mother of school-age (but not preschool) children who is not in the labor force is becoming less the rule and more the exception, the still sizable proportion of mothers at home and the growing numbers of mothers at work continue to live with the effects of ambivalence, insecurity, and guilt. The combination of more mothers working and the attrition of the homemaker role have created threatening options and confusing expectations for twentieth-century women.

The historical relationship between the economic realities and the social roles of women has shaped the cultural imagery attached to mothers and teachers in American society and defined the quality of their interactions with one another. Because women are the central and dominant forces in families and schools, their collective history, contemporary identities, and potential spheres of influences will define the dynamic interaction of these two institutions. Further, improving the relationship between families and schools will have much to do with redefining our cultural images of mothers and teachers and analyzing the sources of continuity and discontinuity between their social identities. Although patterning a constructive relationship between families and schools is an agenda that should be the concern of men, women, and children in this society, I believe that women will be more open and responsive to reconsidering their roles and redefining their relationships and will, therefore, be more central to the process of social change.[26]

Images of the American Teacher

> Sociologists and the general public continue to expect the public schools to generate a classless society, do away with racial prejudice, improve table manners, make happy marriages, reverse the national habit of smoking, prepare trained workers for the professions, and produce patriotic and religious citizens who are at the same time critical and independent thinkers.[27]

When we think about the educational process in a modern industrialized society, we usually confine our visions to what happens *inside* schools and to the teacher as the central figure in the process. The teacher is most often viewed as a woman and she is seen as the *one who makes education happen* for children, the one who transmits the patterns and values of the mainstream culture. In her book, *The School in American Culture,* Margaret Mead describes three images of the American school that correspond to three role definitions of the American teacher. In reality, these three definitions of the teacher do not exist as separate and exclusive entities, but rather our view of the American teacher encompasses bits and pieces of the three images. It is important to recognize that the role definitions of the teacher described by Mead are not only culturally defined and sustained, they also have been the predominant images used in the academic literature. It is for that reason that I think it important to give them explicit attention.

The *Little Red School House* is a reality that few of us have experienced, but it is an image that lingers in our minds and symbolizes the democratic tradition of America. We visualize a rural scene, well-tended farmland, cows, horses, and blackberry bushes surrounding a one-room schoolhouse where big children are responsible for the teaching of little children and where parents and teachers are sympathetic to the same values and cultural traditions.

> This image, the beloved image of the school, crops up in the minds of those who have never in fact seen such a school, so firmly is it rooted in our literature and tradition. Like so many of the symbols of the American dream, it stands both for a desirable state never attained and for a past golden age which has been lost—the school in a world which did not change, a world of rural images, where . . . goodness was literally symbolized by a "clean slate." [28]

In this deeply rooted stereotype, the teacher is viewed as a young girl rather than a mature and whole woman, whose identity is closely tied to her monolithic role as a servant of the community. She is seen as a guardian of the morals and traditions of the community and must reflect the purity and virginity of her nature in her abstinence from lovemaking, passion, or other worldly pleasures. As a matter of fact, this guardian of children cannot even be trusted to guard herself. She lives under the careful and judgmental scrutiny of the community fathers and mothers.

Mead's second image is the historical tradition of the *Academy*. This was an institution established for the privileged where young minds were introduced into the mysteries of the Greek and Latin past. Parents were not content to impart the wisdom of their generation to the children, but they "sought to structure the future in terms of the past, to guarantee the child's future position by the degree to which he participated in the heritage of the past." [29] The Academy was seen as being dominated by male teachers and students. The male teachers not only symbolized a relationship to cultured European traditions, but it was also believed that a male presence would stress clear, rational, and objective thinking in an orderly world. This vision of the Academy is still prevalent today in many elitist private schools. It fosters images of control, order, and superiority among men. The teacher of the classics rejects the confusions and complexities of the contemporary world and creates an environment for students that is stable, predictable, and without tension and emotion. This environment is designed for men and for boys who will grow up to be men in control of their destinies.

The third image of the American school is the *City School,* a place where children are not taught the traditions and values of their ancestors or the realities and constancies of their parents' present. The City School is a scene of acculturation and assimilation, a door through which the estranged children of immigrants, the foreign born, will learn the behaviors and values of the New World.

> They are not only poor, but they are foreign; they have unpronounceable names and eat strange things for breakfast; their mothers come with shawls over their heads to weep and argue and threaten a teacher who is overworked, whose nerves are frayed by the constant battle.[30]

To the urban children of poverty, the teacher in the City School represents hopes for the future, but she also symbolizes the rejection of the cultural and familial values and traditions. The teacher is considered successful to the extent that she manages to alienate the children from the bonds of their family and to the extent that she directs them to an unknown future in a bewildering and changing world. This teacher feels a sense of inadequacy because she feels that what she knows will not necessarily be the appropriate preparation for the children's lives ahead. Her own educational history seems strangely outmoded as she is forced to transcend her past in a desperate attempt to provide a meaningful present for her charges.

Although the three cultural definitions of the teachers often combine to form our conception of the teacher role, parts of the three definitions are often in conflict with one another. Each of these images of the American teacher implies a different set of personality characteristics, social skills, and cognitive faculties. Each of these roles implies a different relationship to parents and community. Each of these roles implies a different kind of adaptation and responsiveness to the changing needs and demands of society, implicitly and explicitly imposed by the world of work in which children will eventually find themselves. Despite all the differences, there is one theme shared by all three definitions; that is the expectation that teachers should be all-giving, nurturant servants of the people whose job expands to adapt to the needs of society.

As cultural definitions of good and bad become more and more ambiguous in our society, as the future becomes less and less predictable, the boundaries of the teachers' role found in social science literature have greatly expanded since Mead's writings of more than two decades ago. Critics of formalized schooling and advocates of strong familial socialization have challenged the all-encompassing influence of teachers on the lives of children. In *Deschooling Society,* for example, Ivan Illich claims that schools have taken total control over the lives of children and the teacher has become a custodian, a preacher, and a therapist.[31] As a custodian, the teacher acts as a master of ceremonies, arbitrates and structures rules and regulations, initiates children into the mainstream social values, and rejects any attitudes or behavior that deviate from the narrow cultural norm. The preacher part of the teacher seeks a more subtle and lofty level of control. She not only works to control their moral and spiritual visions inside school walls, but she expects those visions to extend into their lives beyond the classroom. Finally, Illich sees teachers as therapists who control the personal lives of children, analyzing and directing their motivations and actions in order to direct their psychological growth. The therapist role is thought by Illich to be the most potentially destructive and manipulative force in the lives of children and dangerous to the development of their natural expression and exuberance.

Anna Freud also criticizes the encompassing nature of the teachers' role defined by the literature and expressed through our cultural myths. She is less concerned with Illich's negative criticism of the social and political consequences of using the school as a total institution and more concerned with the psychological experiences of the child who is trying to define and understand his relationship with the teacher as a special person. She describes the psychological transition of the child from the all-encompassing, unmeasured love of the mother to the more circumscribed attention given by the teacher. But more important, Anna Freud talks about the need for mothers and teachers to perform distinctly separate roles in the lives of children.

> The teacher's role is not that of a mother-substitute. If, as teachers, we play the part of mother we get from the child the reactions which are appropriate for the mother-child relationship—the demand for exclusive attention and affection, the wish to get rid of all the other children in the classroom.[32]

Anna Freud, therefore, is proposing that the teacher's role be far more circumscribed, objective, and generalized in relation to children. Teachers should develop a more distant relationship to children and escape the dangers of rivalry with mothers, "who are the legitimate owners of the child," by taking a "more general and less personal interest in the whole process of childhood with all its implications." [33] In the same sense, the teachers must not shift into the therapist role and become dangerously sensitive and responsive to the emotional involvements of the child. Teachers, therefore, should be neutral, objective human beings who avoid creating strong emotional and sexual bonds with children; and teacher-child relationships should be removed from drive-activity and instinctive wishes. Interestingly enough, Freud assumes that the teacher of young children will be a woman, but she feels that the teacher's role must be more circumscribed and defined in such a way that she is less seductive, less entrapping to the expressive instincts of young children. Perhaps she must be thought of as less nurturant, less loving, and even less woman.

Images of Mother

> Don't poets know it
> Better than others
> God can't be always everywhere; and so,
> Invented Mothers.[34]

> Mothers have as powerful an influence over the welfare of future generations, as all other causes combined.[35]

All-giving and all-forgiving, mothers have been pictured in poetry and prose as superhuman. The image of motherhood is particularly powerful, even more encompassing and dispersed than that of the teacher. Motherhood is thought to be the ultimate and inevitable extension of the woman's role in this society. As a matter of fact, women become mothers when their biological purpose is consummated. Mothers live for others, are selfless, nurturant, responsive, and submissive. Their world revolves around their husband and their children, and their status is realized through their husbands' work functions. Mothers are protectors who use their initiative and aggressiveness to fend off the cruel world that might destroy the innocence and joy of their children. Most important, mothers are not thought to have a separate, intact identity. Their identity is shaped by their relations to their family. Mothers do have relations with other institutions—the school being a primary one. In fact, their skills and competence as mothers are often evaluated in terms of how well they have prepared their children for school. The school is the place where *mothers* experience their first public evaluation and scrutiny, where their child is compared with his agemates, and where teachers and other mothers voice approval or disapproval of the mother as reflected through the child.

The mother's work is not valued by society. Things of value in this society are attached to economic reward, and housework, child care, and nurturance are free with marriage. "Though we give lip service to the idea that the mother's work is worthy, hardly anyone believes it. Mothering has 'use value,' but not 'exchange value.' "[36] Those "womanly" qualities of resourcefulness, patience, understanding, expressiveness are also devalued and thought only to be functional in the context of home and family. They are seen as antithetical to the aggressive, instrumental roles needed in the world of men and work. Children become the major focus and source of identification and reward for mothers, and through children the mother establishes relationships with the outside world. When children no longer feel the need for the constant attention of mother, she experiences great loss and abandonment. She will always be a mother, but her active mothering functions slowly but inevitably slip away until she is left with an empty nest, a vacant identity, a useless life.

The cultural images of mother are less clearly delineated but seem to express the mirror images of the teacher. The notion is that there is need for strong teachers when mothers are perceived as being less than adequate. So implicitly at least, a kind of competition exists between who is doing better at their respective social functions. The competition and antagonisms between mothers and teachers is somewhat diminished in homogeneous, "simple" societies where there is a continuity of values, behaviors, and attitudes between families and schools and where the future appears relatively certain. Margaret Mead's Little Red School House, for example, reflects a continuous, fluid relationship between mothers and teachers. Teachers possessed cognitive skills and pedagogical strategies that were superior to mothers, but they followed the same value system and social orientation. The teachers were made in the familial image, and school was thought to be a natural extension of family life. The image of Mead's City Teacher, on the other hand, reflects a discontinuous, negating relationship between mothers and teachers. There is ambivalence on the mothers' part toward teachers because, on the one hand, teachers symbolize the chance for the social mobility and assimilation of the next generation into mainstream society, while on the other hand, they symbolize the repudiation and devaluation of family, history, and culture. The mothers' values and skills are thought to be inadequate for the complex, industrial, and changing society into which their children will grow. The City Teacher mirrors the mothers' ambivalence and expresses their uncertainties through competition with and alienation from the families of children. Because the urban families and communities (especially those of "strangers," minorities, and immigrants) represent the irrelevancies of the past, the threat of difference, and the resistance to change, teachers begin to see mothers as uncooperative and competitive figures who seek—both consciously and unconsciously—to undo and negate their hard work in the classroom. Out of the static and narrow images of mothers and teachers, therefore, grow negative competition, distrust, and alienation.

Idealized Images and Real-Life Status

We all cringe at the oversimplified stereotypes of mothers and teachers. For the most part, the cultural images do not reflect the real, alive people we know who struggle with gracefully combining multiple identities and making sense out of their world.

Even though our idealized vision of the teacher demands the impossible, asks that she be superwoman, mother earth, mind reader, and soothsayer, the teacher's real-life status in the social and occupational hierarchy is dramatically low; ". . . a parent or parent substitute, even a nursery school teacher doesn't rate with a dog trainer." [37] There is a great contrast between the high expectations of our idealized images and the negative realities of the teacher's experience, and there are, of course, differences in the way the teacher is perceived and stereotyped by various subgroups in this society. To those groups who have been systematically excluded from schooling and who view school as the major avenue of cultural assimilation and social mobility, teaching is likely to be considered a lofty and laudable profession. But characteristic of the academic, middle-class community is the expression of disdain for teachers—viewing teachers as servants of the community. These feelings of superiority are reflected in the perceptions and orientations of academicians and researchers. Social scientists have attributed the low social status of teachers to a low respect for intellectual endeavors, the preponderance of women in the profession, the lack of professional autonomy (i.e., lack of power in the gate-keeping function), and the low degree of professionalization.[38]

Beyond the limiting impact of the social and economic factors, the teacher's low status reflects the cultural perceptions of the teacher as woman and the teacher as child. Envisioning the teacher as woman is not simply an indication of the large proportion of women in the profession. These character traits symbolize the psychosocial qualities that we attach to both male and female teachers—the traditional womanly dimensions of nurturance, receptivity, passivity, and the childlike dimensions of creativity, affection, and enthusiasm. One is impressed on the one hand with the multidimensional nature of our great expectations of the teacher and on the other hand with our view of the teacher as a one-dimensional being who is subordinate, passive, and responsive to the needs of children. It would seem that our cultural definitions of the teacher role pose an inherent contradiction that claims that in order to communicate effectively with children, teachers must exhibit the nurturant, receptive qualities of the female character ideal and the expressive, adaptive qualities of the child. Ironically, these same qualities are viewed as inferior and of low status when one conceives of the teacher in relation to the social and occupational structure of society.

It is important for social scientists to probe the origins of image-making—to distinguish between those images of teachers that arise out of history and culture, academic literature, the mass media, and memories from childhood. For instance, Willard Waller claims that much of the hostility between parents and teachers reflects the parents' negative experiences as children in school. The images of a tyrannical, authoritarian teacher figure are carried into adulthood and projected onto the teachers of their children. When parents greet teachers they are not likely to see them on equal terms, as potential collaborators, but more often they respond as children to a feared and threatening authority. Waller asserts that productive and egalitarian relations between parents and teachers will not evolve until children have more positive experiences and perceptions of teachers that they can carry into adult life.[39]

It is not only important to understand the origins of teacher images but also important to emphasize the difference between images of the teacher role and the actual attitudes and behaviors of teachers today. In this chapter, I have been concerned with analyzing the descriptions of teacher images, not with observing their actual behaviors through the eyes of a journalist. In real life, the teacher is more or less affected by the imposition of cultural stereotypes, but she is not hopelessly bound in these traditional modes. In recent years, one recognizes a severe cultural lag between our stereotypic images of "teacher" and real teachers who are demanding the prerogatives and power that other professionals have been accustomed to.

> They want acceptance as working equals, equality of status, and recognition of their competencies in their own areas of responsibility.

> . . . Putting it bluntly, they do not want to be talked down to but they do want to be talked to at eye level. . . . In the dignity of their professional competence they do not appreciate being directed in every detail of their daily function.[40]

It is evident, therefore, that a large proportion of America's teachers today defy the stereotypic images of the teacher presented in the social science literature. We can also identify a small and vocal population of teachers who show a great deal of aggressive strength and political savvy; who find themselves behaving like professional men.

In the same sense, we both idealize and denigrate mothers and have unrealistic expectations of their constancy, goodness, and giving. All mothers are certainly not passive, nurturant, accommodating beings who live vicariously through their husbands and children, although the mass media would often have us believe so. Some mothers are professionals who excel and thrive in a man's world and are perceived by themselves and others as being the outstanding exceptions to the rule. Other mothers are full-time workers who take primary responsibility for family resources, who do not view work as a choice but a necessity, and who do not explore their individual self-definition through their work. Still other mothers seek to create alternative work patterns, perhaps working part-time in order to provide amusement, fulfillment, enrichment, or spending change.

Whether outside work is done by choice or not, whether women seek their identity through work, whether women are searching for pleasure or survival through work, the integration of motherhood and the world of work is a source of ambivalence, struggle, and conflict for the great majority of women. (The conflicts are most often articulated and expressed with great feeling by the more educated, middle class women. We must not assume however, that the relative silence from other women reflects comfort in their life patterns. It may merely reflect what are considered socially appropriate modes of expression and characteristic ways of showing ambivalence and pain in their subculture.) In general, the values and institutions of American society make it extremely difficult, if not impossible, for a mother to comfortably and guiltlessly integrate outside vocations and parenting.

Separation and Integration of Life Roles

Not only has the turmoil and guilt of mothers been institutionally and culturally sustained, but prominent and influential theorists have "objectified" and rationalized the narrow vision of a womanly soul. Whether for teachers or for mothers, psychoanalytic theory, in its efforts to uncover psychic realities, has contributed to the constricted imagery and stereotypes associated with women. "Traditional psychoanalysis shapes women to feel it is 'natural' and 'feminine' to relinquish their autonomy and thereby to suppress any predilection for developing skills that lead to the accretion of power and other resources." [41] The crucial importance of the mother in molding the personality of her child and the necessity of her intense care in the early years were decisively established by narrow interpretations of Freudian theory. Its impact on the mother's sense of responsibility for remaining at home and her sense of guilt for leaving is unending. The studies of Bowlby and Spitz on maternal deprivation, while conducted under the extreme conditions of institutionalization, were exaggerated into another warning against the mother's absence. Later Erikson's theories of identity achievement for women were stated in terms of women's relations to men.

> The stage of life crucial for the emergence of an integrated female identity is the step from youth to maturity, the state when the young woman, whatever her work career, relinquishes the care received from the parental family in order to commit herself to the love of a stranger and to the care to be given to his and her offspring.[42]

The term "psychological parent" created by Jean Curtis in her recent book, *Working Mother,* emphasizes the lasting impact of these theories on the lives of women. Even at a time when traditional roles are being redefined, when more mothers are working and more fathers are participating in homemaking and child rearing, many women find it difficult to relax or to share their sense of primary responsibility for the emotional and physical well-being of their children. "It is the mother," says Curtis, "who is always mindful—who always feels a direct personal responsibility for the whereabouts and feelings of each child, all the time . . . [who] knows what size shoes they wear . . . who their teachers are, what kind of work the first grade does." [43] So ingrained are these attitudes, moreover, that "women find it difficult to relinquish the role even when they are offered the option." [44]

When theorists claim the critical importance of sustained, intense, and exclusive mothering, they are also reflecting prevalent social attitudes toward women establishing a professional identity.

> Although 40 percent of the work force is composed of women, the cultural view is that women do *not* work and are in the home. It is an ideal view and not a real one; but it serves the purpose of forming images and placating discontents. Even the women who are working are convinced that they are not really "workers" and do not think in terms of ambitions, goals, demands, and rights. They may be pleased that they are permitted to work at all.[45]

The woman must justify her choice of life style, and the locus of this justification lies in the family rather than in her professional work. Traditionally, it has been her ability to supervise a household, have a happy marriage, and bring up well-behaved children that has served as the real justification for a woman's life rather than her success and satisfaction in her profession.

> The professional woman with a family meets requirements in her work that are covered by values quite different from those that organize her home life, and she is faced with the necessity of learning to tolerate such contradictions or of extemporizing an integration of her own.[46]

One of the ways women seek to establish an integration of their domestic and professional roles is to find work in the fields traditionally conceived as feminine—work devoted to the problems and concerns that the woman herself faces in her private capacity within the family. Choosing a profession like teaching provides a continuity of this sort because it supports a special form of integration in the woman's life. Lessening the distance between her two roles reduces contradictions in her self-image.

Interestingly enough, the blurring of distinctions between family life and work has provided social scientists with an opportunity to give less attention to the characteristics and qualities of professional and work roles. Such a continuity has led social scientists to assert the lack of commitment and attachment that women feel toward their work lives. Once again the teaching profession is seen as a woman's secondary role, which competes with her primary role as mother of a family. It receives, therefore, only peripheral attention from the social scientists, who do not seem to be interested in the teacher's conception of her work, her professional goals, and her maturation. So there is this strange twist: Mothers and teachers have become natural enemies, yet teachers are inevitably and ultimately (at the very core of their being) mothers. Does this lead to teachers having to magnify their separateness in order not to succumb to their biological, female tendencies to be mothers? As one teacher said to me: "I try my best to be *asexual* in the classroom in order not to be confused with mother or motherly things."

Mothers and teachers are caught in a struggle that reflects the devaluation of both of their roles in this society. Their generalized low status makes them perfect targets for each other's abuse, not daring to strike out at the more powerful and controlling groups in this society who are most responsible for their demeaned social and economic position. Not only do they provide relatively safe and visible objects of discontent for one another and for the rest of society, but mothers and teachers are also involved in an alien task. Both are required to raise children in the service of a dominant group whose values and goals they do not determine. In other words, mothers and teachers have to socialize their children to conform to a society that belongs to men. Within this alien context, it is almost inevitable that mothers and teachers would not feel an authentic and meaningful connection to their task and not completely value the contributions of one another.

While the achievements of an increasing number of women have helped some to a greater sense of self-worth, it is ironic that the positive gains of their success may work as a negative force in their dealings with teachers and other women of lower status. In a society where success is identified with the male domain, the conscious and unconscious assimilation of dominant male characteristics is part of the achievement package. The necessary denigration of female qualities and identifications thus works to separate successful women from their less fortunate sisters.[47] Not only is it likely, if these mechanisms operate, that women who achieve the traditional form of success will have a harder time working with teachers whose status is rising more slowly, but their potential loss of the affective and nurturant qualities, long assigned to women and now in danger of suppression, is a serious outcome.

Establishing positive and productive relationships between woman roles means that the values and goals of our culture, which shape the education and socialization of children, must undergo a profound transformation that reflects more than the competitive and individualistic agenda of a male-dominated society, but also encompasses the special, valuable qualities of women. The redefinition of cultural norms will not only make mother and teacher roles more esteemed and valued in the eyes of others but will also give greater meaning and purpose to those who *choose* to take on those roles—and inevitably clarify the various ways in which mothers and teachers can engage in collaborative and supportive relationships. One of the positive aspects of the feminist movement lies in addressing the transformation of social and cultural values to better reflect the psychosocial needs and characteristics of women. One hopes that the growth of the feminist perspective will have a positive impact on the relationships between mothers and teachers—through the transformation of societal values will come potentials for finding strengths in each other's work. Bonds of strength rather than weakness will generate the most effective and productive interactions.

But the promises and hopes of the feminist ideological thrust must be experienced by a great many women as being depersonalized, overly politicized, and detached from their everyday lives. Perhaps the rhetoric seems far too bold and elusive to those who yearn for tangible evidence of change. It is through immediate and personal contact with economic realities that the majority of women will begin to experience changes in their self-esteem. The present trends of expanded educational opportunities and increased acceptance and participation of women, and particularly mothers, in the labor force will contribute to a greater sense of competence and self-worth for more women.

Conservative attitudes and narrow conceptions of social and cultural roles have been directly linked to limited education.[48] The present and predicted general rise in the educational level of this country, therefore, will foster attitudes more conducive to change. Not only is it likely that increased education will begin to break apart stereotypical role divisions and widen the options and opportunities for both men and women, but also we would expect that women will begin to find satisfaction in their jobs and experience new levels of achievement and mastery. It is a hopeful fact that there is "an extremely high correlation between self-esteem and achievement." [49] When mothers first began working in greater numbers after World War II, the time was ripe to produce evidence of maternal deprivation. But today, studies attest to the positive aspects of a mother's working. "Two variables that have differentiated working from non-working women are their sense of competence and their attitudes toward the woman's role." [50] Far from thinking that mothers need assume total care for their young children, one study revealed "that the more help women had with child care, the more nurturant they could be." [51] Women need not fear, therefore, that achievement beyond the boundaries of home will diminish their mellow, affective qualities in relation to their families.

Other research has indicated the importance, especially for adolescent girls, of the role models these working mothers are presenting. Although there is need for further research before the impact of initial findings can be assured, it is nevertheless significant that:

> . . . for girls, maternal employment seems to contribute to a greater admiration of the mother, a concept of the female role that includes less restrictions and a wider range of activities and a self-concept that incorporates these aspects of the female role.[52]

For boys, the effects of a working mother are less clear.

> Maternal employment might influence their concept of the female role, but what the effects are on their attitudes toward the father and themselves depends very much on the circumstances surrounding the mother's employment.[53]

We must, of course, recognize that all of these findings are subject to the influence of a complex interaction of variables—the motivation behind the mother's work; positive, negative, or ambivalent attitudes of husbands; the presence or absence of social networks and institutional supports; and the social class, racial, and ethnic backgrounds of the families and communities. The impact of the child's personality is a critical factor that is often forgotten. Nor can it be assumed that the children of nonworking mothers will by default experience diminished self-esteem. It is easy to overlook the fact that many mothers enjoy their work at home. "When work is a source of personal satisfaction for the mother, her role as mother is positively affected." [54] Whatever a woman's tasks may be—homemaker-mother, working mother, teacher; married, divorced, or single—she may enjoy her work, and to the extent that she experiences maximum fulfillment and minimum strain, there will be positive outcomes.

Good Fences Make Good Neighbors: Conflict and Collaboration

The pressures of the times for women to be active and achieving, the attenuated functions of mothers whose children are in school or beyond schooling, and the diminished demands of housekeeping are all making it difficult for "nonworking" women to feel comfortable and satisfied with their positions. Ironically, as the chores of housework and motherwork are eased, motherhood assumes burdens of different dimensions.

> As affluence has brought more technological help to the mother, it has provided less personal help to her so that the role of mother has become more difficult . . . it is hard today because of the psychological hazards involved.[55]

In addition:

> Our society makes no provision for . . . emancipation from the mother. And she, with no other engrossing role, clings to the one role that has so far validated her life. Permitted few involvements outside the home, she has made enormous investments in her children. She needs them far more than they need her.[56]

Not only do mothers at home today often experience the psychological threats of a reduced functional role, but they also can no longer depend on their "natural" inclinations and well-socialized patterns of parenting. As the household chores are more expediently done by machines, their emotional, affective role has taken greater prominence—a focus and passion that tends to increase their competition and hostility toward teachers. In an interview I had with a wise and experienced teacher, she spoke of the dangerous repercussions of maternal feelings of loss and isolation on the child's adaptation to the school setting and on the mother's relationship to teachers. Her insightful comments are paraphrased below.

> **Mothers seem to be in subtle competition with teachers. There is always an underlying fear that teachers will do a better job than they have done with their child. They also are somewhat ambivalent about relinquishing control. But mostly mothers feel that their areas of competence are very much similar to those of the teacher. In fact they feel they know their child better than anyone else and that the teacher doesn't possess any special field of authority and expertise. Especially now when mothering is *learned* through books, when educated mothers are reading books about child care, child development, "good" parenting; mothers often feel that their *knowing* and understanding of socialization and development are not primitive and simplistic, not only shaped by intuition and emotion but also reinforced and confirmed by experts in psychology and education. The combined wisdom of their own deep experience with the child and their knowledge of the contemporary child-rearing literature makes them feel (at one level) as if they have a unique and special perspective. On the other hand, the discrepancies between the realities of their daily lives with children and the "experts'" words of advice and warning make them feel great ambivalence about their competence as mothers. The more they know about the potential psychoemotional and intellectual dangers of child rearing, the more inadequate and fearful they feel about their mothering and their child's healthy development. Part of the mothers' difficulty in relating to teachers may reflect the basic feelings of inadequacy and insecurity that they are feeling as mothers. Their self-doubt gets projected onto the teachers. Mothers' feelings of inadequacy are often intensified by the fact that child care may be their only arena of expression. If they fail in this area of socialization and nurturance of children, then they will experience total failure as useful and valuable people. So a great deal of their self-esteem and self-worth hangs on their child's successful transition from home to school and on his achievement and advancement through school. The teacher is a threatening figure because her evaluation of the child can enhance or negate the *mother's* self-image.***

* In the final section of this chapter, all of the narratives, paraphrases, and quotations of teachers' voices are taken from a pilot study entitled "Teacher-Mothers: Conceptions of the Dual Role" that I did under the auspices of the Radcliffe Institute, Harvard University, 1976–77. Narratives appear in boldface type throughout the text. Those quotations that are not taken from this pilot study are given specific reference.

The tremendous growth of Parent-Teacher Associations modestly begun in 1897 to "one of the largest organizations of women in the United States"[57] underscores the fact that schools have been one of the most acceptable forms of involvement for mothers outside the home. Schools are viewed as being legitimately within the mothers' sphere of influence and responsible parenting. Although fathers may be present at public, ritualistic school events, mothers tend to be responsible for the daily interactions with teachers.

> **The ritualistic and institutional structures of the school are not the essence of the parent-teacher-child relationship. For instance, one of the important symbolic exchanges that builds trust and communication between home and school occurs at arrival time each morning. The teacher takes the young child's hand out of the parent's hand, holds it up, and says, "Say good-bye to your mom." That gesture speaks many messages.**

The needs of parents for participation in the schooling process, however, are not always in the best interests of teachers and children. For teachers, the intense overinvolvement of mothers infringes on their sense of professional territoriality and is seen as an interference; and for children, their mothers' overprotectiveness can be a deterrent to autonomous development. The reactions of mothers who do not work outside of their homes and whose central investment is family are complex and often hidden. Deep feelings, moreover, may not be revealed by appearance or conversation. As one study of homemakers reports:

> Although these women present a seemingly self-fulfilled exterior, their replies on projective tests showed that they were actually experiencing considerable psychic turmoil, a depressed sense of emotional well-being, and low self-esteem. They do not feel attractive to men nor competent at anything, even child care and the social graces, let alone work and intellectual functioning. They feel somewhat lonely and isolated . . . uncertain and on the sidelines. Though their lives are working out as expected, they still feel an inexplicable sense of failure and disappointment, of having been left behind.[58]

The profound disappointments of their own empty existence are often translated into strained and burdensome relationships with "the other woman" in their child's life. The mothers that tend to cause the greatest turmoil for both teachers and children are those who express their sense of loss by overidentifying and living vicariously through their children. When the child leaves for school each morning, a piece of the mother goes with him, and it is extremely hard for the mother to "let go" and permit her child to have a separate, autonomous experience. One of the ways the mother might try to share in her child's world is to be continually probing the child for information about school and badgering the teachers about every detail of the child's functioning in school. In some sense, the mother's motives are very immature and self-centered. She wants to relive her own childhood (perhaps more happily and successfully the second time around), and every new encounter for her child inspires a memory of her own growing-up. One mother expressed her vicarious needs by dressing her child meticulously and preciously even when she knew her six-year-old daughter would be tussling with friends, romping in the park, and working with fingerpaints and clay. In a sense the mother looked at the little girl as a miniature version of herself and wanted her to project an adult, ladylike image. The central issue with these overidentified mothers seems to be one of separation from their child. It is difficult for them to disentangle their own motives and needs from those of the child; to see their child as a separate person. Their intrusive presence, their questions, their prodding, their nosiness makes even the most secure teacher feel as if she wants to deny them information; as if she wants to structure an environment for the child that will protect him from the burdensome presence of his parents and give herself some space to establish a new and different adult-child relationship.

Although it seems clear that this overidentification is problematic for teachers and dysfunctional to the development of autonomy in children, mothers who have a more balanced vision of their own independence and their child as a separate being also talk about the agonies of separation and the very authentic and uncomplicated feelings of knowing their child in a way that no other person can know him. We recognize this special kind of knowing in mothers who are also teachers—who speak of the deeper, more intense attachments they have with their own child and reveal how much more energy and passion are involved in parenting one than in teaching twenty-five.

One of the ways Teacher A separates home and school is by defining and experiencing parenting and teaching as very different kinds of relationships. She obviously gets great joy out of mothering her son, Jason, and finds that being with him requires a very different kind of energy and focus than teaching. "I find when I go home with Jason, a very calming kind of thing happens. He is mine, number one. The kids in my class are great, but they're not really mine." It is calming to be with just *one*, who you know so well and who you care about so deeply. But even with all the pleasure, parenting is harder because of the intensity of the relationship and because one expects and wishes for too much from one's child. Teacher A feels that some of this intensity is dispersed among the children in her classroom and that if she does not manage to communicate with a schoolchild, the ultimate weight and concern will rest with the parents, their primary sponsor. For Teacher A, parenting is more profoundly satisfying and more important than teaching, but it is also much harder and more demanding. She can stop teaching at 3:00 P.M., but her head is full of mothering all the time and she'll be a mother for the rest of her life.

Women who have become mothers after several years of teaching often recall how, with the experience of parenting, their visions of teaching were substantially transformed and how their conception of the parents' place in education has changed. These teacher-mothers find it relatively easy to relate to the mothers of children in their classroom who are also teachers. The dual role filled by these mothers makes them more knowledgeable about what goes on in school and also makes them more aware of those things that would be useful for the teacher to know. In general these parents seem less self-conscious and defensive about admitting to the teacher the problems that they might be experiencing at home with their child because they recognize that the information might help to enlighten the teacher about the child's world beyond school. They also know enough about universal patterns of child development so that their child's problems seem less threatening and unique. Mothers who are also teachers not only tend to offer more in-depth, holistic information about their child but they also seem to value the teachers' needs for autonomy and control within the school environment. As teachers they recognize their own needs for distance from parents, and they want to give their child's teachers the same sort of space. Finally, with this parent group, communication is easier because much can go unsaid. In some sense, they seem to share similar perspectives on the definitions of home and school boundaries, and that permits negotiations to be far less wordy and detailed and far more fluid and natural.

Even more striking are shifts that parenting brings in the teacher-mother's perspective on child growth and on her conceptions of learning and achievement in school.

> No longer is Teacher B as oriented toward children achieving goals and following a structured pattern of growth as she was during her first few years of teaching. Neither does she believe that teachers can "teach" intellectual skills to children by hammering out directions and offering consistent encouragement. Now Teacher B sees learning and development as a much more individualistic, fluid process. Children learn to read when they are ready to focus on the task and when the various social, psychological, and intellectual dimensions fall into place for them. Teachers and parents can provide a comfortable and rewarding environment and consistent structured attention, but the *internal*, idiosyncratic mechanisms of each individual child must find resolution with the task. When Adam, a very immature, high-strung little boy, was learning to read, he found himself a cardboard box and would sit in it every day in the classroom as he struggled with his letters and words. Somehow he knew that he needed to escape the distractions of classroom life, and he found some measure of solitude, which allowed him to focus within the physical constraints of the box. Whenever Roosevelt tried to read he had to be sitting next to Teacher B. Sometimes he would literally hang on to her as he worked at sounding out his letters. Teacher B's close physical presence was a solid anchor for Roosevelt and provided him with the comfort and support he needed to venture into the unknown and threatening territories of

reading. Both Roosevelt and Adam sought their own solutions and struggled for their own way of learning.

Interestingly enough, Teacher B's visions of children as critically involved in defining their own learning relieves some of the pressure within both teachers and parents to *produce* results in children. At best, caring adults can provide the environments for learning and present the child with an array of intellectual tools and strategies, but the integration must take place *within* the child in his own time. Teacher B has found that this message, when presented to the anxious parents of first graders, diminishes some of the pressure that parents put on teachers for immediate results and relieves some of the tensions experienced by the child, who needs space and time to find his own momentum and style of learning.

The easier, more fluid communications between teacher-mothers, the more generous visions they have of each other's special role, seem to underscore the great importance of clarity, understanding, and negotiation as elements of constructive relationships. The teacher-mother relationship is made easier because each woman shares a greater knowledge and understanding of their collaborative adult role in the socialization and education of the child and of the *child's* role in his own development. There is little mystery that shrouds either parenting or teaching; there is a profound recognition of the complexities of both roles; and there is a sense of relief that one has a partner and ally. For the most part, these teacher-mothers don't experience exclusion from the classrooms of their own child, but an easing of an all-too-heavy burden. We would expect that other mothers who have fulfilling and satisfying lives (whether inside or outside the home) would also experience some relief and support when their children form strong alliances with teachers and peers in school.

The mutual respect that mothers and teachers can grow to feel for each other's sphere of work is related to clarifying the boundaries of one's tasks and one's involvements and keeping the *child's* education and development as a central focus of the adult relationships. Even when mothers and teachers are knowledgeable and understanding of each other's special competencies and responsibilities, one would anticipate (and even welcome) differences and conflicts in their values, attitudes, goals, and styles. These differences become deeply embedded antagonisms if they are left neglected and unheard or repressed under a superficial veneer of good will. If they are recognized, articulated, and negotiated, then there is hope for resolution.

One of the great struggles between mothers and teachers in American society lies in their inability to recognize their *own* needs and to face the risks and dangers of open confrontation. Women who have been socialized to accept and internalize the "subordinate" role deny the full power of their individuality and unique character and project their needs onto their husbands and children. In *Toward a New Psychology of Women,* Jean Baker Miller describes the profound limitations of the subordinate role.

> A subordinate group has to concentrate on basic survival. Accordingly, direct, honest reaction to destructive treatment is avoided. . . . Another important result is that subordinates often know more about the dominant than they know about themselves. If a larger part of your fate depends on accommodating to and pleasing the dominants, you concentrate on them. Indeed there is little purpose in knowing yourself. Why should you when your knowledge of dominants determines your life? This tendency is reinforced by many other restrictions. One can know oneself only through action and interaction. To the extent that their range of action and interaction is limited, subordinates will lack a realistic evaluation of their capacities and problems.[59]

Teacher C spoke of the subordinate role assumed by the upper-middle-class mothers of children in a private, progressive school. Women who were assertive and aggressive in their daily work lives, who were well-practiced in negotiating institutional structures, became bitter, inhibited, and withdrawn mother figures when they approached the school environment.

> **Their silence often obscures their great anger and conflict with the school and teachers. Some of their rage gets expressed in secret gossipy sessions in the school parking lot or gets focused on the unusual woman among them who tends to take an assertive role with the teachers and the headmaster. They admire this risk-taking woman**

who alone has thrust herself into a visible position (in fact, they want to use her to anonymously transmit their negative and complaining messages to the headmaster), but they are also threatened and turned off by her aggressive behavior—she is behaving in the masculine mode that they dare not reveal in themselves. Instead of confronting the institution, the female teachers, and the male headmaster with their concerns, their anger gets turned back on themselves or directed at the mother who dares to behave differently.

Because mothers often obscure their competition and anger and cover up silent rage in their relationship with teachers, fathers who have daily interactions with teachers are often viewed as unusually clear-spoken, single-minded, and aggressive.

Teacher D remembers one father who was the single parent of two young sons. He was a psychiatrist, a bachelor, and an adoptive parent. Teacher D recalls her feelings of threat and discomfort when he asked questions at the first parent meeting of the year. It was her first year of teaching and his questions felt hostile and confrontative. As she grew to know him better and feel more comfortable in the teacher role, Teacher D recognized that his style often appeared bold and his comments argumentative, but the substance of his questions was *informational.* In essence, he was asking the teacher to be an authority, a professional who could answer his questions. He wanted to know what she thought about the basic issues of child development and education; he wanted to probe her values and attitudes; but it also seemed as if he wanted help in coping with his role as parent; help in understanding and relating to his own child. His questions were authentic and legitimate, and once Teacher D became accustomed to his style and temperament, she found that his probing questions made her ask hard questions of herself. She was forced to reflect critically on her reasons for doing things in the classroom and she became more conscious of her intuitive actions with children. The father's intrusive presence became a welcome force for change and encouraged her to grow as a teacher.

Mothers and teachers, who are closely identified with and constricted by the narrow, traditional definitions of women in our society, have not yet realized the potential strength of their collaboration because they haven't adequately identified their own skills, resources, and needs. They have not been able to be in touch with their own identities or search out their own self-definitions, and that limits their authentic interaction with one another. Clarifying their individuality and potential is made even more difficult because of the structures and institutions that define their cultural purpose. For example, as social and economic institutions, schools have taken on a multiplicity of functions beyond the intellectual development of the child, and teachers embody that expansive and complex multiplicity. Schools are asked to do everything that society has allowed to deteriorate or left undone.

> What do schools do? 1) They educate children, preparing them for public thinking. 2) They hold children out of labor, warehouse them. 3) They provide day care. 4) They "Americanize," teach and embody the political values that hold America together. And 5) they grade children. . . . many of the problems with the education that schools deliver arise from frictions, notably conflicts between the educational and non-educational services offered by schools.[60]

The teacher, as the central figure in the schooling process, therefore, is asked to soften and ease the fundamental *institutional* conflicts. How can she begin to clarify and articulate an already unwieldy role that is shrouded in unrealistic and conflicting cultural imagery? The personal task of insubordination that women must openly confront is deeply embedded in the institutions and structures of our society. Individual redefinition of mothers and teachers must proceed in cyclical and interactional fashion with transformations of cultural values and imagery and the restructuring of social institutions. Through these structural and interpersonal processes, women will begin to see collaboration as emerging out of their own self-knowledge, strength, and open conflict.

3

The Voices of Two Teachers

Dyadic or Triadic Relationships

DOCUMENTING and analyzing the relationships between parents and teachers is critical to understanding the educational process that is experienced by children. Not only are parents and teachers both engaged in the processes of socialization and acculturation, but often they become the major protagonists in a play where the child plays a relatively minor and incidental role. The dynamic interactions seem to be less triadic (i.e., equally including the interests and concerns of teacher, parent, and child) and more dyadic (i.e., becoming the arena for parent-teacher dialogue). I do not mean to imply that the subject of the dialogue is not the child but that in the heads of the adult participants the focus of concern becomes the wishes, demands, values, and attitudes of the other adults. One sometimes wonders whether adults are arguing over the best interest of the child or whether, in some sense, they are hoping to protect their own societal status and image—that children become the projection of their needs to feel competent and successful as parents and teachers.

In discussions with teachers, it often becomes apparent that they relate to children as representatives or miniature versions of their parents' *perceived* status in society. When many teachers are asked to describe children, there is a tendency to talk relatively superficially about the child's character, style, and skills as an autonomous and knowable person and focus their description on the family background from which the child comes.

Part of the focus away from the child as a whole person (and a critical member of the school triangle) reflects the broad social and economic functions of schools in our society. Schools are considered transitory, preparatory environments where the child's *future* status becomes the overriding concern of his adult sponsors.[1] This preoccupation with anticipated potential rather than with the present realities of the child's life, therefore, is symbolic of a more general tendency in this rapidly moving, post-industrial society not to view children as functionally whole until they become productive members of the economic structure. Schools rationalize and reinforce the discontinuities between the contributors and the noncontributors in society, between the independent and the dependent, between the powerful and the weak. Adults, having passed through the transitional school environments, are considered the functional, useful producers, and children are perceived of as dependent consumers. These rationalized and accepted discontinuities between child and adult status are never so exaggerated as in American society where there is no valid and authentic role for the child to play in the highly technological work structure.[2] Teachers and parents seek to contrive tasks that resemble real work, but the perceptive child soon recognizes that the tasks bear no meaningful relationship to functional production.[3] In less complex societies, children are early given the responsibility of participating in the work force; their tasks are essential and meaningful to the community's life, and the work is geared to their physical and intellectual development—the complexities and responsibilities of the tasks becoming greater with the passage of years.

Beyond the structural and economic patterns of discontinuity between adult life and child life in this society, there is also a phenomenon that was recently labeled "childism"—a discriminatory response to children that contributes to their peripheral status in family-school interactions.* "Childism" ironically thrives in a society that often proudly proclaims itself to be child-centered. It is the tendency for adults not to take children seriously—to see them as toys to be played with, pets to be groomed, and innocent souls to be manipulated, rather than as sensitive beings with feelings, dreams, needs, and wishes that are every bit as "real" to them as our adult concerns are to us. Childism, therefore, justifies the child's noninclusion in serious dialogues between parents and teachers about decisions that directly shape and determine his life course.†

Even if one moves beyond the broad societal tendencies to exclude children from economic participation and serious personhood, there are general tendencies of teachers not to see individual children but to see them as members of prescribed sociological categories. Teachers, like all of us, use the dimensions of class, race, sex, ethnicity to bring order to their perceptions of the classroom environment. Initial categorization can be a social-psychological process that helps one be able to anticipate behavior and attitudes and act more efficiently and effectively. But these categories become dysfunctional and potentially dis-

* In *Escape from Childhood* (New York, New York: E. P. Dutton, 1974), John Holt claims that as children have become less economically advantageous to the middle class (in fact, have become a major economic and emotional burden), they have developed another use, as "love objects." People use children as love objects when they "think [they] have the right, or even a duty, to bestow on them 'love,' visible and tangible signs of affection whenever [they] want, however [they] want, and whether [the children] like it or not." (p. 105).

† This noninclusion of children is most striking when parents and teachers engage in conversations about the child in his presence. Their conversation concerns the child deeply but is carried on over the child's head, as if he did not have the ears to hear or the mind to comprehend.

torting if they are not continually contrasted with the realities of the child's observed behavior.* Rather than teachers gaining a more in-depth and holistic understanding of the child, with the passage of time teachers' perceptions become increasingly stereotyped and children become hardened caricatures of an initial discriminatory vision. For all of the above reasons (that encompass cultural, structural, attitudinal, and intrapersonal dimensions), teachers and parents can become the major participants who struggle to clarify the territory of the child's life over which they want some measure of control and determining power. The child becomes the perceived focus of struggle, but the interactions are primarily shaped by the needs of adults.

This chapter will look closely at two teachers whose relationships with parents closely parallel the dyadic and triadic models of interaction. Ms. Powell and Ms. Sarni are first-grade teachers in public elementary schools in the city of Evergreen. They have both taught for four years and view their relationships with parents as relatively comfortable and productive. But at the same time they describe their interactions with parents as *potentially* conflictual, highly charged, and overdetermined by forces beyond their immediate control. First grade is considered the critical period of family-school contact—when mothers are most distressed about releasing their child to the care of a distant person; when school is no longer a world of sand boxes and Playdoh but a place for learning to read and write; where parents fear the external judgments made about the quality of their parenting during the first five years of the child's life; and when the child experiences the inevitable trauma of moving from a relatively egocentric, nur-

* Part of the reason that teachers form rigid and unchanging stereotypic conceptions of children lies not only in the relative ease and comfort of simplifying and ordering their environment, but also is related to the fact that teachers (and parents) are rarely trained to *observe* children. In relating to children, they experience not only the interference of discriminatory visions but also a lack of observational tools for discerning differences in the special qualities and changing behavior of individual children.

turant home environment to the more evaluative, social experience of school.

This narrative will not be symmetric in its description of these two teachers. Rather, it is written to reflect the dominant perspectives and preoccupations of Ms. Powell and Ms. Sarni. Ms. Powell is primarily concerned with describing her experiences with parents as an integral part of establishing relationships with individual children; Ms. Sarni's descriptions focus on her perceptions and interactions with groups and categories of parents, often without mention of the child's place.*

Ms. Powell and the Families of Three Children

Ms. Powell is a black woman in her middle thirties who began teaching four years ago after a long and circuitous route into the profession. She is married with a four-year-old son, and her perceptions of family-school relations are often shaped by her dual (often conflicting) role as mother and teacher. Ms. Powell grew up as the youngest child in an ambitious and loving West Indian family with several siblings. Her father was a carpenter, her mother a seamstress who struggled to make ends meet. She vividly recalls a house filled with warmth and caring, the wonderful smell of West Indian cooking, and the magic of making a little into a lot. Ms. Powell chose to teach in the Tubman School because she valued the mixture of children from various social

* In this chapter, the quotations of Ms. Powell and Ms. Sarni are extracted from several in-depth interviews that I did of two of the teachers who participated in a year-long research project on life in classrooms. The sketches of three children are based on my observations of their interactions with their teacher and peers in the classroom. The study, "First Grade: A Multi-Faceted View of Teachers and Children" (co-principal investigator, Dr. Jean V. Carew), was sponsored by the Office of Child Development and completed in 1977.

class, racial, and ethnic backgrounds. She strongly believes that school should be a place where children move beyond the narrow boundaries of their families and learn to productively relate to children from a variety of backgrounds.

Although the Tubman School is rich with variation in the student population, Ms. Powell is one of only two black teachers in the school, and she experiences the extreme pressures and distortions of her token status. On the one hand, she feels as if her professional skills and views are not taken seriously by her colleagues because she is black, and on the other hand, she is called on to be the great counselor and resource on all issues related to black folks. Her relationships with parents are also shaped by their perceptions of her blackness, and it is often difficult for Ms. Powell to unravel and understand the nature of their hostility (or the origins of their friendship) toward her. Is it a response to her blackness, to her professional status, or to her individual behavior and attitudes toward them? Much of her energy is consumed in trying to decipher the motivations of parents and in seeking to establish a relationship that is not distorted by their stereotypic views of her.

Ms. Powell's perspective on the role of parents and children in the schooling process is a relatively uncommon one. For the most part, she views her interactions with parents as secondary dialogues—relationships that can enhance or inhibit productive interactions with the child. Ms. Powell chooses to focus on the child's *present individuality,* with minimal reference to his future status in the adult world or the family circumstances from which the child comes. Most unusually, she is able to talk with great sensitivity and depth about an individual child's character *within* the classroom. She does not constantly refer to the child's background or origin unless she is asked to move beyond the boundaries of school life (and even then she is likely to recognize the changes in behavior and transformation of character that may occur when the child shifts environments).

The following portraits will seek to uncover the dynamic patterns of communication (or noncommunication) between Ms. Powell and the mothers of Karen, Steven, and Luther, with whom she has established very different relationships. The three profiles reflect the subtleties and complexities of the *teacher's* role in establishing and maintaining a balance between her own needs for autonomy and control and her recognition of the parents' needs for information and involvement. One must keep in mind in reading this piece that the story is being told by the teacher. She tells an unusually balanced and perceptive story, I think, but nevertheless, her perspective reflects *her* visions, her biases, and her values, and can never represent the reciprocal duality of parent *and* teacher. Most important, her observations reveal a teacher whose primary focus is *children,* who strives to build collaborative relationships with parents in order to support the development of children, and who deeply believes that her professional wisdom should be incorporated into the parents' visions of the child. In other words, Ms. Powell clearly supports a parent-teacher-child triangle rather than a dyadic interaction between parents and teachers that effectively excludes the child. In fact, the triangle she seeks to shape has a much stronger line going back and forth from teacher to child and a somewhat weaker and secondary connection between parent and teacher.

Karen's Family: Distance, Distrust, and Conflict

Karen is an aggressive and competitive little girl whose parents are academic types from a Germanic background. She came to the first grade with an enormous vocabulary, advanced cognitive skills, and a superior reading level. In reading and writing exercises she excells and gets pleasure from showing her superiority over the children in her class. It is not only important to Karen that she be good in her work; she wants to know that she is the best in the class and is constantly seeking the teacher's assurance and reinforcement. Although her academic work is far above the first-grade norm, Karen has great difficulty relating positively to her peers. Her social skills are unsophisticated and unpracticed, as if she has rarely had to fend for

herself without the direct intervention and supervision of an adult. With peers, therefore, she does not know how to share, to cooperate, to negotiate, to tolerate teasing—not even to have fun. Her relationships always seem to have a competitive edge. Her posture is always one of superiority and intolerance, and the only sustained alliance seems to be with the teacher. She often assumes the role of teacher surrogate, taking down the names of "naughty" children when the teacher is out of the room and delivering them up for punishment when the teacher returns. (Often her name is the only one not mentioned on the list of troublemakers). When Ms. Powell quietly ignores her tattling, Karen is chagrined and feels unappreciated. She prods and pleads with Ms. Powell to act like a teacher and punish the bad kids, and becomes increasingly isolated and withdrawn from the world of children in the classroom.

Karen Rosen's mother is an aggressive, prominent figure in the school. She is highly educated, meticulously cultured in the Western European tradition, and places the greatest value on the intellectual development of her children. She views her two children as unusually gifted and wants them to move through the early years of school at high speed. Because of her prodding and insistence, Karen's older sister was skipped from the first to the third grade, and she is approaching Karen's first year in school with the same resolve for her rapid acceleration.

Ms. Rosen's relationship with Ms. Powell could be characterized as tense and politely antagonistic. Their conflicts primarily emerge from basic differences in their perspectives on education and schooling. Karen's mother, for instance, strongly believes that the primary agenda of schooling should be academic and that social development is of secondary or negligible importance. Ms. Powell is less preoccupied with intellectual competence and works toward the balanced development of social and intellectual skills—each aspect of learning being essential to the other. As a matter of fact, she feels that the *initial* focus of first grade must be the socialization of children to the norms and responsibilities of group life.

Social development is critical. . . . At the beginning of the year we had open house and I talked with a lot of parents about that. A

> large part of the beginning of the year would be devoted to social kinds of development. Because if the child can socially see where he is then he can function; otherwise he's in trouble. Even if a child comes in reading, if somebody doesn't like him, he is crushed.

Ms. Powell is, therefore, annoyed by Ms. Rosen's continuous attempts to push Karen farther and faster through school and feels that the intense pressure exerted on Karen at home to excel in school is an unfair and inappropriate parental demand that turns Karen off from the educational process. Ms. Rosen undoubtedly views Ms. Powell as purposefully and willfully obstructing the academic path of her daughter and compromising her swift advancement through school.

In an attempt not to duplicate or reinforce the academic pressures Karen is receiving at home, Ms. Powell is concerned about supporting her development in other areas. For example, Karen is perceived by her teacher as socially "unsophisticated" (i.e., lacking in the basic social graces and unable to interact and collaborate with her peers) and very inexperienced in dealing with children who do not come from the same "precious" and protected family background.

> In school, Karen is able to deal with only one class of children—the kind of children that she has been around. She is from a professional background. She went to a very special private preschool so that she came in contact with a certain kind of child, and in this classroom we have a variety of children, some very aggressive, some very mild, meek-mannered children.

Her critique of Karen's inadequacies reveals that Ms. Powell is not only concerned with socializing children to be responsible and caring members of a group but also with the development of a culturally pluralistic perspective in children. In the same voice, she will combine the message of primary socialization (i.e., learning to function productively in a social group) and the message of social and cultural consciousness. But Ms. Rosen does not mingle the messages of schooling. She clearly separates the social and intellectual spheres; she devalues socialization as an educational agenda; and she is not concerned with pluralism or integration as deliberate pedagogical goals. Her preoccupation is with her child's high status and with an academic performance that will mark her child as being better than the others.

These two points of view do not necessarily represent the opposing ideologies of democratic and hierarchical world views —the teacher being the more humanitarian and egalitarian and the mother being more concerned with status and superiority over others (although Ms. Rosen is described by Ms. Powell as being of authoritarian, Germanic origins with a controlling and pushy personality); but they also reflect the different social and cultural roles of mothers and teachers. In chapter one we spoke of the contrasts between the "universal relationships" of teachers and children that stress fairness, order, rationality, and detachment and the "particularistic relationships" of parents and children that are shaped by intense and deep involvement and specialized favors. In other words, the conflict between Karen's mother and Ms. Powell is not merely an interpersonal entanglement or a struggle over educational philosophy and ideals, but it is also (perhaps primarily) a tendency for mothers to seek special favors for their child and to view the child's unique and individual needs as the primary concern, as well as a tendency on the part of teachers to want to give generalized, integrative attention that is adaptive to some universal rules of social interaction. Ms. Rosen wants her daughter to be best and to be ultimately successful in the world beyond school, while Ms. Powell wants Karen to melt into the life of the social group and become less demanding of specialized attention.

Ms. Powell recognizes the different orientations of parents and teachers and strongly suggests that parents become educated in the universal, integrative point of view. She claims that some parents' concerns about the special needs of their child are not only unrealistic and inappropriate demands on a teacher, but they are also detrimental to the child's successful entry into the life of the classroom. Parents, therefore, should begin to see their child as one of many, appreciate the multiple tasks of the teacher, and recognize the wide range of children she must cope with every day.

> Children come in with all kinds of social problems at six and I think the school is the best place to see it. . . . It's so pronounced. Children come in nervous, on all kinds of pills, aggressive, terribly frightened, and I think we could meet with parents more often and *tell* them about the kinds of insecurities, or discuss, not tell. . . . Then parents would begin to see the *whole* picture. . . . I think it would get the parents into seeing what their child is all about and realizing that their child is not the only child in the classroom and that if their child has this kind of thing that he has to deal with and the next child has that plus something else . . .

From Ms. Powell's perspective, if parents became more identified with the universal point of view, they would not only become more realistic in their demands on the teacher, but also they would learn something more about their own child (things that they are not able to observe in the home environment) and eventually begin to interact with him in a way that recognizes the various dimensions of the child's life. Ms. Powell's analysis offers a very interesting and uncommon twist. Parents usually urge teachers to look at the *whole* child in all of his complexities and relate to the child in a way that is responsive to all of the various dimensions of social, psychological, and intellectual development. Here we have a teacher who is asking *parents* to be more holistic, to recognize the differences created by the shifts in social context from home to school. Clearly Ms. Powell views parents as somewhat naive about classroom life and unsophisticated about the incredible range of personalities, abilities, and events that go on there. She is slightly condescending (though she corrects herself) when she suggests that parents be *told*; that parents are learners who should be taught about a child they have known for much longer and with much greater depth and intensity than any teacher could know him. Ms. Powell's tendency toward condescension does not, however, invalidate her view that parents will gain another perspective on their child's development by watching him function in the classroom environment.

Ms. Powell's discussion of the role of parents does reveal some contradictions and ambiguities in her perspective. The basic ambivalence seems to revolve around the nature and form of parental presence. She strongly believes, for instance, that the parents' role should be one of *preparing* their child for school life but not participating in the process of schooling.

> I feel that parents should be more involved with their own children as opposed to being involved in school. . . . If parents deal with their children, we will be able to teach them the kind of academic things that they need to know. If parents deal with their children and get to know them, that is the best kind of role they can play. . . . If there is a relationship between the parent and child *at home,* then we can teach them in school.

These words express the traditional view of territoriality between home and school. Ms. Powell's words urge parents to do a better and more thorough job of *parenting,* which would then prepare the child for productive work in school. But almost in the same breath, she speaks of the value of parents taking on active (though secondary) roles in the classroom.

> Often when a parent comes into the classroom and works, it is amazing the kind of thing that happens to the child. . . . They [the children] seem to zoom up and feel better about themselves because their parents are working in the classroom doing something.

Although Ms. Powell shows some ambivalence about parental presence and participation in school life, she makes a firm and clear distinction between parenting and teaching. Even when she recognizes the value of parents expressing their interest and concern by working in the classroom, she views them as entering her territory and expects them to assume a supportive and secondary role. Parents are there to be sources of inspiration and additional adult resources for children; however, their presence should not substantially transform the classroom environment or redefine the established interactional patterns.

It is not uncommon that teachers must respond to a split between the views and perspectives held by the father and mother of a child. Parents do not always present a unified view, and teachers are faced with trying to respond to basic familial conflicts over child rearing and educational philosophies. As a matter of fact, the parent-teacher conference may provide the setting for parents to publicly express the frustrations and conflicts that they have been hesitant to declare privately to each other. In this case, parents view the teacher as a negotiator and counselor, and their public disclosure of differences feels safer than the potential dangers of private confrontations. The divisions within the family are often disconcerting and confusing to the teacher, who feels some responsibility for responding fairly and evenly to the parents' divergent values and perceptions.

On the other hand, a nonharmonious parental perspective may provide the teacher with some leverage and may help her feel less overwhelmed by parental demands. She does not have to feel outnumbered and overpowered by their collective accord. For instance, when Ms. Powell relates to Karen's parents, she is somewhat relieved that the mother and father do not share the same perceptions of their daughter's abilities and struggles and that the quiet, somewhat submissive father is secretly in alliance with her. Even though the mother's voice dominates the parent conferences, Ms. Powell is comforted by her silent bond with the father.

> When the mother left the interview, left the room, then I got some interesting things from the father. . . . The father led me to believe that he saw some insecurities in Karen. . . . He described how she can get into moods if things aren't done her way. He just said he would try to deal with it at home because he could see Karen in two different lights.

After a certain point, Ms. Powell is unwilling to pursue the resolution of differences and conflicts with parents. She is willing to discuss and weigh their various perceptions of the child and offer her recommendations for the appropriate academic agenda, but if parents remain stuck in their own point of view or unwilling to even consider her perspective, Ms. Powell resorts to institutional solutions and bureaucratic remedies. Ms. Powell's relationship with Ms. Rosen reached this point of no return, beyond which they both seemed incapable of hearing each other's words or modifying their conflicting perspectives. She approached the principal to negotiate the differences and to make a final decision about the appropriate course of action for Karen and was frustrated and discouraged by the principal's response.

Ms. Powell strongly believes that principals should serve a listening and negotiating function with the parents and community, but that ultimately they should present a unified front that assures the protection of the teacher. She views her principal as a weak and ineffectual bureaucrat who makes expedient decisions that reflect his sense of threat. For example, he will usually respond to the demands of parents whom he considers powerful and influential (i.e., upper-middle-class professional types) or parents whom he considers irrational and capable of violence (i.e., lower-class, assertive black parents). He responds out of fear rather than on the basis of some rational plan or deliberate ideology. The whole middle range of parents (who are perceived as neither frightening and outspoken nor lofty and articulate) are usually considered relatively safe and inactive, and therefore not worthy of the principal's alliance. Ms. Powell anticipates that Karen's parents, who exude culture and professionalism, will get an immediate affirmative response from the principal—one that will make her feel exposed, unappreciated, and unprotected.

Steven's Family: Discovery of Shared Values and Perspectives on Education

Steven went to an unstructured, nontraditional kindergarten that encouraged self-expression and free movement. When he arrived at first

grade he had had minimal experience with cognitive materials and did not view school as a place to work. Initially, he responded very negatively to the structured life of school and found it impossible to stop his wanderings through space and stay in one place long enough to focus on a task. Every day, Steven would cry about something. He would break into tears when he became frustrated with writing in his workbook or when he would pick a fight with one of his classmates, and then weep helplessly when the other child began to retaliate. Often he would appear to be the victim rather than the aggressor—his round cherubic face, large blue eyes, and mop of blond hair gave him a deceptively angelic quality. Although he struggled with his peers often, he wasn't unpopular with them. They seemed to enjoy his energy, his imagination, and his daringness. He seemed more willing to test the limits of the rules and to tempt the fates than they, even if he would often end up in a puddle of childish tears. Both his mother and his teacher worked together to change his patterns of behavior in the classroom and to help him become more disciplined in his focus on schoolwork. His mother, who was experiencing the guilts and burdens of being a single parent, had wanted not to destroy Steven's spontaneous energies and aggressive male behavior by being overprotective. At home, she found it difficult to draw the boundaries between self-expression and autonomy on the one hand and wild, chaotic behavior on the other; and she looked to the school to help her establish the boundaries and exert some firm control.

The story of Karen is one of conflict and distrust between family and school; a conflict that reflects profound differences in the values attached to education, inevitable tensions in the social and cultural roles mothers and teachers assume in this society, opposing perceptions of Karen's strengths and weaknesses, and clashes in the personalities and style of the adult participants. Although Steven Gordon arrived at school far less skilled and disciplined than Karen, Ms. Powell sees greater potential for change and development in his social and intellectual abilities because of a consensus of values and goals between home and school. According to Ms. Powell, there is the most potential for a child's smooth development in school when the parents and teacher share a consonant set of values. This is not to say that there should be absolute harmony on how the child is perceived or on the particular curricular adaptations that are necessary for the child's optimal growth, but rather that parents and teachers should feel a consensus about the basic value and function of early schooling—a collective view that supports a productive communication and exchange among the participating adults.

Ms. Powell's relationship with Steven Gordon's mother was not always productive and affirmative. When Steven first arrived at school in September, he was unable to sit still for a moment, tolerate any degree of structure and discipline, or interact happily with his peers. Ms. Powell traced his struggles to his "disadvantaged" status as a single child in a single-parent family who had gone to an overly permissive and structureless preschool and kindergarten before entering first grade.

> In the school he went to last year . . . he did pretty much what he wanted to do and if he didn't want to do it, that was okay. . . . It was difficult for him to just understand that he wasn't the only one in the classroom. I'm sure that's somewhat reinforced at home, being an only child, you know everything is yours, everything that comes into the house is for you, mother is for you . . .

Ms. Gordon privately worried about her son's immaturity and asocial behavior but also enjoyed his energy, exuberance, and spirit. She seemed to have difficulty perceiving and defining the boundaries of appropriate and inappropriate behavior for a six-year-old. Filled with ambivalence and uncertainty, Ms. Gordon challenged Ms. Powell's perceptions of her son's intellectual abilities and social skills. Defensively, she claimed that at home Steven read beautifully, while at school he could not comprehend even the simplest words or form legible letters in printing his name. Why did he thrive under his mother's nurturant attention while at school he fell apart and became a discipline problem? Ms. Gordon's only recourse was to dispute the teacher's perceptions of Steven or to blame her for creating an inappropriate and uncomfortable classroom environment for her child. In the beginning of the year, the tensions and disagreements between Ms. Gordon and Ms. Powell erupted often and were waged openly. Over several weeks, Ms. Gordon's defensiveness and pride seemed to fade as she began to expose her insecurities and feelings of anger about her lonely task of raising Steven alone. Perhaps Steven performed at home because he received abundant individual attention without the constant distractions of playful and competitive peers. School was a different place—a setting that was less tolerant of individual indulgence and more demanding of social cohesion, structure, and order.

Ms. Gordon's initial accusations and frustrated demands reflected her wish that Steven be seen as special by his teacher, even that Ms. Powell should see him through a mother's eyes. At the same time, however, Ms. Gordon recognized how important it was that her child not be left alone or excluded from the classroom group. Without siblings at home and locked into an overly intense relationship with his mother, this was his only chance to move off in an autonomous and independent direction. Ms. Powell seemed to recognize that part of Steven's problem adjusting to classroom life was related to the push-pulls within his mother. Steven would not accommodate to school demands until his mother let him become a separate and independent person. Ms. Gordon's narrow view of Steven as unique and deserving of the special favors of hovering adults would have to shift toward a more realistic and objective view of a boy who is bright and able but also dependent and spoiled. The evolution of Ms. Gordon's more objective views of Steven and her more realistic perceptions of school life seemed partly related to Ms. Powell's firm and aggressive attempts to change her perspective, but also related to winning her own battles of separation from her son. Once this was painfully accomplished, mother and teacher discovered that they shared many values and beliefs about education and child development; that they both wanted first grade to be primarily a place for learning social skills and secondarily a place for cognitive growth; that they both believed in helping children learn how "to be in touch with their feelings" and articulate their fears, anger, and joy; and that they strongly believed that young children from a variety of social class, racial, and ethnic backgrounds should learn to relate to each other within the context of classrooms. Their newly discovered alliances inspired Ms. Powell to speak of Ms. Gordon as an unusually understanding and realistic mother who valued continuity and balance between home and school.

> I think Steven's mother is very interested and concerned about his progress, *but in a very fair way*. She is really more concerned about whether he is comfortable in the classroom than if he is doing the very best in the class. She is concerned about him being comfortable with what he is doing, being comfortable with his peers and how he sees himself. According to his mother, if he isn't enjoying what he is doing, it affects not only what happens here but it also affects him at home because he sulks, he gets moody, and she deals with it by trying to find out about the situation.

Ms. Gordon's ability to permit independence in her son not only allowed for productive collaboration with Ms. Powell, but also seemed to release Steven to establish positive relationships with his friends in school. When Steven secretly spoke to his teacher about his mother "not being around as much," Ms. Powell also noticed a clear improvement in his interactions with other children and in their response to him. This new-found social confidence and reinforcement supported his academic progress.

> Now it seems that, even though it is a one-parent family, it is a pretty fair kind of relationship that is going on between them. . . . It is interesting that since he made some comments about not seeing his mother all the time, there has been improvement. . . . He has been able to get along with the other kids. Then, he has discovered that kids really like him. . . . So he is getting along better out there and I guess he is feeling himself that he is getting along better, which makes it in fact so. And, you know, I see that he is doing pretty good. His work has improved and he is reading.

Before her son's birth, Ms. Gordon had been a teacher herself, but with six years of parenting, she had become totally identified with the motherly perspective. Through frequent and often difficult interactions with Ms. Powell, Ms. Gordon was able to move beyond her primary role as mother and rediscover the teacher within her—move beyond the subjectivity and overprotectiveness to a more objective, distant relationship that encompassed love as well as firm judgments and boundaries. It is not only that Steven's mother was changed by her interactions with Ms. Powell. The encounters with Ms. Gordon also influenced Ms. Powell's visions of Steven and shifted her general expectations of the children in her classroom. Through conversations with Ms. Gordon, Ms. Powell began to empathize with her maternal, nurturant views, and see Steven in a new light. He was not merely a troublemaker, a cry baby, and a spoiled child. He was, in fact, spontaneous and alive, and he should be given some space in the classroom to express that part of his nature.

> There are times when he just has to get up and run and play, scream. You know, anything. Sing out. And I really think he should be allowed to do this. But in a classroom, it's kind of difficult. In the structure of our classroom, there's not much room for that. And I think he does need that little time, that extra room to do those kinds of things.

In fact, it was in her recognition that Steven was bright and able and determined to learn to read, and yet still had trouble accommodating to the classroom structure, that Ms. Powell was challenged to reevaluate her educational strategies and goals for *all* of the children in her classroom.

> I'm beginning to think that first grade should be more socialization than academics. . . . Maybe we shouldn't expect them to do the kinds of things that we expect them to do. It may be good for some, but the majority of them seem to have trouble relating to each other, getting along with each other, and just solving problems amongst themselves. We can sit down and talk about what causes a fight, what makes you angry and how can you deal with it other than striking out. . . . This has to be done over and over again—through discussions and role-playing—before we can expect them to sit down and read.

The constructive alliance that grew between Ms. Gordon and Ms. Powell, therefore, was a hard fought, mutual process—one that demanded the generosity, empathy, and openness of both adults.

Steven's narrative reflects the shifting perspectives of both mother and teacher—the teacher's increasing sensitivity to Steven's special needs and unique character, and the mother's increasing objectivity about Steven's weaknesses and strengths. The open conflict and continuous dialogue between Ms. Powell and Ms. Gordon helped them articulate their differences and build alliances, but their evolving relationship also influenced Steven's psychological liberation and maturation and allowed him to master reading by the end of the school year.

Luther's Family: Empathy and Outrage

Luther is an energetic, passionate child who is the proclaimed class leader. He is from a lower-class black family of several siblings that his young mother raises alone. Last year there was a great tragedy in his family. One of Luther's older brothers stole a car and was chased by police, who spotted him driving wildly through town. His car smashed fiercely into the side of a building and he was killed instantly. Luther is said to be the replica of his older brother in body and spirit. His mother, in her grief, confuses their names and fears that Luther will have the same fate. The abandon and daring with which Luther pursues life seems to hold the promise of self-destruction. He has been so thoroughly identified with his dead brother that he has great fears of death and attraction for it. His role of class leader seems to be related to his good looks (everyone always comments on his cuteness), his style, and his intimate knowledge of worldly-wise things. He is a survivor, older than his years in being able to negotiate the dangers of poor life in the city. His style with his classmates is aggressive, bossy, but surprisingly fair and even-handed. He is in some sense a benevolent leader, and he is valued and admired by his peers. In the morning everyone awaits his arrival. He is every girl's boyfriend and every boy's hero—a source of fear, admiration, and respect. But deep down he is aware of his weaknesses and limitations. He knows he can't read and hates to reveal that to himself, his teacher, and his peers. So he tends to withdraw from academic tasks before he gives himself a chance; he's very impatient with correction and criticism; and he struggles to escape back into the social sphere where he is king.

Luther Jones is the youngest of six children. He is primarily the responsibility of his sixteen-year-old sister, who grows tired of the burdensome care of her little brother and often treats him abusively. Ms. Jones, an attractive young woman, is separated from Luther's father and is often absent from home for several days, leaving the children to fend for themselves. During the parent-teacher conferences, Ms. Jones hardly mentions her son. She tells Ms. Powell of her attempts to "better herself." She has dreams of becoming a meter maid, with a neat uniform, regular hours and salary, and a measure of status and power over others. Right now she augments her welfare checks by driving a cab but finds the work demeaning and grueling. Her dreams seem understandable to Ms. Powell, who recognizes her feelings of deprivation, her wishes for self-respect and personal reward, as well as her need to find work that will adequately provide for her family. But Ms. Powell also sees in Luther's mother a wish to be free of her children and a general neglect of their daily needs. Part of Ms. Jones's desire to run away from the responsibilities of child care may be related to the trauma of her eldest son's death. Perhaps she cannot bear the pain of loving children whose lives might also end in self-inflicted casualties. She seems to search for her dead son's reappearance in Luther, whom she both loves and despises because his nature seems to replicate his brother's . . . and she fears Luther's death.

Ms. Powell speaks about Luther's family life with a great deal of knowledge and empathy. Luther is a boy who intrigues and interests her. She is compelled by his unusual blend of strength and weakness, assertiveness and withdrawal. She also responds, as others do, to his handsome and charming physical presence. But mostly, Ms. Powell perceives that Luther has great *potential* —a potential that will die if she doesn't make a critical intervention. She feels a deep responsibility for this child. Ms. Powell's attitude toward his mother, therefore, is shaped by her unusual (almost motherly) commitment to Luther. On the one hand, she feels a deep concern and empathy for Ms. Jones because she is aware of the oppressive realities that surround this woman's tortured life. On the other hand, she feels distrust and condemnation because she believes that Ms. Jones is not acting responsibly in relation to her children and that her neglect and abuse of them are severe barriers to Luther's development.

> Luther's mother told us that she doesn't have to get up with the kids when they go to school; that they all get up and Luther's brother, who is in the second grade, makes breakfast. . . . And when he comes in his hair is a mess, he is not washed, his pants are two sizes too big and have to be held up with a belt. . . . With all his deficiencies, he's a nice little guy. And I think in another kind of home situation, he would really be a super little guy. . . . He cries, he screams out loud for attention and some kind of warmth and physical touching.

The two times that Ms. Powell has managed to get Ms. Jones to come to school for parent-teacher conferences she has been saddened by Luther's pathetic attempts to gain his mother's approval. As he offers her handmade gifts and proudly displays his schoolwork, his mother tells the teacher that Luther is a born loser headed for trouble. In these situations, Ms. Powell attempts to get Ms. Jones to recognize the damage of constantly bombarding Luther with negative assaults and demeaning self-images. She talks about the value of positive reinforcement and praise and suggests that Ms. Jones should search for the good traits in Luther rather than focusing on his negative characteristics.

> I tried to express to her to think about the positive side of Luther, and that maybe if we just reward him when he is positive we might be able to get him to work with the negatives.

But Ms. Powell's words fall on deaf ears, and even as she says them she recognizes the absurdity of it all. Ms. Jones views her interactions with Ms. Powell as a rare opportunity for self-expression; a time to tell someone in a position of relative power and influence about the harsh realities of her life and her dreams for the future.

> Ms. Jones is busy just trying to survive. . . . I'm sure the responsibility of six kids, having lost one in a terrifying kind of experience, is an awful lot to cope with. . . . The amount of coping and caring

> she gives her children is probably very little simply because she is dealing with herself . . . just feeling that she wants to do her own thing. In my meetings with her this came through very forcibly. There were a lot of things she wanted to do, and she was meeting with all sorts of frustrations.

As a listener, Ms. Powell feels uneasy and ambivalent. She is empathetic and caring, but also impatient and accusing of the mother's immaturity and selfishness. The intensity of Ms. Powell's response is enhanced by her deep commitment to this child, her secret wish to take him over and protect him from further abuse. Mother and teacher never really talk about the value of schooling or the nature of the curriculum, because they are both focused on the issues of survival—the mother is struggling for her own survival and Ms. Powell is trying to protect the survival of Luther. Ms. Powell knows that the answers for the survival of both mother and son lie far beyond the boundaries of the family and school spheres. "Something is terribly wrong" when the school must function as a "counseling agency or therapeutic service" for parents and when mothers are so depressed and deprived that their children come to school unkempt and unfed. Intellectually, Ms. Powell recognizes the impossibility of the tasks that both mother and teacher are being asked to accomplish by an uncaring society. Emotionally, however, she continues to search for resolution and remedies. She struggles to overcome the barriers to Luther's healthy development, and his mother often becomes the focus of her outrage.

With all three of these families, Ms. Powell expresses the wish for continuities between the socialization of children at home and at school. She recognizes that differences in the behaviors and attitudes of parents and teachers often reflect divergent and dissonant value systems and life styles. These basic value conflicts between mother and teacher are further elaborated by the personalities of the participants, the realities of their life circumstances, their educational histories, and their social class, racial, and ethnic backgrounds. Karen Rosen's mother is perceived by

Ms. Powell as overly aggressive, impatient, and unrealistically demanding of her daughter. Her personal style clashes with Ms. Powell's and is reinforced by stereotypes of her Germanic heritage and her upper-middle-class professional arrogance. She seems to view elementary school teachers as lesser beings whose professional opinions are not very precise or useful. Ms. Powell senses her lack of respect and feels demeaned in her presence. Not only have mother and teacher formed rigid caricatures of one another, but they also have opposing views of the goals, expectations, and pedagogy appropriate for the first year of school. Although Ms. Powell and Ms. Rosen claim that they are fighting in the best interest of the child, their civilized but intense battles take on a life of their own, and each becomes the primary target of the other's anger. Eventually Ms. Powell responds by withdrawing from the relationship and delivering the mother over to the higher authority of the principal.

Ms. Powell's conflicts with Luther Jones's mother have different origins. The unspoken clashes between mother and teacher arise out of their different expectations of one another. Ms. Jones needs Ms. Powell's nurturance, support, and guidance, and does not want to share it with her son. In some sense, she is competing with Luther for the small measure of attention from a teacher and authority figure, and she is angered by Ms. Powell's demands that she accept the responsibilities and obligations of an adult. Ms. Powell recognizes, even identifies with Ms. Jones's status as a lower-class black woman in a harsh and unjust society, but she blames her for not using more of her energies to restructure her own life situation. Within the oppressive constraints of reality, Ms. Powell believes that Luther's mother should take mature and responsible action. Ms. Powell's frustrations with Ms. Jones are intensified by her special feelings of affection for Luther. Her feelings for him are strong, protective, and maternal; and she finds herself not only urging Ms. Jones to be a better mother but in some ways wishing to displace her altogether.

With both Karen's and Luther's families, Ms. Powell claims a great disadvantage for the child who is the recipient of mixed and conflicting messages from home and school. The relationship with Steven Gordon's mother has been more satisfying and productive. However, it has not been spontaneous or naturally easy, but has required a great deal of energy, hard work, and conflict. Through weeks of bitterness and misunderstanding, Ms. Powell and Ms. Gordon grew to understand each other's styles of interaction, perspectives on child development, and educational goals for Steven. The constructive interactions between mother and teacher required that they both change; that they both be able to empathize with the other's role and appreciate the differences in their perspectives as necessary and advantageous for Steven's growth. Most important, even in the midst of the most difficult and passionate conflicts between them, Ms. Gordon and Ms. Powell never lost sight of the reason they had come together in the first place. They both cared deeply about Steven and believed he was worth fighting for.

Ms. Sarni and Three Parent Groups: The Voices of Conflict and the Silence of Alliance

In her second year of teaching, Ms. Sarni worked in the Central School, located in the center of a working-class Italian enclave. Ms. Sarni is a second-generation Italian who grew up in a close-knit, Italian neighborhood in South Evergreen. She still remembers the day when the Portuguese, with their large families and aggressive style, began to invade their community. At age fourteen, her parents fled to a nearby exclusive suburb where, at age thirty, she continues to live with them. Although she has lived a suburban life since adolescence, she is still deeply rooted in the memories of her early childhood, and she makes weekly visits back to her "home" in South Evergreen. The Central School was familiar and comfortable for her. She knew how to communicate in Italian, felt closely identified with the culture and values of the community, and experienced the trust, admiration, and respect of the parents.

The Douglass School, where she has taught for the past two years, has an unusually varied pupil population, with children from highly educated, professional backgrounds, children from solid, working-class homes, and children from families of great poverty and disorganization. There are equal proportions of blacks and whites that represent a range of social-class levels. Down the street from the Douglass School is a large graduate student complex for the nearby university, and on the other side of the tracks, but within the Douglass School community, is a large, low-income housing project with poor and minority families. "The projects" is the base of strong black political leadership and increasing criminal activity. Ms. Sarni's experiences with families at the Douglass School have not been as fluid and smooth as her relationships at Central. In this community, she is forced to relate to a variety of parental expectations and demands, and she is forced to confront values, attitudes, and behavior that are alien to her cultural perspectives.

Parents should be seen, not heard. Ms. Sarni's views of parent participation in schools are relatively uncomplicated and unambiguous. She believes very strongly that their primary function should be external and peripheral to the life of the school. They should provide a strong, firm, and nurturant home environment with two sturdy parents who support and uphold the "traditional American values." But parents should not become involved in the educational process *within* the schools; neither should they criticize or undermine the efforts and values of the teacher. Most important, they should not use the school as a social and political arena; a place to unleash their anger and hostilities against the oppressive conditions of society. In some sense, school should be divorced from the dark side of society and reflect the promises of a productive and bright future for children. It should be a place for learning to read and write, safe from the worldly intrusions of political conflict, poverty, and racism.

Ms. Sarni feels great nostalgia for the conforming and appreciative role that parents played at the Central School, a setting where she worked for a year before coming to Douglass. Their cooperation reflected a kind of passive submission and complete trust in the teacher's skills and values. Once inside the school, the children *belonged* to the teacher, and parents relinquished their offspring in exchange for the hope that new worlds and vistas would be open to them through schooling.

> The parents at Central School backed the teacher 100 percent; there was nothing short of hitting the child that the parent would not approve of. There was 100 percent parental support. *The child was there to learn; you were the teacher, you are in charge, you do what you want, and you do what you have to do.* The PTA there is a good size. There are a lot of parents who are involved in the PTA, but they don't run the school. . . . They're vocal in their opinions, but they don't try to tell the teachers what to do, nor do they try to tell a headmaster what is good in a teacher.

Teaching, therefore, is seen as the autonomous and enlightened function of the teacher, and parents participate in their child's schooling by being good *parents* at home and by offering quiet cooperation and admiration for the teacher. Ms. Sarni recognizes this optimal relationship as a rapidly disappearing phenomenon and one that reflects a basic consensus of values and goals between home and school. Most important, parents must believe that schooling is critical to their child's success in this society and that *teachers* know best what the future society will require in terms of skills, competence, and attitudes toward work. In Ms. Sarni's view, the Central School community represented all of the virtues necessary for an unblemished and smooth rapport with parents.

> It is mainly hard-working immigrants . . . a lot of them Italians. . . . Very solid background . . . husband and wife, mother always home, mother always conscious of being a good housekeeper, caring for her

> children and meals on the table, coming well dressed, respect, proud to be an American . . . you know they instill all of these admirable qualities. . . . Husband very solid, hard-working, works long hours, cares for children, never, never on welfare, never on relief, very proud kind of people. And they want their children to get the best kind of education they can possibly give them. . . . Some of them may not have gone to school; some of them may not have gotten out of grammar school; some may have just come over from the old country and just speak broken English. Or like the mother of some of the kids I had—she spoke nothing but Italian. And they believe the children are going to be better if they get a good education and study. If they learn, perhaps they're not going to be the ditch digger that their father was, or the manual laborer, or the factory worker. . . . And whatever the teacher can do to help the child be successful, they want the teacher to do. Any kind of behavior problem is just not tolerated. They're there for one reason. They're there to learn and study and that's it.

In this community, Ms. Sarni experienced a very special kind of resonance with these parents. First of all, she shared their cultural traditions and values; she spoke their language and understood their dreams for their children. She also understood the subtle meanings of cultural nuances and unspoken exchanges so that her interactions with parents and children didn't contain the potential threat of misunderstanding or misinterpretation. Although Ms. Sarni seems to feel that this complete harmony between home and school is supportive to child learning and growth, for the most part she stresses the impact it has on the style and substance of her teaching. In other words, it makes *her* feel good to receive the implicit admiration and trust of the parents, and it increases *her* feelings of status and professionalism when parents view her as someone with special skills and a key to the future. *Her* energy doesn't have to be sapped away by negotiating or sparring with parents over educational priorities or curriculum content. The benefit of unspoken parent-teacher consensus might have an indirect impact on the lives of children in the classroom, but Ms. Sarni focuses her comments on the direct benefits to her self-esteem, her professionalism, and her good humor.

The Douglass School does not offer the same kinds of rewards for Ms. Sarni. Rather than feeling the comfortable and familiar harmony of her Italian roots, she is faced with a widely divergent and outspoken group of parents who do not, for the most part, share her perspectives on parent and community participation in schools. There are three major groups of parents that Ms. Sarni identifies as reflecting different educational histories, socioeconomic backgrounds, family structures, and attitudes toward schooling. At least one third of the children come from middle-class and upper-middle-class professional backgrounds. They live in the graduate student ghetto down the street from the school, and one or both of their parents go to the university. The parents are highly educated and articulate and aggressively push their children to be little scholars. Ms. Sarni feels somewhat threatened by their intellectual status and generally annoyed by their demeaning attitudes toward her. Mostly, she perceives them to be indulgent and overly permissive parents who are preoccupied with their child's intellectual development but do not give careful enough attention to their moral and social development. The "academics" (as Ms. Sarni refers to them) are a relatively transient group who enter the school with high demands for excellence but never become rooted enough in the community to offer any real support or to become deeply committed and involved in community life.

> In my experience I have more trouble with university parents than I have with black or white lower-class parents. My first year I had corrected two papers incorrectly. The father was studying for his doctorate in Chinese literature and he came in very upset and I said, "Well, you know, I have so many papers, I'm bound to make a mistake." And you know, he didn't like me or anything I had to say and he told me off. . . . Then he went to the principal and told him off, told him what he thought of me and thought of the school. And the following week the father brought it up before the assistant superintendent . . . and when he proceeded to tell the assistant superintendent where to get off, they finally threw him out. . . . That was my first year. So I would say most of my trouble comes from the "academics."

The university parents communicate (both explicitly and implicitly) to Ms. Sarni completely different messages from those she received from the Central School community. Rather than feeling special and competent, Ms. Sarni feels criticized and demeaned in the presence of university types. Instead of feeling intuitively knowledgeable about the values and traditions of the families, she sees the "academics" as strangers (often from a foreign country) and transients who hide behind their intellectualism and professional status and reflect attitudes that are alien and irresponsible to their children and the wider society.

> There are a lot of parents who bring up their children to not respect the teacher, and if they feel like telling the teacher off, well, that's their prerogative and they have the right to do it. There are parents who believe that they should not salute the flag and the children won't salute the flag.

Ironically, Ms. Sarni often gets great pleasure out of teaching the children of these university parents because they are usually well prepared academically and highly adaptive to the school environment.

> . . . And then you have a child, very, very bright, and you can spot them, you can spot "academics," you know; very knowledgeable, well dressed, very confident children. They are easy and fun to teach.

The second group of parents that Ms. Sarni views as potential troublemakers and irresponsible citizens are at the other end of the socioeconomic continuum from the "academics." They are poor whites and blacks, often single-parent families, who live in the low-income projects near the school and do not provide a stable, orderly, and clean home environment for their children.

> You have a lot more families where there's only one parent. That's basically the mother. Generally the father has left or died, and usually you find them on some kind of subsistence. So that you find a lot of the kids don't come from solid backgrounds.

Ms. Sarni seems to feel superior to these families and not very sympathetic toward their position in society. Although she recognizes inequality and injustice in this society, she feels that if people work hard enough, they can pull themselves out of the depths of poverty and provide a decent life for their children. She sees a direct parallel between poor and chaotic home environments and the child's poor performance in school. Not only does she view the impact of the home background as damaging to the child's successful schooling, but she also sees this group of poor parents as potentially violent. They are the families that give the community and the school a negative and demeaned reputation. And deep down, she is fearful that if they became angry enough, they might lose control and become violent with her.

> You know the teachers have their tires slashed. My car was walked on the other day and there were big sneaker prints all over it. . . . So all you need to do is look at the neighborhood to see that the school can't do anything about that. That's something you've got to correct in your homes.

For very different reasons, therefore, Ms. Sarni feels uncomfortable and fearful of the "academics" and the lower-class parents on welfare. With the former she feels demeaned, subservient, and relatively powerless. They do not value her role as a teacher, and she is apprehensive of their powers of persuasion and status. With the latter group, she feels disdain, but she fears their tendencies toward violence and brutality. Neither group would she choose to confront. In fact, she tries to find ways to avoid conflict and disagreements, which often means that the interactions between her and the parents are ritualistic and contrived without any meaningful information being passed back and forth.

> You have to be very careful what you say about parents, and you have to be very careful what you say to parents. And also you have to be very careful sometimes what you say to children, because then they go back to the parents and say something that might be offensive. . . . So generally I feel more apprehensive here when a parent comes in, because I'm not quite sure how tactful one has to be in choosing one's words carefully.

The communications are particularly vacuous and tentative with the poor black parents, whom Ms. Sarni describes as racist in their attitudes toward white teachers. The parents suspect that she is treating their children unjustly and not giving them a fair chance in the classroom. They blame their children's failures on her poor teaching and become very defensive about their own life style and meager educational background. At best, the communications between home and school are meaningless gestures designed to secure a stalemate; at worst, they can become hostile outbursts that disrupt and divide the school community.

> I have to choose my words very carefully and I have to make sure that I'm not degrading the child in any way or patronizing the mother. . . . I don't know whether this is always true, but it seems that quite a number of the black parents tend to take this antagonistic attitude toward the school. . . . There have been cases where the child's been brought up in an atmosphere where white obviously is not accepted, and so they might call you "whitey."

This group of parents becomes even more threatening when they are swayed by the political rhetoric of "black radicals" in the community who use the school as a focus for all of their hostility toward society. Ms. Sarni views these lower-class blacks as being highly susceptible to the powerful influence of political leaders who urge them to move toward aggressive and violent action. It is against these black community leaders that Ms. Sarni expresses her greatest outrage.

> She [black radical community leader] lives in this neighborhood and we are "whitey" no matter what. . . . She is a racist bigot. . . . Really, she could turn this whole place upside down and kick all the whites out. She can't stand whites and she hates America. And my opinion is, "Well, if you hate it so much, why don't you get the next boat and go somewhere? Here you've been getting all these benefits and you hate it so much."

Not only does this black political leader offend Ms. Sarni's image of the school as an apolitical, protected enclave, reserved for the sole purposes of teaching and learning, but she also thinks this woman is abusing her responsibility as an American citizen. She doesn't show the appropriate appreciation for the bountiful gifts of American citizenship, and she inspires others in the same pejorative direction.

The only group of parents with whom Ms. Sarni feels a sense of rapport at the Douglass School is the group that very much resembles the Central School community. They tend to be solid working-class or lower-middle-class citizens who have lived in the community for generations, who own their own modest homes, and who have solid, two-parent families. They send their children to school clean and ready to learn, and they view the teacher as critical to their child's future success in society. They are not likely to share the ethnic heritage of the Italian community surrounding the Central School, but they do share the same dreams and the same belief that education is central to those dreams.

> You find some—you can pick them out—who are very well behaved and very well kept and well dressed and they're black. You find that with most of them both parents are at home, the fathers always working and the mother is working or at home . . . a good home, a neat housekeeper.

This year Ms. Sarni has had the pleasure of having in her classroom many children whose families come from this hard-working and solid group. She views them as cooperative and supportive of her decisions and wishes all parents would show the same allegiance and appreciation. She describes the optimal relationship that she shares with Reginald's parents. Reginald is the only child of a working-class black couple who are very concerned that their son succeed in school and move on to bigger and better things in the world.

> Whatever I say, they go along with. . . . Reginald's mother says, "If you have to hit him and take the stick out, you hit him." I wouldn't do that, but she backs me 100 percent. She is constantly telling her son, "You are there to learn and you don't give the teacher any trouble, and you listen to her and you do what she says."

It is interesting that Ms. Sarni perceives a good and productive relationship with parents as being reciprocal, as expressing a kind of equality and exchange. But when one hears her words, she seems to establish herself as the superior authority. The parents are expected to relinquish their control and offer their child to the teacher, whose judgment and wisdom they trust and whose skills and competence they greatly admire. To Ms. Sarni, therefore, the "give-and-take" relationship she refers to is not so much a balanced relationship reflecting equal inputs from teachers and parents but a very one-sided one that reflects the teacher's dominance and superiority in this sphere of the child's life. If the parents accept this basic premise of teacher dominance, then the relationship is likely to proceed smoothly, and the child is likely to experience the relative advantage of the harmonious feelings between family and school.

For the most part, Ms. Sarni has found that her strategies for dealing with these three groups of parents have worked effectively —that is, she has managed to stay out of battles and avoid explicit conflict with them. Her general policy tends to be one of avoidance and careful distance. With none of these groups is real, critical dialogue perceived as necessary by Ms. Sarni because she dares not say anything that might be potentially offensive to the "academics" and the welfare parents. And the "cooperative" parents seem to have such great trust in her capabilities that no explanations are required. Ironically, both the positive and negative relationships with parents inevitably lead to empty silence and ritualistic noncommunication.

Views of Outsiders: The Classroom as a Private Place

The exclusion of families from classroom life provides a kind of clarity and order that Ms. Sarni seems to need in order to focus on the educational process. It is not that she builds boundaries around her classroom only in relation to parents. She also wants to close the classroom door to all sources of criticism, from fellow teachers to reading specialists to school psychologists and social workers. All of these additional adults are not seen as potential resources or helping hands but as interruptions to the smooth and orderly flow of the classroom environment. Ms. Sarni, for instance, works very hard at decorating her classroom and at creating a pretty place for children—one that will be a dramatic contrast to the disorder and chaos in many of their lives. Her Christmas decorations are the most ingenious and elaborate in the school, and they are put up promptly the day after Thanksgiving. She describes herself as a "frustrated interior decorator," and it is clear that much of the inspiration behind her beautification efforts lies in the personal satisfaction of living in a charming environment. The physical contrasts between the inside and the outside of her classroom are symbolic of a much more deeply etched boundary that Ms. Sarni tries to maintain between public and private spheres, community and school domains, and the worlds of professionals and laymen. She sees these worlds as nonoverlapping and often polarized and feels she can do her work most effectively in the privacy of her classroom domain.

To Ms. Sarni, the work of a first-grade teacher is straightforward and indisputable. She is hired to teach children how to read; that is the primary agenda of her classroom and she holds herself accountable to that task. And, in fact, Ms. Sarni's children learn how to read, every single one of them. Some of the children leave her class at third- and fourth-grade levels, but *everyone* reaches the minimal standard of first-grade competence. As a matter of fact, her reputation as a "good teacher" extends far and wide, and parents often work hard to get their children in her classroom. For even the most arrogant university types and the most angry poor folk, reading is their central concern for their child, and Ms. Sarni accomplishes that without question.

There is a strange irony in Ms. Sarni's stereotypic views of parent groups and her universal success at teaching the children of those groups that offend her the most. How is it that she can hold onto her prejudicial perceptions of lower-class parents, even view their children as replicas of their parents, and still manage to teach them without malice or subtly exclude them from the educational process? Ms. Sarni considers teaching a laudable and important profession and takes her professional role very seriously. Central to her view of professionalism is success with *all* children, without excuse or apology or disparagement for the social and intellectual skills they might bring to the classroom. Yes, she does view them as more or less likely to succeed in school because of their socioeconomic and educational backgrounds, but that cannot serve as a facile excuse for the differential success of the teacher.

Ms. Sarni, therefore, looks on most other teachers with some contempt and views them as lazy and unprofessional in their habits and behavior. She cannot understand how teachers can feel satisfied with themselves if their children are not learning. She cannot understand why many teachers do not spend their energies busily decorating their classrooms for Christmas and Easter and creating a pretty holiday environment. Ms. Sarni feels most disgust for her fellow teachers who categorize children as learning problems and assign them to outside specialists in order to be relieved of the heavy burdens and responsibilities of working with "problem" children. If she had her way, there would be no "outside people coming in" to rescue and assist classroom teachers or to cover up for their inadequacies. Teachers would be forced to work hard, as she does, to develop effective strategies for teaching all children. It is not only that outside professionals and school specialists cover up the *teacher's* weaknesses and interrupt the smoothly flowing rhythm and structure of the classroom, but according to Ms. Sarni, they often have an unrealistic perspective on life in classrooms. They come as advocates for an individual child and focus their energies on solving his unique problems or special interests, and they often forget the complex interactions of children in the classrooms. Their personalized interventions interrupt the balance and precarious equilibrium of a teacher's relationship to the class as a whole. Not only does their intrusive presence cause waves of confusion and create inequalities among children, but they also bring an alien orientation that "does not belong in the classroom."

During the year, a psychologist from the mental health center determined that Timothy was "minimally brain damaged" after administering a series of perceptual tests to him. The diagnosis was told to Timothy's mother, who was depressed and overwhelmed by the news, and to Ms. Sarni, who mistrusted and challenged the psychologist's perceptions.

> This Dr. Brown at the mental health center really psyched this mother out! I don't think a doctor has the right to do that. . . . She came in here practically destroyed. She's a supersensitive person and she started crying . . . "What have I done to Timmy? What was it in my genes that made me do this to Timmy?" . . . All kinds of guilt complexes. . . . I don't think the psychologist had any finesse, he just went *bang*!

Ms. Sarni complained about the lack of sensitivity on the part of the psychologist in translating the information to a layperson, but she was equally critical of the diagnosis. Although Ms. Sarni recognizes that in the eyes of society a psychologist is the presumed authority on mental disorders and is generally given more deference than a classroom teacher, she feels that psychologists are often less knowledgeable about a child's response to "real-life" conditions than teachers and are oriented toward identifying pathology rather than health. Despite their lofty status, the psychologist's limited vision often leads to misdiagnosis and mislabeling.

> I don't have a psychologist's degree . . . I'm just a classroom teacher, but I have some knowledge. I'm going back for my master's now. Just from looking at him, he is by no means minimally brain damaged. . . . He might have a perceptual problem. . . . He's very slow on all his papers. . . . He doesn't work up to his ability. . . . He's easily distracted. . . .

Once students have been labeled and categorized by a psychologist, school personnel feel justified in their lack of success with the "problem" children. Ms. Sarni speaks critically of this process of rationalization for failure and views it as an inevitable result of "outsiders'" intrusions into the classroom teacher's domain.

Ms. Sarni's perspective on parent groups, therefore, is part of a more general orientation toward "outsiders." She is preoccupied with the exclusion of all external forces that might bring chaos, disorder, and messiness into her classroom, and that includes parents, colleagues, and outside professionals—groups that many teachers would view as natural allies. It is not so much that Ms. Sarni regards them as enemies (except for the hostile, aggressive types); rather, she sees them as *irrelevant* to the primary agenda of school.

Teachers' Voices: Mixed Messages and Motives

Both Ms. Powell and Ms. Sarni view their relationships to parents as relatively good. In comparison to other teachers, they feel fortunate to have avoided most of the angry outbursts of hostile parents, and they do not feel their interactions with children have been distorted by feelings of threat and defensiveness in relation to their families. But both of them engage in a process of distancing when they interact with mothers and fathers of children. They both feel that ideally the environments of home and school should reflect similar values and norms and that teachers and parents should have a shared sense of educational goals. At the same time, however, they believe that family and school settings should be clearly separable and distinct. Parents can do the best for their children by being good parents (rather than surrogate teachers) and by attending to the child's needs for nurturance, love, and firm discipline.

Ms. Sarni takes the notion of separate environments to its extreme. She values parents who trust her implicitly and completely give over the education of their child to her authoritative care. She wants appreciation and respect from parents who recognize her special professional skills and value the teacher's role in the socialization of their child into the mainstream of contemporary society. Most important, she prefers a classroom environment that is safe from the external influences of parental demands, where she can create and sustain a structure for children that is uncontaminated by the negative impact of un-American values, sloppy habits, and irresponsible and abusive parenting. If she can just guard these children from the harsh realities of poverty, decadence, and political extremism for a few hours of the day, she feels she might be able to start them off on the right foot. But she is not overly optimistic about breaking the generational chain. She deeply believes that, in the long run, there are few interventions *outside* the family that will change the prospect of life for children, and that children will turn out to be just like their parents.

Ms. Sarni's temperamental need for clarity and structure in her classroom seems related to her perceptions of parent groups. The categorization and stereotyping of parents permits her to keep them at a distance. Individual interactions and negotiation with the *real* people behind the stereotypes might cause more confusion than Ms. Sarni could tolerate. Even though her distancing of parents has a negative, often pejorative caste, it does allow for a more orderly world within her classroom. And as long as she is "producing" readers at the end of the year, Ms. Sarni does not feel the parents have any legitimate reason for complaint.

Although Ms. Sarni seeks to establish a comfortable distance from the families of the children in her class, in her interactions with children she carries around images of their families in her head. Even as she relates to a child, she is seeing him as the shadow of his parents. As a matter of fact, Ms. Sarni finds it very difficult to describe the individual nature of the child without reference to the sociological dimensions of family structure, social class, race, and ethnicity. Her descriptions of individual children rarely present the child as a whole and unique human being or portray the child as a member of the classroom scene. We do not hear about the subtleties and complexities of a child's individual personality or his interactions with his peers, but rather we are given the stereotypic and static image of his parents. One of her primary ways of envisioning the classroom social structure, therefore, is by reference to these background variables. Ironically, Ms. Sarni yearns for a classroom setting that is free from the "negative" impact of families and community, but her view of children is shaped by the very forces that she seeks to avoid.

Ms. Sarni's relationships with families, therefore, are dyadic in the sense that they tend to exclude the child as a critical member of family-school interaction and in the sense that she views children as small replicas of their parents rather than as individuals deeply connected but separate from the conditions of their parentage. But the story of exclusion is not simple, and in her classroom, children are not necessarily objects of discrimination because their parents are viewed negatively. There are conflicting themes in Ms. Sarni's perspectives on families and community. On the one hand, her perceptions of children reflect her discriminatory visions of parent groups, while on the other hand, she goes about the task of making children equal in her classroom by resisting distinctions between them and by teaching them all to read. With blinders on she fulfills her part of the bargain and holds herself professionally accountable, but she feels that inevitably her work will be reinforced or undone by the more enduring forces and conditions of the families and communities from which the children come.

For the most part, Ms. Powell also sees parents as peripheral to the primary agenda of school. Their role should be supportive of life in the classroom but not intimately involved in it. Mostly, she is concerned with the correspondence of ideological and educational perspectives between family and school because she believes that the alliance of values is directly related to the child's successful development in school. Her stories of Karen and Luther are told in order to underscore the damaging impact of family-school conflict on the child's chances for intellectual and social achievement within the classroom.

Although Ms. Powell asserts the need for a correspondence of values between home and school, she does not really seem to view the relationship with parents as symmetric and interactional. Yes, she believes parents have an important perspective to offer, but she also views the depth and intensity of their involvement with their child as a source of distortion and misperception. Their great love for the child blinds them from seeing the child *holistically*. From her relatively detached perspective, Ms. Powell feels that she can see the weak and strong attributes, the positive and negative dimensions of the child's personality. Most important, in her teaching role she can recognize the critical significance of socializing children to responsible and caring participation in classroom and peer-group life. She works to move children beyond their egocentric needs to explore the potential richness of group experiences. Their acculturation to group norms is seen as a deliberate preparation for life beyond school. Because parents are usually rooted in the present and rarely share the future orientation of teachers, and because parents remain focused on the superior success and unique needs of their child, they must be prodded by teachers to move beyond their individualistic perspective and become acquainted with some of the other dimensions of the child that are rarely revealed *within* the family. Ms. Powell wants to paint for parents the "whole picture" and make them more realistic about their child's abilities and more modest in their expectations of the teacher. In other words, she sees herself in a teaching role even with parents and often describes conferences where she is "telling" parents what to do rather than listening to their unique perspective on the child.

But in seeking consonance with families, Ms. Powell is consistently able to see the individual child as a whole being. Her descriptions of children are perceptive and insightful, and she gives the full details of the child's functioning *within* the classroom setting. Ms. Powell rarely uses family-background variables as the major descriptors of children but is more likely to focus on themes of psychosocial development. She can easily picture the individual child without reference to his parentage. Parents, therefore, are not central to her perception and evaluation of the child except when they are obstructing the educational process by undoing the skills and attitudes taught in school (as with Karen and Luther) or when their support and alliance are critical to the child's development in the classroom (as with Steven). But even when parents enter the scene, Ms. Powell views them as secondary figures. Her relationships with children are the strong bonds that require her focused and continuous attention.

Ms. Powell's triadic relationship with families therefore includes the dynamic involvements of parents, teachers, and children, with the greatest emphasis put on interactions between teacher and child. Her negotiations with families are far less economical and clear-cut than the dyadic relationships of Ms. Sarni. Ms. Powell's focus is on the individual development and unique qualities of each child and her myriad perceptions of and interactions with the child's parents. Her temperamental style with parents and children is in direct contrast to Ms. Sarni's. She invites complexity rather than clarity, exploration rather than closure, and questioning rather than certainty. Rather than seeking to exclude the external forces of the outside world, Ms. Powell works to understand their impact on the child's growth in school and enter into a process of negotiation and collaboration with families. These myriad involvements consume her energy, increase the range and complexity of her visions and responsibilities, and sometimes distract her from teaching children to read.

4

Black Dreams and Closed Doors

Visions of Liberation and Oppression

THE HISTORICAL and contemporary relationship between American blacks and public schooling has been passionate and ambivalent. Schools have always held out the promise and hope of liberation and enlightenment at the same time as they have been recognized as social and economic vehicles of oppression and denial. The truth is complex and bittersweet. In his recent book, *Inequality,* Christopher Jencks warns us not to put our trust and hopes in schools as effective institutions of social mobility and social change. With some of the most sophisticated methodological strategies and statistical analyses, Jencks et al. try to destroy one of our most pervasive and precious cultural myths—that schools and education will save our black children from poverty and oppression and give them the skills to overcome racism and injustice. The authors claim that we must rather turn our energies to confronting the economic structures of our society if we are to see any real change in the patterns of inequality in this society.[1] Despite Jencks's efforts, the myth of schooling is much too powerful in our history. Like every myth, it is half true, and the truth keeps the promise alive in us.

The value of schooling is as prominent a cultural image as Mom's apple pie, the American flag, or black-eyed peas and greens. It crosses ethnic, racial, and social-class lines. As black people, the promise of schooling has touched us deeply. Although our rational minds tell us that there is no evidence of *group* mobility for blacks through schooling, we know the stories of *individual* mobility—perhaps we ourselves are the proud products of social and economic advancement through schooling. Our heroes keep that image alive. Hank Aaron travels around the country urging young black children to learn to read and write, not to concentrate on hitting balls. James Brown dances the message of education with his slick patent-leather shoes. Even ghetto teachers in black communities, who know all the casualties and failures that they experience daily, cling optimistically to the American dream. A young black very competent teacher that I interviewed voiced this point of view when she spoke of the potentials of the very poor black children in her class.

> You can see some little boy from my class could become the President of the United States or could become anything that he wanted to be if he had the chance. If he had the chance to go to school, I figure he could go all the way.[2]

The contradictory perceptions of schools as institutions of liberation and oppression not only reside in black cultural imagery, but they are also expressed in the academic battles between traditional and revisionist historians who present divergent interpretations of history that are highly political and ideological.

> The dominant perspective, until the past decade, was that the American public schools were the highest realization of the democratic ideal, that they provided equal opportunity to all and rapid

> mobility to the deserving. . . . In recent years, this idealistic and optimistic vision has been dethroned by a barrage of criticism, and a new construct that has been raised up in its place. The new interpretation holds that public schooling has been a capitalistic tool of indoctrination, that it has been purposefully used to stamp out cultural diversity, and that it has been slyly (or brutally) imposed on unwilling masses by arrogant reformers . . . whereas the old concept was oversimplified in its optimism, the new concept is overly simplified in its cynicism. The former too easily proclaimed the inevitable triumph of democracy, equality, and opportunity; the latter too glibly perceives oppression, indoctrination, and conspiratorial behavior.[3]

Diane Ravitch seeks to move beyond the simplistic, politicized images of schools as institutions of good and evil and present a more complex description lying somewhere between cynicism and optimism. Ravitch's analysis underscores the need to study the assimilation and acculturation of minority groups into American society as unique and differentiated stories that reflect the intersection of economic and historical realities and sociocultural priorities and agendas. Although each minority group forged a different path, one must recognize that most groups were not monolithic in their perceptions of education and schooling but expressed a range of dreams and visions.

This chapter will explore the dynamic and complex narrative of black families and schools in American society. It is a story that speaks of political and economic oppression and psychological manipulation on the part of the dominant white majority; and it is a story that expresses the strength and endurance of black family life, the passionate commitment to learning, and the unswerving pursuit of education and schooling on the part of blacks. The intersection of black families and schools is the central focus of this chapter because the interaction of these two primary institutions of socialization and acculturation dramatizes the contradictions and dissonance between the black cultural perspective and family structure and the environmental norms and socioeconomic purposes of school. Not only do we begin to perceive the asymmetric relationship between the dominant and powerful school and the relatively vulnerable and oppressed families and communities, but we also see the kinds of environmental and cultural transformations a child must make as he moves back and forth from one setting to the other. For a young child it can be a journey of shocking contrasts and contradictions. How does he negotiate the tortuous, uneven path? How does he incorporate and understand the contradictions? And how do his adult sponsors seek to prepare him for moving in a world that is hostile and unjust?

Not only do we see evidence of oppression and exclusion in the stark contrasts between black families and white-dominated schools, but a focus on family history further enhances our understanding of the social costs and personal pain of racism in American society. In a very insightful analysis, Christopher Lasch claims that family history can provide the missing link between the study of culture and the study of social structure, production, and power. Family history, therefore, reveals the levels of dissonance and consonance between the macroscopic spheres of politics and economics and the interpersonal and psychosocial spheres of acculturation. The study of families becomes critical to our understanding of the intellectual, cultural, and ideological socialization of children and central to our interpretation of social change.

> The union of love and discipline in the same persons, the mother and father, creates a highly charged environment in which the child learns lessons he will never get over. . . . He develops an unconscious predisposition to act in certain ways and to recreate in later life, in his relations with lovers and authorities, his earliest experiences. Parents first embody love and power, and each of their actions conveys to the child, quite independently of their overt intentions, the injunctions and constraints by means of which society attempts to organize experience. If reproducing culture were simply a matter of formal instruction and discipline, it would be left to the schools. But it also requires that culture be embedded in

> personality. Socialization makes the individual want to do what he has to do; and the family is the agency to which society entrusts this complex task.[4]

Despite the fact that *all* families are engaged in this critical cultural task, social scientists have questioned the goodness and adequacy of black parents and distorted or diminished their educative role. Throughout the research literature black family life is described in contrast to or in opposition to the social, intellectual, and motivational demands of school. The *dissonance* in patterns of interaction, values, structures, manners, and style is the major preoccupation of scholars. Furthermore, the dissonance is thought to reside in the *willful* neglect by black parents of their child's preparation and accommodation to school life. Two themes emerge: one that emphasizes conflict and distrust between black families and schools and another that places the blame for conflict on the family.

This chapter will speak to the issues of contrast, asymmetry, and conflict between black families and schools, but also point to the potential bridges and alliances between schools and families and the critical educational function that families have served for generations. I will also argue that in order for schools to successfully teach black children, they will have to incorporate the cultural wisdom and experience of black families and meaningfully collaborate with parents and community. Black families and communities have been settings for cultural transmission, survival training, moral and religious instruction, role-modeling, mythmaking, and ideological and political indoctrination. But very little of this "informal" education has been systematically documented by scholars because it has been considered distracting and divergent from the formal schooling of black children; because much of it seems incomprehensible and mysterious to white scholars; because it is thought to bear no direct connection to the successful accommodation of blacks to mainstream life; and because it contradicts our sacred myths about the great American melting pot.

A Historical Search: Prelude to Contemporary Realities

A historical search for patterns of interaction between black families and schools is critical to an understanding of the issues of inclusion and exclusion experienced by black parents and children today. Although the contemporary strategies for the domination and control of blacks may be more subtle and sophisticated (may even be rationalized by scientific evidence), they are clearly the dark shadows of an earlier time. In fact, it is important to recognize that the current struggles over school desegregation, integration, and affirmative action in American society are echoes of discriminatory structures and processes that were evident in the early history of this country. Their resolution, therefore, will not be found in remedial social policies, innovative curriculums, or facile programmatic shifts; the patterns of interaction and the institutional structures and norms are deeply embedded in the fabric of society. A more comprehensive understanding of the origins of interaction among black communities, families, schooling, and education will begin to elucidate the resounding themes and patterns that have emerged over time and may point to their modern expression in political, social, and intellectual battles being waged today. An appreciation for the depth and embeddedness of pain and struggle in the black quest for education and schooling may also lead to a more realistic assessment of the potential for social and institutional change in the future.

This historical description will focus on the ante-bellum period in black American history, first documenting the relationship between Southern black families and *education* and, second, describing the experience of Northern blacks and *schools* during the same era. I have chosen to document this very early period of black movement into American society because it marked the beginnings of social and economic patterns that have emerged as dominant themes of interaction between blacks and whites in the two hundred years that followed. The ante-bellum period revealed strategies of oppression and deep patterns of racism with stark clarity—a clarity that helps us analyze the more covert, shadowy forms of oppression experienced in later periods. It is also during this historical era that we are able to document striking and interesting contrasts in the perceptions of schooling and education on the part of Northern and Southern blacks. These contrasts were revealed in the shaping of different social and political strategies for inclusion into the world of education that have endured as divergent themes today. Finally, the ante-bellum period is a potentially revealing period because it has been more thoroughly documented by social historians. (Perhaps its distance from our lives today makes it feel less threatening as a focus of scholarship.) For instance, literature on black families and child rearing at this time, although admittedly limited and distorted, is more plentiful than any other historical period. Yet, for the most part, we must rely on the records of the literate white planters for primary evidence. Their vision of blacks as children and property limited them from seeing the mature, resourceful, and adultlike family structures that blacks were able to sustain. But, at least, historians have recorded the *existence* of the black family as a social form during the ante-bellum period and not expressed the ultimate denial of ignoring its presence entirely, as was the case for other eras in history.

Although the ante-bellum period is a good place to begin in order to understand the origins of interaction between black families and schools, it only reveals a partial and unfinished narrative. In order to avoid the inevitable distortions of overinterpretation from minimal evidence, one must of course trace the story through the centuries and decades that have followed and document the complex changes and subtle shifts in strategies, goals, and dreams on the part of black families and communities. Risking the problematic aspects of distorted interpretations, I will use the ante-bellum period as a historical backdrop; as a source of contrast for present realities that shape social policies involving blacks and schools; and as a focus in searching for the roots of contemporary visions and conceptions of social science research.

Southern Black Families and Education

One of the major arguments throughout the historical literature on black Americans is whether one can even claim the existence of families and schools as viable social institutions. Traditionalist historians and sociologists, notably Frazier and Elkins, have denied the existence of both institutions during the slavery period.[5] However, from the work of recent scholars the evidence is strong and increasing that even during slavery, at least one of these institutions, the black family, had more substance than had previously been recorded.[6]

Most scholars agree that prior to the surge of the plantation system into trans-Appalachia and the Southwest triggered by the ascendance of "King Cotton" (circa 1790), the slave family on Eastern plantations was a relatively stable institution.[7] In fact, indications are that until slavery became a highly profitable business in the lower South, the perception and treatment of most slaves was similar to that of indentured servants—the promise of freedom constantly hovered on the horizon. The slaveowners' support of the black family was regarded as an important step toward what was seen as the eventual liberation of the slaves. However, the reports on the status of the black family conflict following this period. Traditionalists contend that slavery, as it existed in the lower South where the majority of blacks resided during the nineteenth century, at least undermined if not destroyed the family as the "fulcrum of the social order that blacks had known in West Africa, from which most slaves came." [8]

Largely following the pioneering work of Frazier, conventional wisdom holds that slavery prevented the emergence of a strong sense of family and led to a matriarchy that has endured as a feature of the modern black family. To both Frazier and Elkins, slavery was an institution that severely warped or completely destroyed blacks' commitment to family life. Frazier's fundamental thesis is that slavery fostered sexual licentiousness and an indifference to matters of family that extended into the post Civil War era.[9] Elkins went even further than Frazier in his dismissal of the importance of informal slave families by emphasizing that the black family had been irrevocably "destroyed" by the law.[10] Moreover, Elkins's thesis denied the slaves even the dream of an alternative existence by reducing the slaves' aspirations to "catfish and watermelon." [11]

Revisionists, historians, and sociologists have disputed Frazier's and Elkins's evidence and conclusions regarding the status of the slave family. Genovese contends that Frazier and Elkins have been led astray in two ways:

> First, they [Frazier and Elkins] have read the story of the twentieth-century black ghettoes backward in time and have assumed a historical continuity [that did not exist] with slavery days.
>
> Second, they have looked at slave law and at the external of family life and not closely enough at the actual temper of the quarters.[12]

In contrast to traditionalists, revisionist scholars stress the creativity of the blacks in their institutionalization of the family rather than the crippling effect of the law, which prohibited slave marriages, and the slaveowners' disregard for the slave family in their frequent auction of familial members. These scholars have extensively documented the case of the black family as a viable and important institution during slavery. Although a thorough examination of the dynamics of the slave family is beyond the scope of this work, it is necessary to provide a basic portrait of this family for an appreciation of its influence on the education of blacks.

The simple nuclear family is generally regarded as the most prevalent family structure of the slaves.[13] But it should be emphasized that the structure of the family was relatively open and fluid; slaves without kin, who had been usually separated from their own family through sale (or, less often, by death), were often "adopted" into another family and treated with the same affection reserved for close family members. Moreover, the black family is regarded by most revisionist scholars as relatively stable, within the limitations set by the auction block, in that it was usually founded on a monogamous union that endured even with the sale of one of the marital partners. The significance of the family to the slave allows it to be considered the slaves' principal survival mechanism.[14]

The basic, and perhaps only, significant disagreement among revisionist scholars in their description of the black family concerns who was primarily responsible for the relative stability achieved by the slave family. Some scholars credit the white planters with the relative success of the slave family.[15] These authors conclude that the master-slave relationship was essentially a collaborative or accommodationist arrangement in which the slave fulfilled his obligations to his master in return for the recognition of certain "customary rights and privileges," the principal one being the planter's informal recognition of the slave's right to maintain a family. They point out that the maintenance of the family was in the interest of the planter, who in turn benefited from a contented and obedient slave. Indeed, planters often used the threat of the dissolution of the family, by sale of a family member, as the chief disciplinary measure against delinquent slaves.[16] Slave narratives attest to the efficacy and power of this threat.

Other scholars maintain that it was the slaves themselves rather than the slaveowners who were responsible for the survival and the relative stability of the black family.[17] These writers convincingly argue that the legal nonrecognition of slave marriages, sexual exploitation of black women, and economically or punitively dictated separation of family members greatly threatened the survival of the black family, and except for the tenacity of blacks, the slave family would have foundered. Slave narratives collected during the 1920s and 1930s give much support to this thesis of *black* initiative in holding families together. They maintained that the undermining of the familial authority figure and the imposed negligence of the children (through assigning parents to long and arduous work in the fields) testify to the planters' disregard for the family life of the slaves. The narratives further suggest that fear of reprisal against family members and friends, rather than satisfaction with plantation life, is the major explanation for the relative infrequency of slave rebellions and escapes. Thus, it appears that the slaves' commitment to family life is the major, if not the *only* explanation for the survival of the slave family as a thriving institution during the ante-bellum years.

Unlike the family, the school, as an institution, was nonexistent. In fact, education for anyone but the aristocracy was denied during the ante-bellum years in the South. When the Northern states experienced a successful movement for the establishment of free public education, most Southern states steadfastly clung to their traditional belief that education was the province of the privileged, the well-endowed, propertied class. Edwards and Richey, in a persuasive analysis of the reasons for the developmental lag of Southern educational institutions behind those of the North, advance the argument that Southern society was a fundamentally distinct social organization from that of the North in that it was more hierarchically and rigidly stratified; and the planters who dominated every aspect of Southern life were "little disposed to champion the cause of popular education" for the poor whites,[18] much less for blacks, slaves or free. Thus, education was deeply embedded in social-class hierarchies, its primary purpose being to perpetuate socioeconomic inequalities and ensure the status quo. In contrast to the movement in the North, the education of Southern blacks, whether slave or free, was not given even the fleeting attention given to that of poor whites.

Most scholars divide the educational history of the blacks in the antebellum South into two distinct periods.[19] The first extends from the introduction of slavery to the climax of the insurrectionary movement in 1831 when the education, particularly religious instruction, of blacks was gradually gaining increasing support. The second period saw a precipitous decline in this support reinforced by an increasing hostility toward even the idea of religious education for blacks. This period began when the industrial revolution, at the close of the eighteenth century, transformed slavery from an essentially patriarchal to an economic institution.[20]

Knowledge about the education of blacks prior to the mid-nineteenth century is, at best, fragmentary. What available information exists suggests that "the first real educators" of the slaves "were clergymen interested in the propagation of the gospel among the heathen of the new world." [21] Slaveowners not only encouraged the religious instruction of the slaves, but often financed a more secular education, usually in the trades, in the interest of improving the slave's value on the auction block. Prior to the 1830s, an educated slave brought much more money than an illiterate one.

Even less is known about the education within black families and communities during the early years of slavery. Genovese is one of the few investigators who provides even a glimpse of the slave family's educational role. He states that blacks, not whites, were primarily responsible for the acculturation of slaves who were newly arrived from Africa. For example, it was they who "took primary responsibility for teaching other blacks [English] on the plantation. The English they taught was based on that pidgin that had arisen from the slave trade. The principal need of the slave was communication with the other slaves, not with the whites." [22]

The revolutionary fervor that led to the creation of the American Republic spilled over into a movement for the eventual abolition of slavery. During the latter part of the eighteenth century, there was a gradual progression toward the general liberation of the slaves in both the North and South. Blacks were generally allowed to be educated, by the abolitionists, in whatever was deemed necessary (usually religion and agriculture or the trades) to allow them to make a smooth transition from slavery to freedom. Although slavery was finally abolished in its more overt forms in the North, slavery in the South endured and entered upon a new and more repressive era. Technological advancement in England's textile industry led to a tremendous increase in that country's demand for Southern cotton. In response, the plantation economy expanded and became more firmly established. Slaves were perceived as economic property and became valuable to white landowners as a cheap labor source. In this economy, the educated slave, rather than being an asset to his owner as in earlier times, became a distinct liability. One begins to recognize the historical parallels between the economic needs of the dominant class and the incidence, form, and substance of black education. Blacks, and their human needs for enlightenment and liberation, were never part of the dominants' political and economic decision making.

Long before the famous revolts of the early nineteenth century, a few Southern states began to enact laws that restricted blacks' educational opportunities in the interest of securing better laborers, the best of whom were considered the most illiterate. The Haitian revolt of Toussaint L'Ouverture and the slave rebellions in the South (i.e., Gabriel in Virginia in 1800 and Vesey in South Carolina in 1822) led to an extension of restrictions and constraints on the education of blacks. After the slave insurrection of 1800, a Virginia planter remarked: "Every year adds to the number of those [blacks] who can read and write. This increased knowledge is the principal agent in evolving the spirit we have to fear." [23] Nat Turner's insurrection completed the reactionary course and triggered the post-insurrection panic of 1831 to 1832. This movement led to the enactment of severely repressive laws in every Southern state by 1835. The laws not only made the instruction of slaves in reading and writing by whites an indictable offense but also forbade slaves to teach one another and prohibited the assembly of slaves, even for religious purposes, except with the express approval of their master and in the company of five "good" white men. Even the giving or selling of books or pamphlets to slaves was prohibited. Thus, ignorance was viewed as an ultimate and purposeful form of "social control" imposed on blacks.

Most scholars attribute the ante-bellum legislation against the education of blacks to an almost paranoid fear that enveloped almost the entire Southern white population—"the fear of exciting blacks' dissatisfaction by teaching, thus producing insurrection." [24] In defense of repressive education laws, Georgia's Supreme Court Judge Lumpkin succinctly expressed this insidious and overwhelming fear: "Everything must be interdicted which is calculated to render the slaves discontent." [25] However, the apprehension and dread of the slaves' insurrection was only the surface manifestation of a more fundamental and profound fear—the fear that slaves would rise out of the "place" prescribed for them by white Southerners. This overwhelming fear continued to haunt and consume white Southerners beyond slavery into the twentieth century and to motivate their virulent opposition to the education of blacks.

But although the "black codes," as these repressive legislations were termed, drastically curtailed the education of blacks, they did not stamp it out altogether. Indeed, it could be argued that in one sense the repressive educational laws were counterproductive—producing an unexpected and opposing response from blacks. Blassingame contends that "since whites put so many restrictions upon slaves obtaining an education, the slaves themselves invested it with almost magical qualities." [26] The secrecy and dangerous pursuit of education endowed it with supernatural and otherworldly qualities. The quest for reaching this magical dream through the transforming process of education is still evident in contemporary attitudes toward schooling for blacks.

The literature offers considerable evidence that blacks made heroic efforts to obtain an education in spite of the repressive laws and despite the fact that those who violated the law were severely punished. Bullock provides a vivid illustration of the slave's determination to obtain an education during this period.

> Historical literature is replete with cases of slaves who struggled to gain literacy [by defying state laws]. Old slaves give mixed accounts of these education escapades. In the experience of some,

> learning was the expected thing, an apparently formal course, of plantation life; for others, it was a forbidden and clandestine undertaking into which only the young could venture.[27]

Blacks took many routes, often extraordinary, to secure an education. Three institutions of formal education emerged and continued to be available to a limited number of blacks during this period: sabbath schools, apprenticeship training, and clandestine schools operated by literate slaves or free blacks.

The religious instruction of the slaves was circumscribed and closely supervised. Many slaveowners simply did not permit it and of those who did, religious instruction was limited to oral instruction and excluded any "potentially subversive tenets of Christianity (e.g., the brotherhood of man)." [28] The narratives of ex-slaves reveal that only religious instruction that made the slaves more malleable, obsequious, and profitable to their masters was tolerated. William Brown and Lunsford Lane, ex-slaves, recount that their religious training consisted principally of being taught obedience to their white masters and that "God made blacks for slaves." [29]

Another means of formal education available to some, admittedly an insignificant number of slaves, was apprenticeship training. Many talented slaves were trained as artisans or tradesmen because their skills were perceived as necessary to the smooth and profitable functioning of the plantation. The plantation was essentially a self-contained world—one that caused increasing complexity in the slaves' responsibilities.[30] Some of these apprenticeship programs allowed the slaves to develop a rudimentary degree of literacy, necessary to the learning of the trade. William Brown wrote that "I am chiefly indebted . . . to my employment in the printing office for what little learning I obtained while in slavery." [31]

Very little is known about the clandestine schools where literate slaves and free blacks provided interested slaves with another means of formal education. There are indications, however, that such schools were usually located in the towns and cities, as opposed to on or near the plantations, where blacks were allowed a higher level of anonymity and the low visibility necessary for the secretive existence of their schools.

House servants, usually considered the most privileged segment of the slave population, were often able to secure at least a semi-formal level of education. Masters themselves often introduced these blacks to the essentials of reading and writing. (Many of the authors of the slave narratives were among this group.) Some slaveowners formed personal and deep attachments to a few of their servants (quite understandably since some of the house servants were the illegitimate offspring of their masters) and, through early childhood, reared them as their own. Thus, these servants were permitted to enjoy some of the same educational opportunities available to the slaveowners' children; though the privilege was always elusive, guided by the tolerance and whim of the master. And with late adolesence and adulthood, the privilege was abruptly curtailed.[32]

However, for most blacks the formal or semi-formal routes to education remained irrevocably blocked. Pettigrew maintains that slavery "sharply lowered the need for achievement in slaves. . . . Their reward came not from individual initiative and enterprise but from absolute obedience." [33] But the extraordinary, and often desperate means slaves took to secure an education are not only testimony to their courage but proof of their enduring initiative and resourcefulness. Perhaps the *immediate* rewards and creature survival came from absolute obedience to the white master, but the distant promises of education propelled the black spirit toward pursuing a dangerous dream—one that heightened and sustained very clandestine and private achievements.

Many researchers attribute the "greatest efforts" in providing blacks with a rudimentary education to the planters' children, who, in defiance of their parents' orders, taught reading and writing to their black playmates, usually in playschools.[34] Sometimes white children innocently and enthusiastically shared their knowledge. But often black children literally bribed their white peers for the opportunity to learn to read and write. Frederick Douglass, in a most poignant passage, reveals that after his mistress was dissuaded (by his master) from continuing his education, he bribed white children, some of whom were strangers, in order to learn to read.

> When I was sent on errands, I always took my book with me, and by doing one part of my errand quickly, I found time to get a lesson before my return. I also used to carry bread with me . . . for I was much better off in this regard than many white children in our neighborhood. This bread I used to bestow upon the hungry little urchins, who, in return, would give me that more valuable bread of knowledge.[35]

Perhaps the slaves who took the most desperate and dangerous means to secure an education were those who attempted, often successfully, to teach themselves. Household slaves, who had access to their masters' books, were the most likely to use this means. However, field hands, who were able to secure abolitionist literature, also endeavored to learn to read without the benefit of a teacher.

The main question is why so many slaves went to such remarkable lengths to secure an education. According to Blassingame, slaves who acquired an education gained immeasurable status in the slave community because "they had a secret mirror on the outside and could keep the others informed of events which were transpiring there." [36] For example, Henry Clay Bruce observed that in the slave quarter, "a colored man who could read and write was a very important fellow." [37] Furthermore, education invested the slave with a sense of self-esteem in the midst of his adversity and degradation. Bullock contends that slaves who managed to gain an education, no matter how elementary, considered themselves, and were considered by others, "quality people." [38] The ability to read and write often brought feelings of superiority, which in many instances led to a psychological identification with the master.

Perhaps the major explanation of why many slaves pursued education with such energy and vigor can be attributed to a combination of functional and psychological factors that led to a perception of education as *preparation for emancipation*. It is often reported in the literature that some slaves used their education to forge passes for their escape to the North. However, many slaves although highly educated remained enslaved when they could have relied on their intellectual prowess, as others had, to escape their masters' clutch. There are indications, particularly in the slave narratives, that many slaves sought an education in order to be ready to assume the role of freemen when they attained the opportunity. Negro spirituals indicate that many slaves were anticipating liberation not only in the otherworldly, metaphysical sense but also in the more tangible, earthly sense. Moreover, education decreed a sense of psychological liberation to the slave. While learning to read secretly, Thomas Jones jubilantly wrote, "I felt at night, as I went to rest, that I was really beginning to be a *man*, preparing myself for a condition in life better and higher and happier than could belong to an ignorant *slave*." [39]

Undeniably, the greatest threat to the educated slave was the possibility that his master would discover his secret. Lunsford Lane observed that one of the most important things "slaves had to be constantly on guard against . . . is never to appear so intelligent as [they] really were." [40] Indeed, the reprisals against slaves who sought an education were extreme. Jacob Stroyer, cunningly deceived into revealing to his mistress his ability to read, was threatened with a severe beating and finally apprenticed far away from the plantation and his family in order to remove his potentially dangerous influence on the other slaves.[41] "Among the bitterest recollections of ex-slaves were those of whippings for trying to learn to read. Few things so outraged their sense of justice." [42] Douglass, in a strikingly dramatic account, related that after his master learned of his giving reading instruction to other slaves under the guise of religious training, the master and other whites "pushed in upon us with sticks and stones, and broke up our virtuous little sabbath school. . . . They had much rather see us engage in those degrading sports . . . (wrestling, boxing and drinking of whiskey) . . . than to see us behaving like intellectual, moral and accountable beings." [43]

Thus, the literature provides ample evidence that the whites' dread of the education of blacks verged on the pathological and that the whites acted to squelch even the least flicker of light in the blacks' minds. That many slaves, in spite of insurmountable odds, risked their well-being and achieved an education constitutes a tribute to their endurance and strategy and their profound belief in education as liberation and power. The evidence also reveals the fact that slaves, not their masters, were their own educators—it was they who developed ways to adjust to and modify their new environment, maintain remnants of their cultural heritage, and sustain a sense of individual dignity. Indeed, in the final analysis, perhaps the most profound and critical education black children received during this period was that which allowed them to survive the dehumanization of bondage.

Socialization of Children and Familial Education

The status of slave children in the plantation economy and conceptions of the nature of childhood during this period were very much entwined with the role that slave parents played in the education and socialization of their young. Some black children enjoyed an idyllic childhood barely aware that their social status and destiny differed from that of their white playmates. However, their situation was the exception. Most black children began working irregularly at light tasks by age ten [44] and were usually not sold on the auction block until age twelve.[45] It can be assumed, therefore, that much of slave children's basic education was acquired while they were at their first home and had extended free periods to observe and interact with their parents and other members of the slave community.

There is much controversy concerning the slave parents' role in the education of their children. Frazier and Bernard argue that black parents, after long hours of excruciating labor and psychological humiliation, had little if any time and energy to attend to the personal care of their children.[46] Henry Bibb and Booker T. Washington reveal that they only rarely saw their mothers during the day. Even at night, their mothers barely managed to find the energy to attend to their care or respond to their childish demands.[47] These recollections seem to indicate that the socialization of young slave children became by default, if not by conscious design, the province of the planters. Planters usually consigned the care of young slaves to the old black women of the plantation who, it is reported, often neglected their duties.[48] However, Genovese contends that, for the most part, "children raised each other. The nurses did not so much attend to the younger children as supervise the older ones who attended them."[49]

Given the above, it is understandable why there is so much controversy concerning the slave parents' role in the education of their children. Nevertheless, both Blassingame and Genovese maintain that black parents did not assume peripheral roles but were primarily responsible for their children's socialization. Black parents communicated to their children "African traditions in the form of folklore, music, and beliefs about the supernatural."[50] However, as is indicated by many of the slaves' autobiographical sketches, the most important education parents provided concerned the strategies of survival. Parents drilled two main lessons into the heads of their youngsters. First, the etiquette of race relations was hammered forcefully and ritualistically into the child as soon as he could understand. Deference and courtesy to whites were essential qualities in the slaves' behavioral and psychological repertoire if they wished to avoid brutal beatings and survive to adulthood. Second, parents also emphasized conformity and obedience to the planter's will, however irrational. Parents, in recognition of whites' "overwhelming power . . . taught [their] children unconditional submission."[51] Above all else, they were expected to defend close relatives who were unjustifiably victimized by whites. Finally, slave parents endeavored to infuse in their children a sense of morality and ethics. Religion was perhaps the cornerstone of the parents' training, especially those teachings concerning the deception of despair and the promise of hope. Many of the slave narratives are replete with acknowledgment to parents' enduring sense of purpose and an unwavering faith in God despite great adversity.

From minimal evidence concerning child rearing during slavery, we can begin to trace patterns of socialization and adult-child relationships that have survived in modified forms today. Informal education of children in the slave community was less focused on adults as the central figures of socialization. Older women, too weak to be functional and useful in the field, were given the caretaking role for children who were too young to bring economic benefit. Although some of the literature claims that these elderly women were negligent, even cruel in their punishment of children, the intergenerational distance between young child and weary grandmother created a kind of detachment and space that may have encouraged autonomy and responsibility in children. The old women's mode of child care, whether consciously defined or benevolently inspired, promoted a different kind of interaction among the children—one that emphasized mutual responsibility and caretaking among peers.

The scholars' evidence, often dependent upon the planters' perspective, also does not tell us about the other side of the double life of slaves. Yes, slave parents were preoccupied with the notion of teaching their children to be obsequious, obedient, conforming, and always childlike and smiling in the eyes of white folks. But beyond the watchful eyes of the overseer (and the scholar), we do not know enough about the internal and intimate relations within the black community. We certainly do not gain a realistic picture of the *range* of behaviors, feelings, skills, and competencies that black parents taught their children far out of the range of the manor house—behaviors and emotions that were not revealed to hostile external visions but reserved for the darker side of the double life of slaves.

Northern Blacks and Schooling

Education in the colonial North was the product of the "sixteenth-century religious and political reformation in Europe."[52] Consequently, what few schools existed were founded by churches for the propagation of their religious doctrines. The concept of education for any but an exclusive group of white males—destined for the ministry—was rarely entertained. Thus, when the first blacks arrived in Jamestown in 1619, their subsequent exclusion from the educational process was not unusual because most of the whites were themselves consigned to illiteracy. Education became somewhat secularized by the beginning of the eighteenth century, but it was not until much later that secular education became available to other than the privileged class. The American Revolution spurred a more universal interest in the common man —the rights of man movement—and led eventually to the establishment of free public schools in the North designed to ensure the preservation of democracy.

> . . . there was a widespread acceptance of the view that popular education was essential to the preservation of republican political institutions. This argument was tellingly used over and over again by intellectuals, publicists, and spokesmen of labor. Schools, it was also asserted, would teach respect for law and authority, they would make labor more productive, they would alleviate pauperism . . . in short, they would promote the general welfare.[53]

The revolutionary era also had an unsettling and transforming effect on the status of slaves. Heretofore, they were treated principally as chattel or at best indentured servants. But the revolutionary fervor, which spawned the abolitionist movement, eventually culminated in the general liberation of Northern blacks, which was accomplished by the early nineteenth century. By 1830, a system of free public schools was the right of all white children, "but the products of Horace Mann's famous crusade for the common school seldom included blacks."[54] Mier and Rudwick maintain that from the beginning of the establishment of free schools, most Northern whites sought to "explicitly ignore or limit the accessibility of black children to white schools."[55] Whites restricted blacks' participation in the common school by confining them to either separate schools or separate classrooms within the whites' schools. Initially, though, blacks' participation in the public school system was simply not considered or taken as a serious issue.

There was a fundamental difference, however, between the attitudes of white Northerners and Southerners with regard to the right of blacks to be educated. White Northerners tolerated the education of blacks as long as black parents did not demand their children's right to be educated in the same classroom as whites. Warner is, therefore, correct in his assertion that during the antebellum years, the right to be educated was not the dominant educational issue for Northern blacks as it was for the Southern slaves. Instead, Northern blacks focused on the quality of the schools and whether such quality could best be realized through segregated or integrated schools.[56] It is in their response to whites' opposition to the right of blacks to attend the purportedly free public schools that we begin to examine the relationship of Northern black parents to schools.

Unlike the slave family, which in recent years has been the subject of extensive research, there is practically nothing written on the free Northern black family. Gutman has indicated that the Northern black family enjoyed a high level of stability, most likely surpassing that of the slave family, whose vulnerability was dictated by bondage.[57] There are also impressions in Frazier's work that the Northern family was part of an extensive social network that involved intimate and deep ties with other black families.[58] This cohesive network not only helped the black family survive the oppression of Northern whites—which was just as virulent as that of white Southerners though more subtle and covert in form—but also played a central and critical role in the development of educational opportunities for blacks.

It is here that we recognize the need for scholars to analyze patterns of interaction among black families and the development of strong social networks within the community if we are to begin to comprehend the relationship between blacks and schools and the underlying power of their efforts for change. In other words, it would be misleading to characterize the individualistic relationships between nuclear families and schools as reflective of the meaningful patterns of interaction that led to social and institutional change. The dynamic relationships had a much broader base in the perceptions of both blacks and whites. In fact, a pattern emerges as one traces the development of blacks and schooling—a pattern that reveals a relationship between the existence of strong social networks, the crystallization of a sense of community, and the active and aggressive pursuit by blacks for quality education. During periods of dislocation and migration, for instance, the black assault on schools was minimal, fragmented, and weak; but when people became rooted and community bonds developed, then blacks initiated demands for inclusion in public schooling. For the most part, then, black parents' relationships to the educational institution must be analyzed in terms of the collective activities of black community groups, both formal and informal.

Bond delineates three distinguishable phases in the process of Northern blacks' struggle for an education: first, the creation of public schools for all white children; second, the provision of separate schools for black children at public expense; and, finally, the prohibition of separate schools on the expressed grounds that they were *undemocratic* in principle, a legal abstraction that was rarely practiced.[59] It is important to establish that there was a lengthy pause between phases one and two. That is, the availability of public schools for whites was a clear and explicit social and economic agenda; only as an afterthought was minimal schooling offered to black children. However, it is during this period that black parents played a significant and very interesting role in procuring educational opportunities for their young.

The initial response of blacks to their exclusion from the public school system was to establish their own schools, without the benefit of public funds available to white schools. Thus, during the last decades of the eighteenth century, there was a proliferation of private schools maintained by black churches and mutual-benefit societies. Some scholars [60] give much of the credit for the establishment of these institutions to white religious and benevolent associations, but the evidence supports Mier and Rudwick's conclusion that "even where white philanthropic support was solicited, the initiative came from blacks." [61] In fact, in the few cases where white abolitionists took the initiative in trying to establish schools for blacks, they often failed because of the local white hostility (e.g., mid-1830s in New Haven and Canterbury, Connecticut). When white allies were forced out through threats and violence, groups of black parents assumed leadership roles and directed their schools.[62]

According to Mier and Rudwick, the institutional organization of the black urban community took two forms, the church and the fraternal or mutual-benefit organizations. "Historically, the two were interrelated as the distinction between the sacred and the secular was not closely drawn." [63] Black mutual-aid societies were particularly fascinating organizations, performing a variety of socioeconomic functions that allowed blacks to adapt to and survive in the often hostile urban environment.[64] Black ministers assumed the chief leadership role in these organizations, even though the mutual-benefit society often preceded the church in the community by many years.

One of the first important functions of these societies was the establishment of free schools. Religion, culture, and learning became closely entwined in the educational curriculum and became interrelated themes in the building of cohesive social networks among blacks. Although the societies were closely identified with the white Protestant ethic, they were also institutions that affirmed black identity, independence, and self-respect. During the late eighteenth and early nineteenth centuries, these organizations, more than any other, played the central role in the development of blacks' educational opportunity.

Mutual-aid societies flourished wherever there was a sizable black population (Newport, Rhode Island, New York City, Baltimore, and Washington, D.C.). The Free African Schools of Boston and Philadelphia perhaps most prominently exemplified the fruits of mutual-aid societies, playing a significant role in the educational, social, and political spheres of the black community. Sometimes brave and determined individuals, not operating under the auspices of any mutual-aid society, also sought to develop black schools. The most well-known example of this situation is the establishment of the first school for the education of blacks in Washington, D.C., in 1807—the Bell School—which was founded by three illiterate ex-slaves (George Bell, Nicolas Franklin, and Moses Liverpool).[65] They built the school with their own hands and employed white teachers to staff it.

In spite of their valiant and persistent efforts, black parents were often financially unable to maintain their schools. When there seemed no viable alternative left *within* the black community, parents initiated the struggle to enroll their children in the white schools. Their efforts for inclusion often resulted in white hostility frequently coupled with outbursts of mob violence.[66] Often the hostility of whites to the presence of black children in the same classroom as their own was so overwhelming and violent that black parents were forced to withdraw their children from school and acquiesce to the formation of separate schools. By the middle of the eighteenth century, most Northern communities had provided blacks with separate schools, although not with funding equal to that allowed white schools. In time, the disparities between the black and white schools grew at an alarming rate, lead-ing to further appeals by parents for the equal public funding of black schools. Many school boards, fearful that blacks would demand admittance to white schools, succumbed to black parents' requests. Equality between black and white schools, however, was rarely achieved. In the end, black parents in most Northern cities acquiesced to the existence of separate schools as a "necessary evil." [67]

The Boston narrative is probably the most notable example of black parents' refusal to adjust to the resultant inequalities between black and white schools—a story that would find its historical parallels in the political and legal spheres of subsequent periods. As in other cities, whites' racial prejudice had initially prompted blacks to request a separate school—the Belknap School—established in 1820. In less than twenty years, however, blacks discovered that segregated schools failed to provide their children with educational equality. By 1849, the parents, believing that court action was their last resort, unsuccessfully petitioned for their children to attend integrated schools. When the Massachusetts State Supreme Court upheld the legality of segregated schools, the first recorded case of the separate-but-equal doctrine entered the law books. The adverse ruling, although damaging to their spirits, failed to smother the parents' determination to achieve quality education for their children. Black parents effectively boycotted the separate schools (often transferring their children to distant schools) until in 1855 the state legislature prohibited segregated schools. The following scenario would be repeated time and time again throughout American history [68]—a chain of events that revealed the iron will of black parents and community and the profound depth of interpersonal and institutional racism:

> White prejudice—black acquiescence to the maintenance of separate schools—development of structural inequality between white and black schools—black demands for integrated schools to achieve educational equality—legislative and/or judicial prohibition of segregated schools.

Some scholars support the thesis that the development of many Northern segregated schools was "probably the result of a deal between the [black] administrators of schools for Negroes who agreed with antagonistic and powerful benevolent and parochial societies for selfish reasons" (i.e., to secure employment as teachers).[69] It is difficult to assess the validity of this argument because of serious gaps in the literature. The majority of researchers, however, overwhelmingly support the argument that separate schools in the North arose primarily as a "function of the caste-like structure" of Northern society.[70] The inferiority of separate schools was merely another symbol of the low socioeconomic status of blacks and the general perception of blacks as lesser beings not to be mixed with. Black parents fought for an education that would allow their children an opportunity they were denied—assimilation into American society. Although Northern whites were a shade more subtle in their patterns of resistance, they were in accord with Southern whites that blacks should be kept separate and unequal and that all possible avenues of assimilation should be denied.

Next to the separate schools, nowhere was the manifestation of the inferior status of blacks more apparent than in the type of education to which they were directed. Abolitionists, who were initially the primary planners of the curriculum for black schools, believed that an industrial education (that exposed blacks to agricultural training, mechanical arts, handicrafts, etc., with emphasis on the religious and character-building courses) was the only way free blacks could be accepted into white society.[71] Little, if any, consideration was given to the educational needs, choices, or aspirations that black parents had for their children. It is not surprising that when blacks established their own schools they implemented a curriculum that they perceived to be similar to that employed by white educational institutions (i.e., classical or liberal arts education). But even when blacks successfully completed their classical training, they still found themselves locked into their caste-like identity. Administrators of the New York African Free School, in the 1820s, complained that many young blacks, upon graduation from the schools, "were idle because they could neither find jobs nor enter the trades" and that educated blacks often had "no alternative" except to seek employment in the menial occupations (e.g., common laborers, servants, coachmen, etc.).[72] Ironically, the South, where most blacks were legally denied an education, employed proportionately more black skilled artisans than the North, where blacks were allowed an industrial education.[73]

In conclusion, it can be said that the historical roots of many of the issues that would confront twentieth-century parents and educators of black children were well established in the antebellum period. The history of Northern blacks tells the story of blacks confronting institutional structures, demanding their inclusion in schools; while the narrative of Southern blacks is the passionate drive for education, enlightenment, and liberation. The first was a calculated political battle designed to gain resources (whether material or human) that would ensure educational equality for their young. The goal of their political and legal pursuits was assimilation into mainstream society—not necessarily a relinquishing of their cultural heritage and "blackness," but definitely a chance to taste a substantial piece of the American pie. The strategies were politically and legally shaped and the orientation was toward structural and institutional inclusion.

Southern blacks, on the other hand, yearned for the "magic" of education—a magic that would bring self-esteem, adulthood and manhood, liberation on earth, and identification with the white world. There was an otherworldly quality attached to education, almost redemptive in its meaning. The struggle was more deeply personal than political, springing from psychological needs for fulfillment and hopes that knowledge held the key to freedom of body and spirit. In both the North and South, however, blacks recognized that their forced ignorance and exclusion from schooling had economic origins; that their chattel status and subservient role was necessary for the smooth functioning of a hierarchical economic order. Inclusion or exclusion of blacks turned on their economic function to the dominant society—their use and abuse as workers.

Both of these traditions endure today. Blacks fight political battles for inclusion in dominant school structures, and they fight psychological battles for education in the broadest sense, an education that will help to sustain their sense of culture, brotherhood, and community as well as teach the skills and competencies necessary for economic and political survival in mainstream society. The first tradition has taken different forms and revealed various strategies depending on the historical context; but the second has endured, strong and deep.

Patterns of white Northern and Southern resistance to the black struggle for education during the antebellum period took superficially different forms that extended through the decades that followed. Southern whites were overt and unambivalent in their intention to maintain an uneducated black population, because they feared that knowledge and skills would bring an erosion of the caste-like economic framework on which they depended so completely. Northerners did not seem to deny blacks a minimal education, but they did not want to mix with them in schools and communities. If a few "exceptional" blacks were to gain a high level of education, they were to use their skills and competencies to serve their community, not assimilate into the upper stratas of white society. The black sphere was to be a separate world with high, impenetrable boundaries that enclosed an inferior group of people. Although the institutional racism in Northern and Southern territories seemed to take different forms, the underlying theme in both was resistance to the right of blacks for an education. Whether the strategies were building walls of institutional separation and exclusion in the North or prohibiting access to learning in the South, the oppression was deeply rooted and often fiercely violent, and basic human rights were being denied to black parents and children.[74]

Historical Reflections in Social Science Research

Social science research on blacks and schools has echoed many of the historical themes of racism and oppression. Researchers have created theoretical and methodological strategies that have given scientific validity to racist assumptions. In the late nineteenth and early twentieth centuries, numerous studies appeared that flagrantly exposed the researchers' discriminatory visions of blacks. In 1902, for instance, Frances Kellor said, "The Negro child must be trained from infancy, his surroundings improved and the standards of his home life raised. Only then can the question be dealt with, 'what effect has education upon the Negro?' "[75] In 1911, the Hanus Survey, which was carried out as a part of a larger study on mentally deficient children, concluded that the poor performance of Negro children in school was caused by deprivation in the uniquely debilitating Negro home. In 1913, M. J. Mayo, using school marks as an indication of mental ability, concluded that "there seem to be no statistical grounds for holding to the view of substantial racial mental equality. Our data point clearly to a measurable degree of mental difference." And in 1921, an issue of *The Annals of the American Academy of Political and Social Science* devoted to child welfare classed the black child with "the lame, blind, orphaned, and illegitimate as special groups needing attention."[76]

Although the preceding excerpts are blatant and crass in their prejudicial language, imagery, and conceptualization, one recognizes the unbroken thread between historical forms of social control and oppression of blacks and the research evidence used for justifying inequalities. "Racial mental inequalities," measured by careful statistical techniques, seem a strong echo of (and justification for) legal and institutional inequalities based on race. Further, the history of political and legal conflicts between black families and schools emerges as a central conceptual theme in the early research on blacks and education. Black family life is described as chaotic, disorganized, and structureless; and black parents are accused of willfully ignoring and inadequately preparing their children for social and cognitive adaptation to the school environment.

The focus on the deviance and pathology of black family life is an exaggerated extension of a more general moralistic tone that pervades the sociological and anthropological literature on family structures and functions. The static pictures of the family found in popular American imagery do not correspond to the real-life patterns of the vast majority of people in this society. In *All Our Children,* Kenneth Keniston destroys any remaining illusions of the perfect, symmetrical nuclear family when his data reveal patterns and structures of family life, across all socioeconomic, racial, and ethnic groups, that do not conform to the stereotypic image of father as breadwinner, mother as homemaker, with two lovely, clean, and well-behaved children.[77] In an essay entitled "Youth Deferred," Joseph Featherstone speaks sensitively of the moralistic tones that bias the literature on family life—a bias that does an injustice to the adaptive, resilient structures of families that do not mirror the plastic media images of television commercials, children's books, or introductory sociology texts.

> Discussions of the family are bedeviled by moralistic norms. Just as there is the statistical norm of the American family—Mom, Pop, Sis, and Bud—there is also the moral norm, the father at work, the mother at home taking care of the kids, all parties happy in their roles. The moral norm has never done justice to the diversity of family styles; it has overlooked working mothers, female-headed families, families in which fathers contribute substantially to child-

rearing, and many other variations on the theme of family living. It is one reason American families, whatever their make-up, do not get the kind of support they need for child-rearing. The norm has also been an agony to those who for their own good reasons find the family and its commitments oppressive. One of the best things the women's liberation movement has done is to publicize the truth that not everybody needs the family.[78]

Divorce, separation, remarriage, and adoption all may mean that there is little correspondence between the social, psychological, and biological definitions of family. The unit described as the household often does not resemble the unit that is socially defined as family. And when one introduces the dimension of time, one recognizes changes and transformations in the constellations of family and in the evolving relationships and interactional patterns among members. Beyond changes in the structures and patterns of households, it is critical that we not conceive of the family as a closed system, but as part of a wider social system that is open and responsive to a myriad of external influences. The family must be seen within the broad context of numerous significant external relationships.[79]

> Research on kinship has shown that relatives outside the nuclear family may exert significant influences, even in urban, industrial societies in which the nuclear family is presumably "isolated" from contacts with kin. Grandparents, for example, not only can and do play a role in the education of their grandchildren, they may also play a role in defining the ways in which parents perform their own educative functions.[80]

Coupled with the distorted vision of isolated nuclear families are equally narrow perceptions of child-rearing patterns within families. Throughout the literature on cognitive development, for instance, investigators have focused on the *dyadic* relationship between mother and child as the only critical determinant of learning, and assumed an asymmetric, one-way influence from parent to child rather than a dynamic, two-way interaction. The preoccupation with mother-child dyads excludes and negates the other powerful participants in the child's socialization; assumes that parents do not learn from their children; and gives the burdensome responsibility of child care and growth to a single female figure.

The exclusion of significant others from the analysis of child-rearing patterns has a particularly distorting effect on our view of black family life and the socialization of children. From the slavery period, for example, we find evidence of the critical caretaking role performed by older siblings and peers, and the powerful influence of grandmothers and women elders in the rearing of young children. Reflections of these more extended patterns of child rearing are found today in black communities where children seem to be less focused on the *adult* as the central figure for sustenance and guidance and seem more likely to seek help and support from agemates. A comprehensive description of the educative function of families, therefore, would have to include socialization and learning that are not supervised or controlled by adults; would have to document *child-inititated* interactions with significant others; and would have to reflect patterns of communication and behavior extending far beyond the boundaries of the nuclear family or household.

In critiquing social science research on black families, Robert Hill identifies a major methodological and conceptual fallacy that obscures the experiences of black children—the tendency to impute function on the basis of structure.[81] Knowledge of the fact that a family is headed by a single parent does not necessarily tell us anything about the living patterns and daily experiences of family members. Moving from a family of two parents to a single-parent form may be a structural adaptation, not necessarily a sign of deterioration and disintegration. The preoccupation with prototypic nuclear structures in social science literature is coupled with the tendency of researchers to offer differential explanations for deviance and difference in white and black communities. Single black mothers are more likely to be perceived as unwed, irresponsible, and promiscuous; while white mothers, expressing similar behavioral and attitudinal patterns, may be described as engaging in liberated, alternative life styles. Even though researchers are often making social-class as well as racial differentiations, their descriptions are more a reflection of their value-laden perceptions than they are revealing of differences in behavioral, empirical data.

Recent experimental research on the intellectual development of young black children has continued to be preoccupied with the inadequacies of their family life and with the negative conflicts between black families and schools. Researchers have searched for the source of the black child's low achievement and poor acculturation in school by focusing on the dissonance between family life style and the school environment. Much of the literature on the early cultural deprivation of black children rests on unquestioned and long-standing assumptions about child development and the socialization of cognitive modes in children. Hess and Shipman's experimental work on language development and expressive styles of black children reflects these basic assumptions and is a classic example of the modes of inquiry used by social science researchers. The authors claim that lower-class black children experience irreversible cultural deprivation because there is a lack of cognitive meaning in the mother-child communication system. They distinguish between the communication styles of lower-class and middle-class mothers, asserting that middle-class mothers offer a range of alternatives for thought and action (elaborated verbal cues) while lower-class mothers give predetermined solutions and few alternatives for consideration and thought (restricted verbal cues). Hess and Shipman use these two examples of a middle-class and lower-class mother preparing their children for the first day of school:

Middle-Class Mother:

First of all I would remind her that she was going to school to learn, that her teacher would take my place, and that she would be expected to follow instructions. Also that her time was to be spent mostly in the classroom with other children and that any questions

> or any problems that she might have she should consult with her teacher for assistance. To tell her anything else would probably be confusing for her at this age.
>
> Lower-Class Mother:
>
> Mind the teacher and do what she tells you to do. The first thing you have to do is be on time. Be nice and do not fight. If you are tardy or if you stay away from school your marks will go down. The teacher needs your full cooperation. She will have so many children she won't be able to pamper any youngster.[82]

According to Hess and Shipman, these excerpts reflect a disparity in the quality and style of language and in the amount of instructional vs. imperative information. More important, on the basis of this early experience lower-class children are poorly prepared to approach the task of learning in school while middle-class children develop into assertive and reflective learners.

The Hess and Shipman data were gathered in a laboratory setting where black mother-child dyads were directed to engage in pre-established cognitive games and their patterns of language interaction were recorded and analyzed. Mothers and children were asked, therefore, to enter an unfamiliar and alien setting, given an experimental task of meaningless social significance, and observed and evaluated by strange adults. No observations were taken in the naturalistic settings where mothers and children usually interact with one another, and the data show correlations, not causality, between child-rearing practices and achievement.[83] Even if we ignore the many ideological and methodological problems connected with this study, we must ask to what realities the mothers are socializing their children. It would appear that both mothers are equally oriented toward the constraints and demands of school for their children. In schools, it is more likely that lower-class children will be rewarded for passivity and compliance while middle-class children will be rewarded for being creative, resourceful, and assertive.[84]

The problem of language difference created by schools is intensified when one recognizes that language is not only a way of discerning intellect and communicating information; it is a medium of culture, a way of signifying one's membership in the community. In an article entitled "Illiteracy in the Ghetto," Jane Torrey makes this point by distinguishing between the *structural* aspects of language (i.e., phonology, grammar, and semantics) and the *functional* aspects of language (i.e., the personal and cultural functions of language).[85] Torrey asserts that the functional aspects of language have far more serious implications than the structural ones. The language of black children, therefore, is symbolic of social and cultural deviance and becomes the basis of hostility on the part of teachers and rejection of the whole educational process by children.

Kenneth Clark's work provides an important transition from focusing on the inadequacies of ghetto life to looking at the structural and interactional patterns *within* schools that do not provide supportive, nurturant, and receptive environments for poor black children. In *Dark Ghetto,* Clark focuses on the rejection and hostility that poor children suffer in white, middle-class-oriented schools and proposes changes in teacher behaviors, attitudes, and competencies that would be supportive of the child's self-concept.[86] Most important, Clark rejects the class-bound, pejorative tradition of social scientists and recognizes the danger of thinking of lower-class life as a self-contained system, which would draw our attention away from the imposition of wider society. Despite his compassionate and insightful analysis, however, Clark still does not present the Harlem community in terms of its own social order, cultural idiom, or life style. Harlem is described less in its own right than by comparison with everything that is nonblack and nonslum.

Although we recognize a shift of *blame* in Clark's analysis of family-school dissonance in black communities, he continues to be preoccupied with explaining the deviance and deficiencies of poor black children. The focus remains on the damaging impact of familial socialization and the resultant inadequacies of lower-class black children. The success and accommodation of middle-class black children is given minimal attention in the literature on racism in schools. The range and variety of human values, attitudes, and behaviors within black culture is neglected by focusing on the poor and by defining their behavior in individualistic and motivational terms. In his book, *Culture of Poverty,* Charles A. Valentine talks about the tendency for social science researchers to enmesh cultural difference with poverty and deviance.[87] Culture begins to take on a pejorative connotation as it becomes linked with poverty and race and the whole essence of inequality. By attributing a distinctive cultural system to the poor, researchers have tended to isolate poverty cultures and focus on the alleged motivational peculiarities of the poor (self-indulgence, inability to delay gratification), rather than consider the various responses of people to the structural characteristics of the stratified social system as a whole.

Contemporary Conflicts Mirrored in Research

The abundant research on the dissonance and tension between black family life and white-dominated schools in the early sixties paralleled the increasing and more visible conflicts between black communities and schools in major urban areas throughout the country. The period following the historic *Brown* v. *Board of Education* decision in 1954 evidenced a tenacious but relatively peaceful struggle by black communities to achieve implementations of the school integration mandate . . . until the tumultuous mid-sixties. Blacks became increasingly disenchanted with their previously more moderate strategies to obtain decent schooling for their children and began to feel betrayed by the unfulfilled promises of the educational establishment. The smoldering resentments that had festered under a superficial veneer of polite distance and civilized requests became unleashed, and the conflicts between school and community became dramatically apparent.

Several factors contributed to the more forceful demands and visibility of black parents in the educational arena. The school populations of many large cities became increasingly black as white middle-class families fled to the more peaceful suburbs and working-class whites became more strident about protecting and insulating their ethnic enclaves and sent their children to parochial schools. As blacks became majority populations in many city school systems, desegregation within urban boundaries seemed an unreachable and unrealistic goal. Segregated minority schools seemed inevitable. Black parents soon recognized that their communities would become more and more isolated from financial and human resources and become the colonized enclaves of a dominant society who feared their potential violence and who turned their backs on their legitimate demands, needs, and dreams for the next generation. As doors began to close to mainstream life and channels of communication and resource exchange slowly deteriorated, as black parents began to recognize that the schools had systematically failed their children (as evidenced in high truancy, dropout or "push-out" rates, high proportions of school failures, low standardized test scores), the polite distance and civilized exchanges between communities and schools grew into angry outbursts of discontent and frustration. The heightened cohesiveness of black communities during this period allowed a pooling of frustrations, resources, and initiatives—much of which was focused on the school as the battleground, the most visible and vulnerable social institution within the community that was perceived as the only avenue that their children could take out of the hopelessness and poverty of ghetto life. The sixties was a decade, therefore, in which black parents in practically every region of the country clamored for their piece of the educational pie by seeking to acquire direct input into the functioning of schools in order to take hold and shape their children's educational destinies.

It was in the confrontations between the educational system's inertia and resistance to change and the more forceful black initiative that the dissonant themes between black dreams and white patterns of exclusion took a more visible form. The conflicts were not new. They had been deeply etched in the institutional foundations of racism described in the historical section of this chapter. But they were more dramatically apparent. The media brought the violent and threatening confrontations into our homes every night; close-ups of rage, fear, frustration, and hatred forced everyone to take notice.

One of the more distant and "rational" responses to the conflicts came from the ivory towers of universities barely out of reach of the sound and fury, where researchers searched out the origins of the black child's failure and pointed to the dissonance between black families and schools and the need for a restructuring of black family life to better accommodate to the norms, sanctions, and culture of the school environment. What kinds of conflicts and differences were the researchers seeking to describe and objectify in the midst of the heated political and ideological debates and the outbursts of street violence concerning schools? Were their explanations and analyses rationalizations for maintaining the status quo; were they reflecting the fears and biases of dominant, mainstream groups in society; or were their perspectives on the conflicts between majority schools and minority communities dispassionate, balanced, and fair?

One of the clearest patterns of conflict between lower-class black communities and white controlled middle-class schools concerned parents' and teachers' opposing views of the educational needs of black children and the appropriate curriculum and pedagogical strategies to use in classrooms. During the sixties, increasing numbers of teachers came into ghetto schools filled with liberal political ideals, progressive educational philosophies, and a missionary spirit. Their approach was not intentionally condescending or patronizing to the black community. As a matter of fact, they worked very hard at identifying with "the people" and becoming partners in the struggle for social change. Some of the most committed idealists moved into the black community so that they would be able to better understand the lives of children in their classrooms and so that they could personally and symbolically establish links between families and schools. In their classrooms, many of these young teachers followed an open-classroom model, encouraged children to call them by their first names, focused on building positive self-images among the children, and supported the use of black dialect as a legitimate language in school. For the most part, parents did not see the value of these more liberalized rules and structures. All they saw, when they looked into classrooms, was chaos, sloppiness, and uncivilized behavior in their children. More important, it all looked like "play," not work. School was a place for learning to read and write, and black children were being surreptitiously denied these basic skills by the whites who professed to care the most. In the idealism, zeal, and compassion of these "progressive" teachers, black parents perceived the unconscious threads of racism. They did not want these "do-gooders" coming into their schools to work on the affective, psychosocial, and cultural dimensions of their children's lives. The family was the place to explore those more expressive qualities. Parental conceptions of good schooling were much more traditional and conservative. For their children, parents wanted the "classical" education that had been historically denied. Many of these young, committed, and misdirected teachers, therefore, became the targets of parental complaints and criticism and the visible expression of the community's outrage against the entire school system. Black parents often worked to get them fired and demanded the hiring of more black teachers and administrators who might share their cultural views of education and who might bring order and structure to the school environment. What irony, that those who wanted to identify with the community so thoroughly had misperceived the values and concerns of parents so completely, and had continued the subtle denial of education to their children.

Another one of the critical themes of dissonance that became visible during this period of heightened crisis in the sixties concerned the conflicting values attached to education by black parents and teachers. Interestingly, most studies that examine and document the educational values of these two groups reveal that there are no significant differences in their perspectives. Lower-class black parents and middle-class white teachers, for example, both show a high regard for educational attainment and value schooling as the most critical arena of the child's intellectual life. In fact, black parents seem to voice a more passionate concern for the value of education in their child's life chances.[88] Indeed, the literature shows overwhelmingly that blacks (regardless of social status) universally view education as the most promising means for attaining higher socioeconomic status.[89] The dissonance between black parents and teachers, therefore, does not lie in the conflicting values attached to education but in the *misperceptions* they have of one another.

Despite the passionate and often unrealistic dreams of black parents, teachers continue to view them as uncaring, unsympathetic, and ignorant of the value of education for their children and unconcerned about their children's academic success in school. Often they perceive the parents' lack of involvement in ritualistic school events and parent conferences as apathy and disinterest and rarely interpret it as the inability to negotiate the bureaucratic maze of schools or as a response to a long history of exclusion and rejection at the school door. Their lack of success in effectively participating in the relatively superficial and peripheral roles allowed ghetto parents is perceived by teachers as a lack of interest and concern in their children's education. The irony, of course, is that they care too much—a kind of caring that limits their view of alternative strategies for moving forward; a blinding preoccupation that makes black parents and children more vulnerable to the modes of subtle and explicit exclusion they face in relation to schools.

On the other hand, what black parents view as the uncaring regard that the teachers have for their children is related to the teachers' projected feelings about the "realistic" chances black children have for educational and occupational success in this society. Parents see teachers as not valuing schooling for black children while claiming to be at the center of that critical educational process. In the eyes of parents, most teachers seem to believe that their energies will be wasted on the inevitable failure of the vast majority of black children, and they assure that bleak conclusion by engaging in custodial (rather than teaching) functions and by demeaning and degrading the black intellect and spirit. Parents' and teachers' perceptions of each other as uncaring about children and as devaluing the educational process lead to distance and distrust and the need to blame one another. Misperceptions, rarely articulated and confronted, always nurtured by hostile stereotypes, lead to increasing disregard for each other's place in the lives of black children. Rather than search for the origins of conflict and find effective strategies for real (rather than contrived) participation of parents and teachers in a collaborative task, schools develop more sophisticated methods of exclusion; parents draw farther and farther away from parental responsibilities in the schooling process; and children fail—often experiencing the failure as their own individual inadequacy, incompetence, and lack of motivation.

Clearly the more contemporary struggles and tensions between black families, communities, and schools are related to the preoccupations of social scientists eager to describe and understand the dissonant patterns. In fact, the historical and contemporary perceptions of black families and communities are intertwined with the discriminatory visions of social scientists eager to justify the unequal nature of society and the relative powerlessness of blacks and minorities. The scholars' documentation of selected pieces of reality reflect their values, fears, biases, and professional training. Their perceptions shape the questions asked, the data collected, the interpretation of evidence, and the remedies recommended. Herbert Gutman identifies three research questions related to black life that reflect the different ideological perspectives of scholars and reveal divergent patterns of data.

What was done *for* blacks?
What was done *to* blacks?
What was done *by* blacks? [90]

Daniel P. Moynihan popularized the first orientation when he boldly proclaimed, "The Negro has no value and culture to guard and protect." [91] This stance is racist in its assumptions; the notion being that blacks are lesser beings to be feared, coddled, and controlled. There is no attempt to systematically and dispassionately describe the patterns of life and experience for blacks in an oppressive, unjust society; only to focus on their inadequacies and deficiencies relative to mainstream society. This external, comparative view of black families presents a picture of black life that is seen as a grotesque distortion, an ugly and incomplete mirror of white life, rather than as its own unique combination of elements reflecting culture, history, and experience.

The second research orientation documented by Gutman, though more benevolent in its imagery than the first, does not give a comprehensive and holistic description of the sociopolitical processes and institutional structures that have victimized blacks. These researchers show a blinding preoccupation with the exploitation of victims, which negates the humanity and diminishes the power of blacks. In other words, the researchers have spoken passionately about oppression and degradation and its damaging effects on the afflicted people, and have neglected to point to evidence of the strong and enduring responses of the oppressed and have failed to document the active, *initiating* strategies that they have used for survival and accommodation.

The final question has been given minimal scholarly attention compared to the other two. It represents a dramatic ideological and methodological shift—one that requires comprehensive and subtle description and analysis and the liberated minds and perspectives of scholars. The objective visions must also incorporate an empathetic pursuit of another truth; a truth told by those who have been denied a historical voice. (Alex Haley's *Roots* stirred the passion of black Americans not because he had meticulously reported the factual evolution of history but because he researched a story that had been untold and hidden, and because he searched with discipline, endurance, and empathy.)

In seeking to understand the relationship of blacks to schooling, therefore, one must respond critically to the basic sociopolitical and ideological visions of researchers that shape the questions they are likely to ask and frame their construction of reality.

Toward New Conceptions of Family-School Collaboration

In order to begin to capture the daily life experiences, capacities, and resources of black families and communities, investigators must not start by searching for pathology and deviance; rather they must develop research strategies that will reveal holistic, complex, and longitudinal descriptions of life patterns. In *All Our Kin,* an insightful and well-documented ethnography of black family life in a Midwestern city, Carol Stack asked how it is that black families have survived so well in the face of oppressive and hostile environmental forces. Her orientation, toward tracing adaptive patterns and strategies for survival, revealed resources and strengths within the black community that have been neglected and ignored by most investigators. She found powerful and supportive social networks and bonding patterns among families that gave shape to strong communities—giving sustenance to families that would never have survived in isolation and offering multiple role models and sources of identification for young children.[92] Informal adoption patterns, mutual-aid networks, pooling of resources, and extended families that knew no biological boundaries seemed to echo the cohesive and protective community structures found during slavery.

Our visions of family-school relationships would be substantially transformed if researchers and educational practitioners would begin to recognize the powerful and critical role of *family as educator*. Social scientists have offered a very narrow definition of learning *within* families—a definition that measures those parental behaviors and attitudes that are thought to be related to the child's school achievement. There "has been a certain vagueness about the processes by which parental behaviors are linked to educational efforts; the process is often implicit and assumed rather than explicit and observed." [93] Even when researchers have broadened their perspective to include a concern for more general personality characteristics as outcome measures of family education (i.e., independence, assertiveness), they have been interested in these qualities only in relation to the child's ability to function and produce (by some measurable standard) in schools.

> Apart from the questions one might raise about success in schooling as a sole measure of educational outcomes, it is clear that the conception of the outcomes of familial education can fruitfully be enlarged. If one defines education as the deliberate, systematic, and sustained effort to transmit, evoke, or acquire knowledge, attitudes, values, skills, and sensibilities, numerous suggestions come to mind. Knowledge, for example, may be viewed from the family's point of view rather than the school's, with private or specialized knowledge, such as information about ethnic customs or languages not used in school, taking on particular importance. Attitudes and values can be associated with religious beliefs, which are often deliberately excluded from the school curriculum. An almost limitless list of skills can become relevant, depending on the traditions, the interest, and the concerns of particular families. Some of these skills, for example, the ability to organize material in space or activities in time, may have useful carry-over into schooling, while others, for example, the ability to clean fish in a family of fishermen, will assume their value whether or not they carry over into schooling.[94]

If one recognizes the initial social and cultural task assumed by *all* families and their primary *educative* function, then it becomes clear that in order for schools to be productive and comfortable environments for children, they will have to meaningfully incorporate the familial and cultural skills and values learned in homes and communities. When families and schools share similar values, cultural perspectives, educational goals, and modes of expression, then the transposition from family education to schooling is more fluid and less conflictual for the child. On the other hand, when schools and families support dissonant values and goals, and when families and communities are perceived as inadequate and chaotic environments by arrogant and threatened school personnel, then education within families is devalued and systematically excluded from the school culture. Children experience the cultural dissonance between home and school, recognize the sharp contrasts and the forced choice they must make for successful accommodations in both worlds, and develop more or less functional strategies for relieving the environmental tensions.

Children seem to learn and grow in schools where parents and teachers share similar visions and collaborate on guiding children forward. For a long time, we have understood that the magic of suburban schools is not merely the relative affluence and abundant resources of the citizens (nor their whiteness), but also the consonance between what the parents want for their children and what the teachers believe is educationally sound. When their perspectives begin to diverge too widely, suburban parents become vocal and demanding and teachers are forced to respond with explanations and clear goal setting. The furor over the new math a decade ago reflected the parents' fear of change, lack of understanding, and feelings of exclusion. Teachers had to explain the new curriculum direction and justify new math as a more adaptive, potentially productive conceptual tool for young children. Many parents remained unconvinced, believing it was another bit of educational whimsy and faddishness; but the battle was open and the arguments were visible and articulated. The *unspoken* consonance that the parents and teachers in suburban schools share may be more critical to their understanding of one another than their *spoken* conflicts. In other words, the arguments arise out of some shared and sympathetic understanding of one another, a sense of consonant values and cultural traditions.

There is a common language for waging battles and negotiating differences.

In most predominantly black urban communities, schools are easily distinguishable from the ghetto housing that surrounds them. Architects build windowless structures so that teachers and children will not be distracted by street life and urban decay and so that community residents will not be able to peer in to discover the mysteries and secrets of school life. In these communities, black parents and teachers are not likely to experience a comfortable feeling of unspoken alliance or a common language for articulating their differences. Rather parents and teachers are likely to come from different racial, ethnic, and social-class backgrounds, and schools are the symbolic expressions of the more powerful and dominant white middle class. In order to reduce the distance and begin to uncover and appreciate their differences, black families and schools must begin to come together in a much more deliberate and self-conscious way than in suburban communities. Because besides learning to relate and finding ways to communicate, urban parents and teachers need to get to know each other in a more intuitive sense, which only arises out of the hard work and experience of coming together.

The process of coming together may seem trivial and meaningless at first; unrelated to the education and growth of children. The recent history of the Liberty School, a predominantly black urban school where teachers encouraged and welcomed parents, reveals the slow and vulnerable process of building parent involvement. For months, even years, only a handful of concerned and loyal parents would show up to plan a cake sale to raise money for school trips for their children. Hours would be spent haggling over the various tasks, the price of cupcakes, the decorations for the sales stall; and finally the cake sale would yield a miserable profit. In retrospect, these beginning stages of gathering together, in small groups around a task, laid the groundwork for more meaningful and productive forms of interaction among parents and participation in school life. Momma-made cupcakes may have been delicious interludes in the child's school day, but few would argue that their consumption would change his reading scores or alter his attitudes toward school. But the cake sale was a prelude to more substantial contributions by parents. From selling cakes in the traditional volunteer role, mothers began to work in the library, finding readable books for children; in the lunch room, managing the traffic of hungry children; and in the halls, keeping track of wandering children or having private conversations with children who needed special attention. Finally, mothers began to work actively *within* classrooms and became actively involved in the schooling process.[95]

It is important to recognize that the presence of parents in the school not only provides more adults to teach reading or offer help and support to children but also transforms the *culture* of the school. With these black mothers present, there is no way that the curriculum and environment could remain unchanged. Even if the content of the lesson appears the same on paper, the transmission of the lesson takes on a different quality and character when presented by the mothers. Even if the concepts are unfamiliar and alien to the child's experience, the mother-teacher's style of interaction, her face, and her character are not strange. It feels like home.

Not only does the working collaboration of parents and teachers transform the educational environment and cultural medium of the school, it also changes the adult perceptions of their roles and relationships. In a group interview I had with the mothers of the Liberty School, they spoke of the evolution (not revolution) toward a participatory role that was meaningful and critical to the life of the school and the development of their children.

> The mothers reported that many behavioral and learning problems in school seemed to disappear when 1) their child experienced an alliance between mother and teacher; 2) they were able to help teachers become more perceptive and responsive to the needs of their children; 3) their participation in classroom life helped to reduce the workload of teachers; 4) they were able to directly

perceive and fully comprehend the complexities and burdensome nature of the teaching role; 5) they could teach some of the teachers, who were not parents, something about nurturance and mothering; 6) they began to perceive of the school as belonging to them.[96]

The infusion of parents into the school on a daily basis is a far cry from the celebration of Negro History Week once a year. The continuous presence of black parents brings sources of identification for children that are real and reachable, that are strong and vulnerable, and that reveal the scars and endurance of human struggle in this society. Negro History Week offers images of Paul Robeson, Marion Anderson, and Frederick Douglass, amazingly talented and great leaders who were bigger than life. They are sources of inspiration, people about whom we can feel deeply proud; but they are unreachable, distant heroes, and their pictures will come down from the classroom walls at the end of the week—only to appear next year, the same unchanging faces, a bit more tattered and worn.

There is recent convincing evidence that family-school collaboration in minority and poor communities has a powerful effect on teachers, parents, and children. Herbert Walberg found increases in the reading scores and intellectual skills of young black children in a large urban school where parents, teachers, and children drew up written contracts of participation and responsibility in the educational and schooling process.[97] *Time* and *Newsweek* magazines have reported stories of progress and transformation in all-black schools in Chicago's ghettos where principals and teachers began to demand the active and critical participation of parents in their child's learning and in school policy. With the support of parents, teachers were encouraged to adapt their styles of interaction and behaviors to the cultural idiom of the community.[98] And in the King School, a public, elementary school in New Haven, parents and teachers tell a long, tortuous, and inspiring story of getting to know one another, growing to trust one another, learning to fight productively, and finally building collaborative partnerships. Not only did the reading scores of children soar to new heights, but the essence of education was transformed by the presence of families within the school.[99]

Schools will only become comfortable and productive environments for learning when the cultural and historical presence of black families and communities are infused into the daily interactions and educational processes of children. When children see a piece of themselves and their experience in the adults that teach them and feel a sense of constancy between home and school, then they are likely to make a much smoother and productive transition from one to the other. Black familial and cultural participation will require profound changes in the structural and organizational character of schools, in the dynamic relationship between school and community, in the daily, ritualistic interactions between teachers and children, and finally, in the consciousness and articulation of values, attitudes, and behaviors of the people involved in the educational process. The irony of the academic and sociopolitical assaults on black families lies in the fact that historically black families have been the central sustaining force of black culture; that black families have been productive educational environments, teaching children survival strategies and the ability to negotiate dissonant cultural spheres; and that the collaboration of black families and schools is the only hope for the successful schooling of black children.

5

Looking Beyond Fences

Sociohistorical Interpretations of School Culture

ONE OF the dominant themes that weaves through this book points to the determining power and momentum of social and cultural imagery. The individuals involved in negotiating the bridges and boundaries of families and schools are greatly influenced by the sociohistorical and cultural forces that incorporate their lives. This is not to say that parents, teachers, and children are the helpless victims of a predetermined fate or that individual initiative and interpersonal exchange are meaningless and hopeless gestures, but rather that interpersonal and intrapsychic issues exist within the context of encompassing belief systems and enduring structures. It is, therefore, misleading to offer an isolated analysis of the complexities of parent-teacher interaction without considering the cultural boundaries within which people function. Ironically, a recognition of those forces beyond the control of individual temperament and action can be a source of liberation from personal blame and guilt as well as a more realistic way of perceiving potentials for change. Parents who experience the competition and anxiety of encounters with their child's teacher may be able to feel some relief in knowing that their struggles are not simple constructions of their own ambivalence and insecurities but are part of a much broader social process that is universally endured by all parents.

This section will look at the varied perspectives of social historians who have sought to analyze the dimensions of school that have had a powerful impact on how teachers and parents perceive their roles, define their territories, and shape their interactions. As one begins to uncover the different perceptions of the historical origins of school culture and the unique dynamics of community culture, one can view the profound dissonance of structure and process that has given a predetermined and limiting cast to productive interactions between families and schools.

Although social historians disagree about the origins, evolution, and purpose of schooling in American society, they do agree that the schools have emerged as self-contained cultures. The magnitude and benevolence of this culture remains debatable, but it is agreed that schools substantially dominate the culture of most local communities. It is in the evolving tensions and controversies between the relatively dominant school and the surrounding community cultures that historians have sought to answer questions about the explicit and implicit goals of school and have tried to document whose interests are being served.

In her account of *The Great School Wars: New York City, 1805–1973,* Diane Ravitch presents a view of school culture that is dynamic and transforming—a shifting compromise of competing interest groups. She perceives the structures and functions of schools as evolving out of numerous cultural wars in which disenfranchised elements of the community rose to seize the power of the school. The subsequent reorganizations were never quite what the fighting faction had hoped for, but they did usually incorporate some modifying concessions. In both the Ocean Hill-

Brownsville controversy in the late 1960s and the Catholic campaign against the public school society in the 1840s, for instance, Ravitch claims that the protesting groups were granted some input into the decision-making process, but "on terms that did not permit the inculcation of a particular ideology." [1] It was feared that total and ultimate control of the school by a dissenting community group would allow a separatism unresponsive to population shifts and cultural reorganization.

Ravitch views schools as volatile political arenas that inevitably support values and norms that are objectionable and alien to someone. "The city's melange of classes, races, religions, and ethnics guarantees ever-present potential for conflict." [2] Most important, the author claims there is no ultimate mode of schooling; and to suppose as much would be misleading and presumptuous. Recognizing the productive uses of conflict for the resolution and compromise of cultural differences, Ravitch makes an appeal for "comity—that basic recognition of differences in values and interests and of the desirability of reconciling those differences peacefully." The aim of schools becomes the promotion of this quality throughout society.

> Respecting common values and common humanity need not imply the pursuit of homogeneity; no one wants to be a faceless figure in a mass society. The school can applaud individual and cultural diversity without resorting to the extremes of separatism and chauvinism.[3]

This vision of schools as complex and dynamic settings that support cultural heterogeneity and integration is supported by Robert Coles's interviews of children, teachers, and parents from several Northern city schools. In *The South Goes North: Volume III, Children of Crisis,* Coles observes that schools are much more complex and diverse environments than most modern critics would have us believe. He describes the school culture as organically changing and highly varied in character and temperament. The norms and values of each school system are clearly reflected through the school experiences as teachers express a different sense of time, different imagery, and a different tone of voice in accord with the school's ideals. Not only does Coles view the school culture as complex and unique in its constellation of values and assumptions, but he observes that the relationship between the school and community cultures is deeply entangled. There is an interactive process between them, with each culture constantly molding and feeding the other. This dynamic is conceived of by Coles as the school's greatest promise and potential misfortune.

> My "conclusions" are not sweeping, categorical, or easily translated into one or another "program." I can only say some things that are distinctly modest. No school, no teacher, no pupil exists in a social and political vacuum. What a school system does (or does not do) a teacher and a child can recognize—and either defy or acquiesce in. Children (and teachers) vary in "background," in character and purposefulness and temperament, but so do school systems—which are, of course, complicated social institutions that have strong links to the political arena, to the marketplace, to the religious, philosophical, and ideological forces at work in a community.[4]

There are other social historians who are not content with the ambiguities expressed above and vigorously pursue the identity and form of those "influencing forces" that Ravitch and Coles allude to. David Tyack, for one, draws out the momentum of the "modernizing" social and economic forces that have shaped the character of schools. Tyack describes this thrust in his history of urban education, *The One Best System.*

> As village patterns merged into urbanism as a way of life, factories and counting houses split the place of work from the home; impersonal and codified roles structured relationships in organizations, replacing diffuse and personal role relationships familiar in the village; the jack-of-all-trades of the rural community came to perform specialized tasks in the city; the older reliance on tradition and folkways as guides to belief and conduct shifted as mass media provided new sources of information and norms of behavior and as science became a pervasive source of authority; people increasingly defined themselves as members of occupational groups—salesmen,

> teachers, engineers—as they became aware of common interests that transcended allegiance to particular communities, thus constituting what Robert Wiebe calls "the new middle class." [5]

In this zeal for technological progress, the "traditional ideology" of schools emerged and began to take on a life of its own. There was "wonder and excitement" over unifying the country as the cultural qualities of "efficiency, rationality, continuity, precision, impartiality" [6] were heralded as the foundation for a good society and essential for sound education. The coordination and efficiency of factory production, business, and transportation brought a favorable outlook and positive response toward such consolidation. Swept up in the process of centralization were village schools, which lost their local identity and became organized under large bureaucratic organizations.

The transition from diversified rural or village schooling to the consolidated, corporate model offers insight into some of the contemporary struggles surrounding schools. For one, the history illuminates a part of the rationale for the prevailing "professionalism" of teachers. The professional ideal slowly crept into the classroom as teachers felt the need to move beyond their personalities and establish identifiable, respected roles and more distant relationships. For a long time, the success and admiration of the schoolmaster had depended on his person, his character, and his style (and the community's sometimes whimsical reponse to it) rather than on his institutional role or positional status. The consolidation, efficiency, and rationality of school systems, therefore, decreased the opportunities for spontaneous interaction and familiarity between teacher and community and increased the teachers' need for institutional support and a more narrowly defined role.

The surge toward professionalism was also accompanied by a more universal curriculum. MacDuffy readers began to filter into village classrooms, bringing the first hint of an outside world that offered an existence less dreary than the hard work of farm life. Children's fantasies reached far beyond the local boundaries of their communities; and professional teachers, more worldly wise than their charges, could help defeat many "self-delusions" about life. More important, the teacher offered skills that could move the child off the farm and toward the new possibilities of an uncharted future.

Tyack claims that it was not until the late 1960s that this "traditional ideology" began to receive harsh criticism from those who feared the social and cultural repercussions of a single, monolithic system that would not respond to diversity and variation among people. Critics argued that the professionals did not have the "expertise and empathy to design a school appropriate for all groups." [7] They began to question the assumptions and practices of a system that failed to accommodate the needs of various subgroups of the population and did not deliver the equality of opportunity it professed to offer. Tyack's analysis underscores the betrayal of pluralism and variation in schools that were impelled by the "cult of efficiency." Benevolent in intention but naive in practice, centralization and consolidation of schools sought to conserve social cohesiveness; but the homogenized Americanism it offered more often undermined the diversity of cultures inherent in our society. Schooling took on a momentum and life of its own as the social forces of urbanization and modernization generated an ideology that gave shape to a school culture of "middle-class efficiency."

In order to make schools more responsive to cultural variation and reverse the patterns of exclusion, Tyack concludes that it will be necessary to curtail the quest for the one best system. In this evolutionary conception, schooling has numbed the diversity that education should support and encourage. Rather than suggesting a more encompassing inclusion of competing pressure groups as Ravitch suggests, Tyack recommends a deliberate and active accommodation to local culture.

> Effective reform today will require reassessment of some cherished convictions about the possibility of finding the one best system, about the value of insulating the school from community influence, about the irrelevance of ethnic differences. To succeed in improving

the schooling of the dispossessed, educators are increasingly realizing that they need to share power over educational decision-making with representatives of urban communities they serve, that they need to find ways to teach that match the learning styles of the many ethnic groups, that they need to develop many alternatives within the system and to correct the many dysfunctions of the vast bureaucracies created by the administrative progressives.[8]

Revisionist historians offer a third, more extreme and pessimistic, interpretation of the structure and purposes of school culture. In what Tyack refers to as an "excavation for conspiracies," they search for the sinister and malicious forces behind what appears to be a benevolent and democratic process, and they reveal schools to have monolithic proportions and static purposes. Schools were not so much an outgrowth of benevolence and good will as the results of "coercion." They stand as symbolic expressions of the triumph of an imported "bourgeois morality," and they have served as a mechanism for managing the influx of immigrants who were perceived as a threatening and potentially dangerous social problem. Such is the "traditional ideology," which Tyack exposes, turned sour.

The school bureaucracy stands as a rigid, hierarchical, impenetrable authority that dictates who teaches, what shall be taught, how they teach, and to whom they teach. To sustain itself, the bureaucracy builds walls of exclusion and annihilates any forces that oppose its regulation and order. Michael Katz describes this insular, immovable character of the school culture when he traces the emergence of school bureaucracy.

> Because they built the rationale for their own existence and their increasing command of community resources upon an implausible ideology ever more divorced from reality, educators had to turn inward; they had to avoid a hard look at the world around the schools and at their own work; they had to retreat into an ideology that became a myth. By the 1850's educators had helped set the stage for the rigid sterile bureaucracies that soon would operate most urban schools.[9]

Although there were several other models of educational organization and purpose vying for supremacy in the 1850s, Katz claims that the "incipient bureaucracy" prevailed because of the strong class interests it served.[10] The system, with its "reasonable" order and "social balance," managed to perpetuate the power, wealth, and prestige of America's elite while placating the poor. Much as C. Wright Mills does, Katz views the course of events as controlled and directed by a presiding power elite who are unresponsive and malicious toward the more lowly constituents. The power remains solidly in the hands of the upper class, and any semblance of reform is merely a purifying illusion designed to pacify the excluded and powerless groups. If community cultures are ever to find expression in schools, this mode of bureaucratic and hierarchical supremacy must be overturned.

In *Schooling in Capitalist America,* radical economists Bowles and Gintis combine in a similar historical analysis, but claim that schools have resisted change not only because of the "structural restraints" that Katz identifies, but also because of the "systemic" nature of the capitalist economy. Schools have not so much withdrawn into a protected self-justification; they have become the instruments for capitalist supremacy. The attitudes and norms promoted in schools are not merely those convenient to bureaucratic professionals; rather, schooling values are the creed of the industrial workplace. As students punch in and out, receive grades as pay, perform uniform tasks, and gulp down bag lunches, they are thoroughly internalizing the social and technological skills necessary for passive accommodation to the workplace. Their complete and irreversible socialization decreases the potential for explosive class reaction, and the emphasis on isolation and competition among students diminishes the chances for collaboration that would support the kind of political organization that Ravitch claims as a vital part of the school culture.

> We take our stand with the critics . . . the range of effective educational policy in the United States is severely limited by the role of

> schooling in the production of an adequate labor force in a hierarchically controlled and class-stratified production system. Capitalism, not technology or human nature, is the limiting factor.[11]

Each one of these visions of the historical transformations of school culture offers a different perception of the cultural, economic, and political purposes of schooling and therefore a different perspective on strategies for social change. Bowles and Gintis's analysis is a sinister appraisal of calculating and malicious forces at work, preserving the superiority, affluence, and power of the dominant class. Mere rearrangements of the structure of school systems, changes in curriculums, or redesigning teacher training are only superficial attempts to obscure a hierarchically arranged society that leads purposefully and inevitably to a harshly unjust end. Only radical transformation of the social and economic structure of society will have any lasting impact on the creation of a more equal and democratic school system.

Ravitch's analysis reveals a more dynamic interaction of groups competing for power and the inevitable compromise that results after the painful, often violent struggles. She also emphasizes the transforming power of the oppressed groups. They are not merely viewed as helpless, passive victims who are being silenced and abused by a monolithic bureaucratic system; but in their fight for inclusion and participation, they have had a significant impact on the nature and direction of the once-impenetrable and distant institution. The oppressed and excluded groups are viewed as actors and initiators who do more than respond; they engage in forceful, focused action.

Finally, Tyack documents an evolutionary history, not guided by sinister forces or shaped by competing interests, but one that grows slowly out of shifting values, modes of living, work patterns, and population changes. Most important, Tyack speaks of the dangers of a single system designed to accommodate all people and suggests a more pluralistic and differentiated model for schools that is more at one with the community of which it is a part.

These historical analyses of school culture look through different ideological and interpretive lenses and suggest different models of family, community, and school interactions. Chapter 4 on black families uses each of these interpretations of school culture to describe the complex relationships between community and school that shape different strategies for initiating change. The pessimistic and harsh words of revisionist historians offer little promise for gaining a measure of control and influence within middle-class-dominated schools. Their analysis asserts a direct correspondence between the economic hierarchy of society and the structure and functions of school, and suggests perspectives on social action that do not focus exclusively on schools. Schools mirror much more pervasive and entrenched economic structures that must be directly confronted if schools are to ever become more inclusive and democratic. Our narrow focus on schools as the panacea for social change will only lead to misleading illusions of reform, and revisionist historians help us refocus our perspectives and redirect our energies toward these more deeply rooted economic inequalities.

Ravitch's historical description is useful in presenting a picture of the school as an environment of conflict and concessions—a place where vigorous and productive fights have given way to responsive and pluralistic settings. Her analysis underscores a major theme of this book; one that claims the inevitability of conflict and the productive elements of open and direct expressions of conflict. Also, her emphasis on recognizing the more subtle influence of powerless groups points to the need for people who have experienced oppression and silencing (be they minorities or women) to begin to view *themselves* as active, vocal, and initiating. In order to begin to design effective strategies for change, the powerless groups must develop political and personal moves that are not merely defensive and reactive but reflective of their own needs, interests, and goals.

Tyack's more benign picture of school history leads to yet another expression of family-school collaboration. In order to reverse the momentum of bureaucratization and consolidation, Tyack proposes a conscious dismantling of this "natural" historical process and the restructuring of schools as an integral part of the community culture. Once again, this conception of social change within and around schools echoes the more optimistic interpretations voiced at the close of chapter 4, which stress the need for families and community social networks to be recognized as active and critical participants in the educational process and important collaborators in life within schools.

As we seek to develop constructive communications between families and schools, therefore, we should not search for social-policy remedies that reflect a single vision of school culture. It is not a matter of choosing one sociohistorical interpretation, or asserting a single truth; rather, it is a matter of recognizing the multiple visions as pieces of an immensely complex narrative. In an article that searches out the relationship between social science and social policy, Cohen and Weiss claim that improvements in research on social policy concerning schools have not led to greater clarity about policy or consensus about interpretations, but to more variety and divergence in the way things are seen and more controversy in the way realities are interpreted.

> The improvement of research methods tends to increase divergence in the treatment of evidence and to multiply mystification in the interpretation of findings. . . . as research on a social problem matures, the angles of vision multiply.[12]

These myriad visions and interpretations are potentially useful to our analysis of the interactions among families, schools, and communities. Although the combined (and often competing) perspectives do not reveal a simple, uncomplicated story, they do reflect the varied and complex views of a highly differentiated society; and they do form the rich tapestry of "truths" that holds the promise and despair of our children's futures.

Issues of Conflict

The sociohistorical interpretations of school culture reviewed in the last section offer different views of family-school-community interaction, and more specifically of the role of conflict in defining the interaction. Throughout this book conflict has emerged as a persistent thread, raising its ugly or beautiful head depending on the content, the purposes, and the strategies used in expressing the conflict. In fact, the chapters may appear to present a basic contradiction in our views of conflict as a vehicle of oppression and as an expression of liberation and interaction.

For instance, there would seem to be a basic contradiction between my assertions in chapter 1, "Boundaries and Bridges," that relationships between families and schools would be more productive if the spheres of influence and territorial boundaries were made more clear and differentiated, and those in chapter 4, on black families, where I suggest that the culture and values of families and communities must be deeply embedded in the substance and medium of schooling. In the first case, I seem to be supporting a deliberate distance between families and schools that reflects their different social and cultural purposes in our society. Schools are environments that must support and encourage the child's movement away from the emotional and dependent constraints of family. Teachers build relationships that are qualitatively different from parent-child interactions; that are based on different criteria of evaluation and judgment. Their adult role is more neutralized and restrained as they apply generalized, universal expectations and visible rules.

But the differentiated roles served by parents and teachers, the alternative environments that are established in which children can discover different parts of themselves, are only workable and productive as parallel and intersecting systems if the institutions have balanced and equalized authority and if there is a shared sense of values, culture, and goals among the adult participants. If, for example, the school negates and demeans the family's central educative function and believes that the community culture is meaningless and uncivilized, then the separation between family and school will not reflect alternative environments for children or differences in the cultural purposes of those institutions, but rather isolation and rejection of the less powerful group.

In his book, *Asylums,* Erving Goffman makes a similar point when he refers to the issues of balance among the various social systems to which one belongs. Every institution has "encompassing tendencies" that capture something of the time and interests of its members and provide something of a world for them. A person can live within several social structures at once (i.e., families, schools, peer groups, workplaces, churches, and communities) and often not experience the competitive loyalties, conflicting norms, and ambiguous identities that can cause a great deal of personal pain and anxiety. But when one of the major social systems to which an individual belongs demands exclusive attention, builds walls that prohibit free movement, and negates the meaningfulness of life beyond its boundaries, then that institution can take total hold of the individual within and separate him from spontaneous interaction with the "outside" world. Families and schools both have "encompassing tendencies" that effectively and differentially shape the nature of the environment, the quality of relationships among people, and the development of adult-child roles within their boundaries. Schools will not become negatively exclusionary of parents and community or overly limiting of child movement if they recognize the need for balance and interaction with the other social forces in the child's life. There is, in fact, an incompatability between the all-encompassing tendencies of a total institution and the vital processes of family life. "The formulation of households provides a structural guarantee that total institutions will not be without resistance." [13] In other words, distinction of roles and environments between families and schools can lead to productive exchange only when there is a basic level of balance and consonance among family, school, and community cultures. Families and schools can feel comfortable and unthreatened in their separateness only when they know each other well, when there are no hidden mysteries behind the walls, and when communications and interactions can be spontaneous and substantive.

The greater the difference between family and community culture and school norms, the greater the need for parents and teachers to work hard at knowing one another. Because they come together as strangers who share in the common task of education and socialization, they must engage in a relatively self-conscious and painstaking task of discovering each other. The process of learning about each other's values, styles, and modes of communication may take relatively obscure and trivial forms at first, as parents, teachers, and children begin to feel each other out. But the real message is not trivial; it is the initial phase of learning to act and interact in an authentic and meaningful way. It is the painful and laborious beginning of understanding and feeling comfortable with people who had seemed like strange and threatening intruders. In sum, conflict is potentially constructive as a way of clarifying and resolving differences in culture and ideology between families and schools when there is open expression of ideas and views and when people feel able to risk the repercussions of misunderstandings and anger. Also, with positive conflict, the process of exchange must lead toward increased balance and symmetry between the two institutions. When the qualities of conflict increase asymmetry and support the imbalance of power between family and school, and when open, critical dialogue is silenced or suppressed under a superficial veneer of good will, then dissonance is dysfunctional and leads toward more destructive and threatening interactions. Finally, productive conflict must arise out of some level of harmony and unspoken consonance (which must be consciously developed and deliberately nurtured if families and schools are culturally divergent). In other words, a common language of communication (reflecting empathy and understanding for one another's values, assumptions, and goals) must be learned before both sides can engage in constructive fighting.

Even as we claim the potentially productive uses of conflict for clarifying and resolving family-school dissonance, it is important to realize that conflict is a relatively unusual (and often ritualized) form of social interaction—one that even the most assertive and open people tend to avoid (both consciously and unconsciously) in the course of their everyday experiences. If conflict were the predominant mode of human intercourse, its force would be diminished and less meaningful as symbolic of change. Because conflictual processes are so dramatic and explicit, we tend to overestimate their importance. In "The Power of Nonconflict," Kenneth Boulding confirms the relative infrequency of conflictual and dialectical processes as part of the evolution of interpersonal relationships and social systems.

> I would be extremely surprised if more than 10% of human activity goes into conflict. The other 90% goes to essentially nonconflictual activities consisting of production and consumption, sociability, communication, travel, eating and sleeping, teaching and learning, sex and so on. Some of these activities may have conflictual elements, but on the whole these are small. Collectively these nonconflictual activities are what I would call "nonconflict." They do not involve threat; they are nondialectical; and we overlook them because they are so commonplace. Furthermore, it is these nonconflictual activities which are the major source of change; whether in biological evolution or in human history.[14]

Within the realm of human interaction, therefore, conflictual processes are significant insofar as they stress the boundaries and limits of a social system (i.e., a school, family, or community) and push the system over "some kind of watershed into a situation in which the parameters of the evolutionary system are substantially changed." [15] Conflict may be thought of as a "facilitator or limiter" rather than the everyday stuff of social interaction and social change. Boulding claims that because of the spectacular qualities of conflict, in our descriptions and analyses of historical processes and events, our perceptions tend to be distorted by the "dramatic fallacy" that exaggerates the power of conflict simply because it is shocking and visible and underestimates the significance of the "great, quiet invisible changes that go on underneath." [16] Mothers giving cake sales in order to become "visible" within schools, the everyday, mundane (or highly charged) interactions between teachers and parents at the end of the school day, the way the mother manages the separation from her young child during the first weeks of school are all part of the "regular" scene of family-school dialogue. These cumulative, gentle, evolutionary processes produce the invisible changes that may or may not lead to conflict.

Although conflict emerges as a central theme in this book, therefore, it should not be seen as the primary mode of productive interaction or the major force in social change. We can recognize both its healthy, dramatic impact as well as its relative infrequency and minimal incidence in everyday living. It is in this modest approach to the perception and uses of conflict that we are likely not to abuse it as a vehicle of oppression.

Cultural Compromise and Personal Pain

Even when families become meaningfully related to the school culture, it is important to recognize the implicit bargain parents must make with their children when they send them to school—especially to a school that does not mirror the values and traditions of the child's family and community life. All parents, of course, experience great anxiety when they must relinquish their dominant and pervasive control over their child and trust that he will thrive under the supervision of a stranger. Feelings of anxiety and threat are accompanied by deep feelings of competition and concern that the "other woman" might do a better job and might capture the heart and attachments of the child. So the feelings of loss and detachment are intense as mothers send their children off to school for the first time—to be publicly evaluated, judged, and categorized, and perhaps to be abused and unappreciated.

But where there is almost perfect consonance between the perspectives and goals of communities and schools, families experience less anxiety in relinquishing parental control. In *Crestwood Heights,* John Seeley describes an upper-middle-class suburban community where nuclear families of parents and children are isolated from their kin, where each family is anchored in its own separate dwelling, and where the family is dependent upon the success of the father's career for its status and its future. Most important, in its orientation toward the future, the family is perpetually poised for mobility and relatively unattached to the past—a flexibility that permits change of residence, jobs, and friends if the move promises enhanced status and economic well-being. In Crestwood Heights, there is a direct relationship between the family's way of life and the norms of the outside, public world. Seeley describes the "massive centrality of schools" that serve as an organizing and cohesive force for the community. Schools and families both support the values of independence, mobility, and hope for the future, which point toward the need for the child's successful separation from the family. The family's job, therefore, is to equip the child with a psychic attitude and the social and cognitive skills for a solitary and successful climb to the top.[17]

In this upper-middle-class suburb, community networks are transient and relatively superficial, families are isolated in their pursuit of status, and the school serves as the single institution of cohesion and permanence in a rapidly shifting world. Parents, recognizing the critical social and economic functions of school to their own status and their child's future, gladly (though not without some ambivalance) relinquish the control and grooming of their child to the greater authority of the school. However, in other communities, where social networks among families are enduring and deep, where the traditions of the past loom larger than hopes for the future, and where schools represent a distant cultural perspective, the child's movement to school is viewed as abandonment of family and community and is anxiously feared. As these parents relinquish their child to school life, they are also risking a great loss of cultural cohesion and familial harmony. In Laura Lein's anthropological study of Boston area working-class families from homogeneous ethnic enclaves, mothers spoke of fearing the ominous "outside forces" that would control the minds of their children and seduce them away from the safety and comfort of their community.[18]

In Herbert Gans's *Urban Villagers*, members of Boston's Italian West End saw the school as a threatening, overpowering external institution that taught opposing values and dangerous habits to their children. Gans describes the social structure of what he labels "the peer-group society," in which one is defined by his relationship to the group, that is, "to persons of the same sex, age, and life-cycle status." This strong and cohesive social network structures the entire life of the community and stands as a mode of ordering one's world. The perceptions and rankings of the "outside world" bear little significance to the dynamics of this community culture.

Rather than submitting to this outside world of public institutions, there is frequently conflict with it. There is mistrust, suspicion, and even rejection of the professionals who attempt to educate, serve, and direct community residents. The "missionary caretakers," as Gans refers to them, display middle-class attitudes of condescension as their service often becomes a character-building attempt that implores residents to adopt "mainstream" values. The schools in particular force a direct confrontation with the peer-oriented society as they evaluate and rank neighborhood children by criteria that are meaningless and alien to the community. The aspirations and hopes that teachers arouse offer distant promises that tend to pull the children away from the community and away from their sources of comfort, structure, and stability.[19]

The message being conveyed by the school to community residents is both humiliating and threatening, but parents painfully recognize the implicit bargain that they must make if their children are to be prepared for life in the world beyond the boundaries of their community. They understand that survival for this generation of children will mean moving beyond their tight cohesive social network into the more varied and complex world, but they also want to cling to all that is good and familiar, to the rituals and patterns that have endured for generations.

Between the two worlds are the children, who must experience the painful bargain—the discomforts of not belonging in either sphere and the guilt of abandoning those one loves for vague promises of a better world. One can imagine how these daily assaults on a child's vulnerable status might inhibit his learning in school and have a distorting influence on his self-image. The personal struggle of negotiating the opposing institutions of families and schools has been a dominant theme in autobiographical literature as the authors present the underside of "Americanization." For instance, in Norman Podhoritz's best seller of several years ago, *Making It,* he argues that in order to thrive in the New York literary world, he had to try to turn himself from a Jew into something like a WASP. This bitter process of denial and transformation began in school, where teachers pressured him to make himself over.[20] Other writers from various cultural backgrounds repeat the tortuous theme of the homogenization of school, the relinquishing of one's precious connections to family and community, and finally the recognition, after assimilation and denial of one's parentage, that one has become disconnected and rootless.

Perceptions of Community

Part of the way of reducing the personal pain and enhancing the self-image of children caught between the dissonant structures of family and school is to consciously change the *perceptions* of the communities they come from. Chapter 4, on black families, underscores the need for social scientists and practitioners to look at families as part of cohesive social networks and to view communities in terms of their own cultural style and social idiom. As long as social science and the popular vision construe poor urban communities as degenerate and destructive settings for children, productive interactions between families and schools will not emerge. Constructive conflict and dialogue between parents and teachers demands institutional symmetry, and this balance is only created and sustained when communities are recognized as viable, integrated expressions of life patterns—when there is some attempt to understand the internal logic and meaning of the cultural idiom and community life.

For the most part, when there have been disparities between schools and communities, social science literature has viewed the school as the redeeming institution of stability and opportunity and neighborhood life (particularly in poor urban communities) as a decadent subculture of immorality and despair. Where schools have been naively esteemed, communities have been abusively and blanketly maligned. Black urban neighborhoods, particularly, have been the focus of biased and moralistic visions and labeled "cultures of poverty." James Conant's *Slums and Suburbs* paints a dismal picture of slum life and reflects the prejudicial, external perspective of many of his colleagues.

> These Negro slums seem to vary considerably with respect to the social mores. In some there are very bad gangs with gang warfare among boys. There are also vicious fights outside of school between Negro girls. . . . The streets are full of unemployed men who hang around and prey on the girls. The women are the centers of the family and as a rule are extremely loyal to the children. The men, on the other hand, are floaters and many children have no idea who the father is.[21]

Conant views the disorganized and desperate slums in stark contrast to the orderly and serene suburbs. The uneducated youth grow dangerously volatile, like the "piling up of inflammable material in an empty building in a city block." [22]

More recently, community sociologists and urban anthropologists have criticized this disparaging perception of the lives of "strangers" and probed behind the stereotypes of city neighborhoods to find ways of life with an integrity and purpose of their own. Their studies uncover cohesive social networks that order and regulate community life and informal educational processes that sustain the values and ideals of the culture. In *Blaming the Victim,* William Ryan claims that the analyses of social scientists have not only been painfully shortsighted but also misdirected. It is the social injustice and inequalities that perpetuate these oppressive economic and social conditions that should receive our scrutiny. "Slum life" is frequently evaluated and judged on the basis of a "middle-class ideology," the same mentality that Tyack found dominating schools and limiting the perceptions of teachers. In fact, Ryan asserts that the jaundiced, discriminatory views of researchers and practitioners may be more debilitating to the child's learning than the city decay.[23]

Other social scientists, who have criticized the characterizations implied in the "culture of poverty," present the urban black community as a frustrated adaptation to the dominant white culture rather than a despairing perversion of it. The street corner men in Eliot Liebow's *Tally's Corner* are described as frustrated, often hopeless; but never so completely lost that they abdicate their quest for dignity. Many of their expressed attitudes and behaviors are "a way of trying to achieve many of the goals and values of the larger society, of failing to do this, and of concealing the failure from others and from oneself the best he can."[24] Sophisticated (often self-deprecatory) humor and bittersweet fantasies are acceptable and dignified expressions for the deep feelings of failure and hopelessness. Although to the outside observer, the community at first appears fragmented and the people seem isolated and detached, closer and more sustained observations reveal social networks of close friends that support each other through crisis periods.

In Liebow's observations, the community culture does not exist as a self-sustained enclave with clear boundaries from the outside world. Instead, it sustains an intimate, beguiling contact with the dominant society, which Liebow describes as "a shadow system of values . . . constructed out of public fictions." [25] Instead of maintaining its own value structure, the community has "stretched" and distorted the prevailing norms of the dominant society into an alternative value system that helps them survive their deprived conditions. The mirrored distortions of the dominant white world are reflected in the social behaviors of the community, which often appear ambivalent, paradoxical, and to some degree contradictory.

More humanistic and ecological descriptions of inner-city neighborhoods reveal a comprehensive and distinctive cultural idiom and moral order in these communities. In *The Social Order of the Slum: Ethnicity and Territory in the Inner City,* Gerald Suttles explores how "distinctive styles" of living emerge within different ethnic groups. A practical morality prevails that accommodates the oppressive life conditions.

> Addams area residents are not engaged in an attempt to create an illusory world that merely denies the one which the wider community has established. The residents are impelled by a far more basic task of finding an order within which they can secure themselves against common apprehensions. So basic is this burden that few slum residents can ignore it or retreat into sheer fantasy, opportunism, or defeatism.
>
> The moral order created by Addams area residents does not meet either their own ideals or those for the wider society. The local people recognize as much and view their way of life as a practical exigency. For all its shortcomings, however, the moral order they have developed includes most, if not all, of their neighbors. Within limits, the residents possess a way of gaining associates, avoiding enemies, and establishing each other's intentions. In view of the difficulties encountered, the provincialism of the Addams area has provided a decent world within which people can live.[26]

Suttles shows this culture to be a "personalistic" one—personal relationships give shape to one's world and people rely on "public definitions" of one another rather than on professional roles or status. Interaction becomes predicated on person rather than position; "friends are above principle." Community residents virtually memorize the character of those they encounter, because subtle and accurate character assessments are crucial to making wise and immediate transactions. "These personal relationships require a massive exchange of information and cannot be extended beyond the immediate participants." [27] From this perspective, the active street life that characterizes these neighborhoods can be interpreted as vital rather than vagrant. Circulation and interaction are crucial to establishing one's personal identity and sustaining strong social networks. In Suttles's analysis, this personalistic culture is interrelated with the conditions of community life rather than reactive to the values of outside society. Because the personalistic morality thrives on face-to-face interactions, its boundaries are circumscribed and its numbers are limited. What Suttles refers to as "segmentation"—social units based on bonded territories—emerges as a means of limiting group membership to a knowable number of persons.

Gans's description of a "peer-oriented society" recalls Suttles's analysis of the segmentation of personalistic cultures. Both authors claim that the vulnerability of these community social networks is due to the assaults and intrusions of the dominant society. In Gans's history of the West End redevelopment, the peer-oriented society loses its struggle for cultural preservation because the residents are unable to understand "the bureaucratic behavior and object orientation and they thereby fall prey to its imposition." [28] And Suttles points out in his notion of segmentation that the personalistic culture is not amenable to institutional organization and therefore has difficulty resisting intrusions from the bureaucratically organized and powerful institutions of the dominant society.

The ethnographic descriptions of Gans and Suttles imply that it requires a "selective perception" to look beyond the shocking and harsh realities of these communities and discover the virtues and cohesiveness that are present—a perception that the "professional class" of the school culture has not allowed itself to develop. In building constructive family-school relationships within these communities, it must be recognized that the indigenous culture is not necessarily enlivened by the same American dream that sustains most school officials. In fact, the community residents may have little regard, and may sometimes have contempt, for the conventional bureaucratic symbols of success and professional status that mark success and advancement for the suburban upper-middle class in Seeley's Crestwood Heights. The community folk of Boston's West End and the Addams area are not simply a desperate collection of frustrated status seekers of middle-class virtue, but individuals with a vital and distinctive culture and a threatened and ambivalent relationship with the wider society.

The community's system of informal education is crucial to sustaining this unique culture, since formal education often undermines it. The urban child of today is faced with circumstances similar to those of the farm child of the 1800s. The "modernizing" education that Tyack describes continues to denigrate and negate one world as it opens up the possibilities of another. The life of the farm was often "harsh and drab"; the opportunities were spare, but the children quite naturally and ritualistically learned, from their families and neighbors, the values and skills needed to sustain their immediate existence. "A child growing up in such a community could see work-family-recreation-school as an organically related system of human relationships." [29]

Robert Coles offers his more contemporary version of the organic social networks that Tyack describes by referring to the personalistic culture as one that is rooted in the "spirit of individuals" as well as in the conditions of life they face. Informal education sustains the cohesive and organizing forces of life and provides children with the powers of subtle and sophisticated perceptions and behavior.

> Life is grim and hard, and the child simply has to find that out. He does, too; he learns it and learns it and learns it. He learns how to survive all sorts of threats and dangers. He learns why his parents

have given up on school, why they may have tried and fallen flat on their faces. He learns about things like racial hatred, about the state of the economy, about technological change. He learns whether he is an insider or an outsider, whether people like storekeepers or property owners or policemen treat his family with kindness and respect or with suspicion if not out-and-out contempt. By the time a child of the ghetto first arrives at school he has learned so much that his knowledge might perhaps be credited to an account called "the intelligence of the so-called unintelligent as it appears in sly, devious, and haunting ways." [30]

For children in contemporary urban societies, therefore, it is important for the school to recognize the value of the informal education of community life as a critical part of the child's learning and an important ingredient of the school culture. In order to understand the significance of informal education, the "professionals" must be able to perceive the coherence and integrity of the culture of which it is a part. Teachers need to become responsive to the profound differences between the organic conceptions of a personalized culture and the more regularized forms and professional practices of school bureaucracies. This will require individualistic changes in knowledge, perception, and styles of interaction as well as structural changes in the institutional arrangements of schools that have reflected a single, monolithic middle-class ideology.[31]

Finding Faces in the Crowd

At the same time as it is critical to recognize families as part of larger, cohesive social networks if one is to understand the dynamics of family-school interaction and collaboration, it is also important to be aware of the individual variations of values, beliefs, and styles within these communities. Community members and teachers will only begin to dismantle their stereotypic roles and reveal their individuality if the social settings in which they gather provide opportunities for interaction. For the benefit of teachers, children, and parents, schools must be small in scale—not overwhelming, impenetrable structures that make people feel small and insignificant but scaled-down settings where people can negotiate easily and feel a sense of control over their environment.

For teachers, parents are threatening in large crowds; but when they can identify their faces and build workable relationships with most of the parents they see, then the parents begin to be perceived as individuals and some of the intrusive and negative images begin to fade. There is a discernible shift of expression when teachers move from relating an actual experience with a parent to speaking about generalized issues of parent involvement in school. For most teachers, the descriptions tend to become less complex, flexible, and subtle (i.e., reflective of the unique character of individual relationships) and more stereotyped and defensive. For instance, Ms. Powell, who was profiled in chapter 3, talked sensitively about building and sustaining relationships with individual parents, but she responded with dread and rigidity when she thought of parents as a group of faceless intruders. Rather than using her own skills of interaction, negotiation, and good judgment in relation to parent groups, she looked to the administration to protect her from parental intrusions. When the physical environment of the school is intimate, therefore, it is less likely that parents will be seen as strange groups of people to be avoided and feared; rather, they will become individuals to be reckoned with.

Not only do intimate settings increase the chances of teachers and parents making positive contacts, but they also provide more supportive environments for teachers' relationships with children. At one small inner-city school, for instance, several of the teachers mentioned the importance of school size in creating a viable sense of community and shared responsibility. They claimed that the small scale of the school (about 200 children) permitted the teachers to know all of the children, not just the pupils in their individual classrooms. Teachers, therefore, felt a sense of caring and responsibility for *all* the children in the school, which had a positive impact on the children's sense of safety and comfort and the teachers' feelings of mutual support.

Young children seemed to thrive in an environment that they could more easily comprehend and negotiate—where they could move independently throughout the whole building, embracing the space rather than fearing it, instead of having to take one route from the school entrance to classroom while the rest of the building remained imposing, distant, and unexplored. Also, children's misbehavior was greatly reduced when they soon recognized that *any* teacher, not just their own classroom teacher, demanded their good behavior and citizenship. And finally, children were able to enjoy a rich variety of relationships with several adults and feel comfortable about visiting other classrooms.

A collective sense of knowing children and feeling responsible for their well-being is highly unusual in school settings. More often, the relationships between teachers tend to be isolated and competitive and teachers only feel a commitment (mostly inspired by the public shame and disgrace they would feel if their class got out of line) to controlling their own charges—and only when their children are under their immediate supervision and jurisdiction. In *Complexities of an Urban Classroom,* Smith and Geoffrey describe the more common experience of competition and peer evaluation that teachers fear in relation to one another. In this large, impersonal environment, children were seen as "belonging" to the teachers, and teacher-teacher interaction was mutually dependent upon teacher-pupil interaction.

> Pupils do belong to a teacher, but if they don't behave this does not necessarily cause questions to be raised regarding the "owner's" classroom control. The critical thing is the owner's reputation. . . . some teachers . . . have excellent classroom control and yet their kids can raise hell elsewhere—playground, gym. *This in no way* reflects upon the teacher. Rather it raises her status—after all, she can control those problems and I can't. Also, one *might* ask if the

> very fact of her strong control of students under her thumb might have some bearing on their behavior while in someone else's hair. No, I would say that a student's bad behavior while absent from his owner casts no cloud upon that teacher. A teacher is judged by what happens in his teacher-pupil interaction, which is 90 percent of the time. He is not judged by what his kids do in the 10 percent of time they are away from him.[32]

The exclusive ownership these teachers must feel restricts their spontaneous interactions with colleagues, who are viewed as competitors. The possessive teacher not only maintains her reputation by competing with other teachers, but she is also likely to view parents with the same threatened and competitive concern. The classroom is seen as her exclusive domain; she owns the children while they are with her, and parents are to remain far away—beyond the boundaries of the classroom. These defensive adult relationships must be perceived by children, who are not given the opportunity to build a variety of healthy and responsive relationships with a range of adults but become preoccupied with pleasing a single one and neglecting or abusing all others.

Like their children, parents feel more comfortable trying to negotiate with a school that is small in scale, simple to comprehend and visualize, and does not resemble an impenetrable, bureaucratic maze. Almost immediately, parents can begin to discern the authority structure and role allocation within the school and understand where and to whom they should go for particular problems and concerns. Parents can also more easily become acquainted with the people behind the roles and begin to find effective strategies and styles of communicating with people of different temperaments and character.

For those parents from lower-class and minority communities it is especially important that they be able to find faces in the crowd. Because they have had minimal experience in negotiating dominant, external institutions or have had negative and hostile contact with social service agencies, their initial approaches to the school are often overwhelming and difficult. Not only does the school feel like an alien environment with incomprehensible norms and structures, but the families often do not feel *entitled* to make demands or force disagreements. Jean Baker Miller's notion of the hazards of subordination (referred to in chapter 2) is relevant here. The enduring historical experience of exclusion and oppression has made it difficult for the oppressed (be they women, minorities, or the poor) to identify their *own* needs, desires, and goals. In order to survive, they have been forced into a preoccupation with sustaining the well-being and scrutinizing the subtle behaviors and demands of the more powerful. The risks of identifying and asserting their own needs are great, and they fear that the enduring pain of long years of silence might explode into uncontrollable rage if they let it be exposed and released. And one always risks the brutalities of the oppressor, who will become threatened by the unfamiliar and aggressive ways of the subordinate.

The mothers at one inner-city school spoke to me of their beginning moves into their children's school. Although the environment felt alien to the mothers, the school personnel welcomed their coming and strongly believed in parent involvement and participation. But even in this relatively open and intimate environment, it was difficult for the mothers to overcome the fears and defensiveness derived from a long history of exclusion and to really believe that the teachers were authentic in their welcoming gestures. A piece of my impressionistic record follows.

> The second woman to speak in my conversation with this group of mothers was someone I had been keenly aware of during my travels through the classrooms. I had seen her teaching a reading group, her voice patient and caring, and her demands strong. Children in one of the first grades had shown me the puppets that she had helped them make. She is a beautiful and elegant lady who spoke with soft control. She has four children, two at this school, and she has been involved in the school since the first year it opened, six years ago. Her mother had been a school custodian and so she spoke of being used to having her mother around in school—to watch out for her, to form alliances with her teachers,

> to punish her when she got out of line. (She was the only mother in the group who said that her parents had been involved in her schooling. Most of them claimed their mothers didn't care, were too busy, and didn't think it was appropriate for parents to be in school. They defined their roles very differently from their mothers before them and seemed to feel some resentment toward their mothers for their lack of involvement—often implying that they would have been more successful in school had there been collaboration between their teachers and their mothers. So these parents seemed to view themselves as pioneers in this work, as contemporary women who had found a different way of defining their motherly responsibilities.) The elegant woman had become involved in the school because in the school's first chaotic year she had heard terrible rumors about the disorder and confusion in the classrooms. One day her oldest daughter arrived home from first grade with her hair chopped off. One of her classmates had chased her around the room with scissors and had managed to cut her ponytail off. Of course, her mother was furious. She came up to the school the next morning in great anger and she has been there ever since. Many of the mothers spoke of initially coming to the school in order to *protect* their children in response to some injustice or abuse done to them and then remaining in the school in order to ensure continued well-being for their children. I was very much impressed with their descriptions of beginning their involvement in response to negative circumstances and being able to transform their involvement into something productive and positive. For most this was not an immediate or easy transformation, but one that required that they "hang in," that they tolerate a certain level of discomfort in feeling unwelcome, and that they continue to be assertive about carving out a meaningful role for themselves.[33]

These women had begun to conceive of themselves as shapers of their own destiny; people who takes risks and make demands. Their action came out of intense frustration and anger (their children were being abused in school) and required that they consciously recognize their "pioneer" role. With the mostly affirmative experience of their work in the school and the visible changes their presence seemed to have on the school environment, their anger subsided and grew into productive action and positive feelings. After years of pioneering work by a small core of brave parents, children began to *ask* their mothers to come to school. "Rodney's mother is always in school. How come you never come?" School became a place for mothers.

The initiating actions of risk-taking parents must be matched by a shift of perceptions and relationships on the part of teachers and school personnel. Just as inner-city parents must become more aggressive in moving into schools, so professional educators must become more restrained and modest in their moves out into the community. As these families from different cultural backgrounds become meaningfully incorporated into school life, there is a need to change the traditional conceptions of social service that have dominated the middle-class ideology of schools surrounded by urban decay. As we have seen, middle-class schools in poor communities have blamed their casualties on the chaotic, uncaring, and disruptive home life of the children. When teachers are not able to effectively communicate with minority children, when reading scores of children rapidly decline as they grow in years, when social control rather than education becomes the preoccupation of teachers, then schools displace the origins of failure onto families. Social workers, school psychologists, and teachers may even go out into the tenements and projects (in pairs for safety) to talk to overworked mothers and "absent" fathers about their poor parenting and structureless households. The message being conveyed is that only when they get their own house in order will their children be able to successfully function in school.

This missionary zeal of the helping professions not only inspires fear and dread in the social worker who arrogantly (or politely) invades the privacy of a stranger's household, but it also angers the parents who constantly face the intrusions and judgments of welfare workers and other petty-powerful people who determine their fate. Most important, the moves out into the community reinforce the asymmetry of the relationship between home and school (i.e., reinforce the power and dominance of the school and the vulnerability of the family) and distract our attention away from *the school* as the setting that needs to be restructured and changed to adapt to the strengths, weaknesses, and skills of the children it serves. Professional educators must redirect their focus to life inside schools, a setting that includes the responsible participation of parents, rather than searching out the origins of pathology beyond the school walls. This turning inward (with welcome arms spread wide to receive and include parents) helps teachers look at their *own* behaviors and institutional norms as contributing to patterns of disruption and failure with children and uses parents as colleagues in helping to develop alternative classroom structures and interactional strategies that will better meet the child's needs.

Ms. Miller, a school social worker in an inner-city black school, supported and encouraged the "radical" and comprehensive changes in skills, ideology, structure, and roles that took place *within* the school as teachers slowly and painfully struggled with finding new ways to interact with families and children.

> Ms. Miller was trained as a social worker but has taken a very non-traditional view of her professional role in this school. Instead of conceiving of her function as one in which she engages in clinical, individualistic interactions with troubled persons or as a family therapist who goes out into the home and community to search for the sources of pathology and deviance within families, Ms. Miller has created a much less directive and intrusive function. Not only has she defined her relationships with teachers and parents as facilitative rather than directive, but she has also been guided by a different ideological framework than the one usually employed in the practice of social work. Her concern has not been so much with identifying and curing pathology as with looking at the organizational and interactional *origins* of perceived deviance. For instance, when the teachers first approached Ms. Miller for assistance, they came wanting help in controlling "problem" children who were disrupting their classrooms. They consistently located the problem *within* the child and often imputed hostile and negative motivations to him. Frequently, they referred to the unruly child's disruptive home environment and wanted Ms. Miller to investigate the sources of family disorder and initiate contact with the ultimately *responsible* parents. The need for teachers to point to a single child

> as the source of classroom chaos shifted as Ms. Miller began slowly working to help them look at deviance in a different way. Most important, Ms. Miller worked on the notion that deviance must be defined *interactionally* and it must be seen in *social context*. In other words, the teacher must view herself as participating in and sustaining deviant patterns, as being partially responsible for defining the deviant label, and as creating a social structure in the classroom that could not accommodate or respond productively to disruptive patterns. Ms. Miller pushed teachers not to focus on their individual problems but to depersonalize the phenomena and talk about the struggles of coping with *difference* in the classroom and providing appropriate limits for children. Also she urged them to explore their own behaviors (in concert with viewing the misbehavior of the child) and search for pedagogical strategies, interactional styles, and intellectual content that would include and accept (rather than exclude and negate) the child. The work with teachers required profound shifts in perspective and a whole new way of seeing the classroom scene. The process of change was slow but teachers began to move from accusing individual children of malice, to discovering some of the problems they *all* faced in teaching, to constructing different kinds of classroom scenes that accommodated more variation among children. Amazingly enough, the school boasts no major behavioral problems for the past two years. Initially, Ms. Miller had purposefully allowed teachers to focus on what they perceived to be their central concern, behavior. Then she had helped them redefine their perception. In the process, teachers began communicating with one another, talked about some substantive educational issues, and moved from their lonely and isolated position behind closed doors. Once there were no more major struggles with behavior problems, teachers were free to move onto the task of teaching social and intellectual skills.[34]

Finding faces in the crowd, therefore, is a very difficult search. It requires that school environments be created that encourage direct and continuous interaction among teachers, parents, and children; that parents dare to initiate action, make demands, endure conflict, and responsibly participate in defining their children's education; and that teachers consciously reshape their stereotypic perceptions of community, use the knowledge and competencies of parents, redesign classroom settings, and learn new skills and strategies for relating to children.

The Child's Place

Throughout this book children's voices remain unheard. Although children are perceived as the focus of all the action, the very reason for all of our concern, the stories told are about the adult participants in the family-school interaction. When children are characterized, they are seen through the eyes of teachers and parents. The exclusion of the perceptions and perspectives of children is not an oversight but an intentional strategy to narrow an already overwhelming task of exploration and to underscore the dominance and significance of the adult sponsors in defining the quality and character of the family-school relationship. There is also an implicit assumption throughout this book: that productive relationships between families and schools will increase the likelihood of the growth and development of young children in both spheres and that sustained negative dissonance between families and schools will be dysfunctional to the child's self-definition, maturation, and movement from one environment to the other. Perceptions of children, however, seem to be at the center of the adult relationships. Conceptions of the nature of childhood shape and determine the interactive process of parents and teachers. More specifically, the extent to which parents and teachers are able to see themselves as differentiated and separate from the child and are able to perceive of the child as a *whole* person has a great deal to do with the degree of tension and competition that the adult sponsors experience.

In chapter 2, on mothers and teachers, mothers who were overidentified and deeply connected with their children were described as creating the most turmoil in the lives of teachers. In some sense, the mother's wish to remain attached and not let go of the child when he went off to school made her an intrusive presence to teachers and disrupted the child's movement toward autonomous development. Because the mother was not able to differentiate the child's separateness and wholeness (or reestablish her own self-hood), she became locked in a struggle with the teacher, whose purpose it was to support the child's independence from family and provide an alternative environment for learning and growing. All mothers seem to experience some degree of pain, ambivalence, and loss when their child moves into the school world, and teachers and schools often structure periods of transition and consultation with parents to relieve some of the anxiety and make the separations less jarring. But for mothers who cannot relinquish control because they are unable to separate their child-adult identities, the "normal" rituals of transition from family to school are made more complicated and burdensome for the teachers and the child.

In a similar sense, teachers who are unable to perceive the individuality and wholeness of the child are likely to be overly focused on parents as potentially intrusive forces and therefore are prone to building walls of silence and exclusion in relation to parents. The profiles of Ms. Powell and Ms. Sarni, presented in chapter 3, reflect different perceptions of the individuality and wholeness of children that inevitably have an impact on how they view their relationships to children's parents and on how they use sociocultural and familial information to construct their visions of children.

Ms. Sarni resists describing and analyzing individual behavior because it is not part of her *consciousness*. Her descriptions of individual children are rather superficial accounts of their visible behavior or amusing and interesting anecdotes about how they handled a specific event. She does not give subtle or comprehensive accounts of their individual life *within* the classroom and when she talks about their development or growth, she is usually referring to the cognitive domain. The child's social and psychological development are not of central importance to Ms. Sarni and are often viewed as a distortion to the primary agenda of academics. She thinks that if she spends her energies worrying about those murky areas of personality and motivation, she will neglect the teaching of basic skills. In fact, her focus on the teaching of basic skills to the exclusion of "emotional involvements" has given her the proud reputation among many colleagues and parents as one who "makes education happen" and who "produces readers" by the end of the school year.

When Ms. Sarni describes the individual child, therefore, she is not likely to refer to his whole being or to the unique aspects of his social and psychological growth. She does differentiate children, however, on the basis of dimensions that are *external* to the classroom environment. She is very knowledgeable and judgmental about the family backgrounds of each child and often perceives the individual child through the lens of familial stereotypes. The sociological categories of race, social class, ethnicity, and family structure become the primary factors of differentiating among children.

> Michael comes from a very solid family. They expect certain behavior. . . . They live in a two-family house on North Street, two parents, a good home, well dressed, well kept. He has loads of uncles and aunts who love him and take him on trips. *He's going to go into school solid and he's going to come out solid.*
>
> If you get a class that has a lot of "academics" in it, you have a good class. . . . Parents are very concerned about their education. The children come in brighter because they have the opportunity. They have the environment, they have their parents. They have books, they have parents who sit down and read with them.
>
> The family has all kinds of problems. The mother especially. She's alone, she's on welfare, she's completely disheveled. . . . Anthony will come to school with pants not fitting, undershirt inside out, shirt not properly buttoned, hair not combed, sometimes a dirty face . . . how is he expected to survive in school? [35]

Ms. Sarni draws almost perfect parallels between her stereotypic pictures of parent *groups* and her judgments about the *individual* potential of children. She speaks unselfconsciously and without guilt—her perceptions are almost always confirmed in the end. Even though she "saves" first-grade children from the dangers and threats of the external world for one year of school and starts them off on the right foot by teaching them to read, Ms. Sarni believes that the stronger life forces that shape the child's future are predetermined by parentage. Her words speak of the inevitable entanglements of myth and reality that continue to reaffirm her stereotypic visions of the family's powerful and irreversible impact on children.

On the other hand, the individual nature of each child is a constant source of interest, dismay, and struggle for Ms. Powell. She approaches the task of discovering the temperament, style, and skills of each child as the primary agenda of her teaching. Her descriptions and diagnoses of children reveal details about how they function socially and intellectually in the classroom and often refer to the psychological dimensions of motivation, self-concept, anger, and anxiety. Learning and development are considered very complex processes by Ms. Powell, who describes the subtle interactions of the socioemotional and intellectual spheres in a child. She often talks about how poor development in one sphere may inhibit or distort functioning in the other. Even with the most highly skilled children in her class, Ms. Powell is aware of some very basic limitations in their development. Karen Rosen, for instance, reads at third-grade level and is quick to learn, but she is also a very threatened and insecure little girl who has difficulty working with other children. She insists upon being the center of the stage when she initiates something but retreats into shyness and withdrawal when the teacher calls on her without warning.

Part of Ms. Powell's understanding of a child's individuality recognizes the power of the environment on the child's expressions of self. In her descriptions of children, she often distinguishes between the part of the child that finds expression in school and that part of the child that is revealed with family members and peers. In other words, Ms. Powell is aware of the constraints and demands of the social context, and she recognizes that her vision of the child is not holistic but a partial one that is situationally defined. She also criticizes parents for not recognizing the limitations and biases that shape their perceptions of their child. Neither teacher nor parent knows the whole story, and part of each's job should be to become acquainted with the other "lives" of children. In a sense, Ms. Powell's broad perspective gives a very generous thrust to her statements about children. Even if children are not functioning well in school, they may be thriving in other environments. They are not thought to be total losers; neither is their self-image totally defined in terms of school criteria. When Ms. Powell speaks of Christine, for instance, she describes her shy, withdrawn character in the classroom and her aggressive, assertive behavior with her older siblings. "That is not the Christine we see in class."

Ms. Powell's interest in the family backgrounds of the children in her class seems to be related to her concern with understanding the other powerful influences on their lives and the potential impact of these forces on their development in school. Her interviews are rich with details about the families from which her children come, information that she believes will give her a more realistic perspective on their behavior and attitudes in school. Family background material, therefore, does not merely seem to be a way of rationalizing stereotypes and labels of children. Rather, Ms. Powell uses this information to draw a more complete and comprehensive picture of the child.

In other words, for some teachers social-background data is used to simplify and categorize a complex scene, but for Ms. Powell it seems to elaborate and expand her repertoire of behaviors toward a single child. For instance, Ms. Powell has abundant information on the disruptive and sad life of Kenny that helps her understand (and value) his highly complex imagination and his expression of dreams and fantasies through highly sophisticated drawings. She also feels that her knowledge of his background gives her more patience in coping with his negative behavior.

> . . . knowing about Kenny, I can deal with him. I can grin and bear it a little longer. I can look at it and see the other side of Kenny, not the repulsive side.[36]

Ms. Powell and Ms. Sarni express very different perspectives on the nature of childhood and the expression of individuality, which reflect divergent conceptual and philosophical orientations toward the process of learning and growth in children. Ms. Sarni's relatively narrow definition of learning and success in the classroom, her denial of the importance of the social-psychological dimensions, and her view of children as shadows of their parents seem to be part of an ideology that is concerned with social order and control and fears the possibility of the social disintegration that might follow expressions of individuality. In her view, schools are transitional, preparatory settings that are designed to shape children for their place in society—a process of socialization and accommodation that must proceed smoothly and uneventfully toward an inevitable conclusion. In an extreme sense, schools must smother the unharnessed, spontaneous nature of the child and produce a cooperative and civilized citizen. Ms. Sarni's ideological orientation echoes the themes and values fundamental to structuralists' conceptions of the functions and purposes of schools described in chapter 1, Boundaries and Bridges. Parsons's and Dreeben's analyses of family-school differentiation, for example, underscore the precarious balance between individual autonomy and expression and the need for social cohesion and productivity. This tension between collective norms and individualistic needs must be resolved in the direction of maintaining social order if society is to function without major social upheaval; and the structure and experiences of schools are designed to impart to children the norms necessary to sustain this "organic solidarity" in society.[37]

On the other hand, Ms. Powell views education as a process of *discovering* one's individuality and special purpose. Children come to school not as wild creatures to be tamed but as young and inexperienced beings whose educational experiences should enliven and enrich their variability. Her orientation toward child growth and individuation seems closely identified with the themes that appear in the ideology of humanists[38] and the theories of developmental psychologists.[39] Developmental theory, for instance, views education as an orderly process of growth but values individuality and freedom. It sees man as confronted by his environment, but not at its mercy. The child is not only acted upon, but acts on his surroundings, modifying them continually. Education, therefore, has the capacity to reform society, as the individual—empowered and activated—can not only survive but transform. Growth is a "disciplined" process that has direction, but not a culminating, inevitable end of normality. The educational philosophy of Dewey has given shape to this ideological and conceptual orientation.

> We have been occupied with the conditions and implications of growth. . . . When it is said that education is development, everything depends upon *how* development is conceived. Our net conclusion is that life is development, and that development, growing, is life. Translated into its educational equivalents, this means that 1) the educational process has no end beyond itself; it is its own end; and that 2) the educational process is one of continual reorganizing, reconstructing, transforming.[40]

Ms. Powell's descriptions of and interactions with children in her classroom reflect this ideological and intellectual orientation toward child growth and reveal these broad and fluid conceptions of the educational process.

Teachers' perceptions of parents and families, therefore, become an extension of their philosophical and ideological perspectives on child growth. If, on the one hand, a teacher views growth as limited to the development of cognitive skills, sees children as replicas of their parents, and perceives the social structure of schools and society as "normal" and static, then she will not be inclined to explore the individual nature of the child or search out relationships with families that enhance the expression of the child's wholeness. If, on the other hand, the teacher views family and culture as powerful forces in shaping a child's nature, she will seek to develop a relationship that incorporates the child and the parents. In Ms. Powell's classroom, individuality is discovered and nurtured through close description and analysis of the children's social and cognitive interactions *within* school as well as through learning as much as possible about the other enduring environments that surround them and the other powerful people with whom they interact. Family background, environmental variables, and personality structure all contribute to Ms. Powell's perception of the child's individuality, and parents become important informants in this process of learning about the unique nature of a child. Her insights offer a view of family-school interaction that revolves around the *child's individuality* and give great emphasis to the integration of these two spheres of socialization.

The place of the child, *in the adult perceptions,* can have a critical influence on the shaping of relationships between families and schools. The recognition by both parents and teachers of the child's autonomy, individuality, and wholeness can be a major source of communication between families and schools. Teachers who recognize the process of individuation in the child will search for a triadic relationship of balanced interaction among parents, teachers, and children—a relationship that is primarily established, sustained, and nurtured *because* of the child (i.e., in the best interest of the child). In a similar way, parents who seek to encourage their child's autonomy and individual nature will more easily be able to see the teacher's significant place and critical function in the child's experience. Exclusivity on the part of either teacher or parents does not permit productive exchange between them. Competition for control, territory, and the child's love will develop into negative conflict.

Teachers and parents who view each other as collaborators often seem to ask similar questions of each other. Food and nurturance sometimes become a vehicle for discovering the hidden mysteries of what is happening in the other sphere of the child's life. Teachers wanting to expand their knowledge of the child's health, life style, and family rituals will ask parents what their child had to eat for breakfast before coming to school. Mothers who fear that their children will experience deprivation when they are far from their loving gaze most often inquire about what their children ate in school or search their lunch boxes at the end of the day for evidence of the child's life in school. Food becomes symbolic of love and caring—one way that *adults* can perceive integration and continuity between the child's worlds. An insightful teacher told about food as a vehicle for adult communication.

> Food is essential and it's the ultimate way for them to know if you are nourishing and taking care of their kid . . . and I like to know in the morning if he ate breakfast. Those are the things that are easy to find out from parents, questions that are usually not threatening . . . and they reveal so much about the quality of life for the child.[41]

Another teacher described the kind of information she asks of parents in order to do a more effective job as a teacher. Her holistic vision of the child incorporates knowledge of the world beyond the classroom.

> What a kid's day is like in the morning has an immense amount to do with how he or she functions at school in the most productive part of the school day, which is the morning. And if he or she has a forty-minute ride on a school bus, that is important for me to know. . . . Tommy is the biggest balker in the whole world; I'm always behind him, pushing. I remember when his mother shared with me what it was like just getting him out in the morning. It was a real relief to know that this was not only my problem. This was Tommy and the way he arranged people's lives around him. It was crucial for me to know in the classroom that he balked and was like this. And for the rest of the year it was crucial for me not to push him; because he would just dig his heels further and further into the ground. . . . I want to know even what the day is like

> for him after school because I want to know maybe if we are pushing him too hard at school. A kid comes home wound up like a clock and running up on the ceiling and hitting his baby brother, and I feel we have to look at the school day and give him either more space to let go at school or make him less driven and anxious.[42]

It might be said, therefore, that teacher and parent merge in the domain of "the education of the child." They are related in the common experience in which they engage. Parents and teachers might know each other through their occasional face-to-face interactions, ritualistic PTA meetings, grade reports and evaluations, or scheduled consultations; but more important, they are linked through their mutual relation and experience with the child.

The experience of the *child* includes both parents and teacher. In his eyes, the role of the teacher and the role of the parent may appear essentially as one realm of adults who control and order his environment. To fully acknowledge or empathize with this child's experience, one must respond to the parts of the child's world and experience that include the other adult. As the teacher encounters the child, she is also addressing the parent. The parent, likewise, confronts the teacher as she accepts the whole child and supports his individuation. What is sometimes interpreted in sociological terminology as "role conflict" might be reinterpreted as misperception or exclusivity on the part of either the teacher or the parent. The disagreeing and possessive parents may not be able to recognize the fact of the teacher's place in their child's life. They may be imploring the teacher to see the child as they do, that is, only in part. Threatened and noncommunicative teachers may also be suffering from the same partial vision of the child's experience. To be fully engaged with the child and involved in a holistic process of education, the teacher and parent must accept the relationship they hold in the child's experience. Ultimately, a more comprehensive and inclusive consideration of the child's perspective may be necessary to enlighten the parts of teacher and parent.

But Anna Freud's uncompromising warnings about differentiating the mother's "child care" role and the teacher's "child education" function still resound with meaning. She too claims to be speaking "in the best interest of the child," for a clarification of roles and territories, for boundaries that provide alternative settings for autonomous development in children.[43] Despite the fact that recognition of the child's place and experience in both spheres will serve as a critical bond of communication between teachers and parents, I would still argue that relationships between parent and child and teacher and child are qualitatively different and are established and sustained for different reasons. Perhaps the sociological labels that differentiate their functions as "primary" or "secondary" are too categorical, static, and ultimately distorting. Certainly a child can feel, at one time or the other, more in touch with his teacher than with his mother, and teachers can provide alternative role models, sources of identification, and love objects for the child; but the relationship is time-bound, often interrupted by or disbanded with the arbitrary limits of the school year. And only fond memories or exaggerated fantasies of the teacher remain.

But mothers, until their death, remain mothers, and the relationship has to be *worked with* and endured (no matter whether it *feels* nice or not or whether others judge her to be a good or a bad mother), and is transformed over time. The structure of schools, the arbitrary time dimensions, the presence of numerous others of the same age, the regularized space and environment, all make it a very different kind of experience for the teacher and child than the enduring, lifetime bond of mother and child. These differences should not be denied as negative or dysfunctional for child development and productive interactions among parents and teachers. These differences may be an expression of the range and rich variety of relationships that can be developed among human beings. "Teacher" can be a very encompassing, dynamic, and meaningful role that incorporates a range of behaviors, dimensions, and feelings; but it is not the same as mothering—and it should not be.

Not only is it important to recognize that in order for parents and teachers to relate productively they must be able to see the significance of the other's relationship to the child, but each of them must be aware of the universal "other" *within* themselves. For instance, teachers must be able to recognize and incorporate the mothering, nurturant qualities that they have within themselves and view those as a dynamic part of their experience with children. This does not mean that mothering or parenting should become the dominant function, but that it should be a conscious part of the teacher-child relationship; and that the recognition of its presence and use will enhance (and make more understandable) the teacher's visions of parents.

Chapter 2, on mothers and teachers, spoke of the more generous and enlightened visions that teacher-mothers (who live the dual role) have of their adult colleagues, because they have experienced both spheres of interaction with children and they can identify the "other woman" (her struggles, challenges, despair, and hope) *within* themselves. Their intimate knowledge of the dynamic nature of both mothering and teaching, their overlapping spheres of influence, and their critical place in the child's experience support productive exchanges between them.

> . . . The easiest parent to work with, the optimal parent to work with was the parent or parents who were also teachers. . . . we could talk as real equals and with real understanding of what we each needed to know about the child. . . . I remember little Danny who still wet his pants though he was quite old. His mother was a teacher and was less scared of sharing with me matters that a parent might consider shameful or terribly private. She knew there was nothing so foreign about school and teaching that she should be afraid to say to me: "Well, maybe you don't know that Danny is still wetting his pants and we are still having a problem with that." So there was that part of being a teacher that made it more possible for us to communicate that kind of information to one another.[44]

Productive collaborations between family and school, therefore, will demand that parents and teachers recognize the critical importance of each other's participation in the life of the child.

This mutuality of knowledge, understanding, and empathy comes not only with a recognition of *the child* as the central purpose for the collaboration but also with a recognition of the need to maintain roles and relationships with children that are comprehensive, dynamic, and *differentiated*. The child as the center and purpose of the adult experience points to another vision of family-school interaction—one that stresses integration, holism, and cohesion between these two institutions of socialization rather than one that underscores their boundaries, territories, and spheres of influence.

Notes

Introduction

1. Sara Lawrence Lightfoot, "An Ethnographic Study of the Status Structure of the Classroom" (doctoral dissertation, Harvard University, Graduate School of Education, June 1972), pp. 33–80.

2. Sara Lawrence Lightfoot and Jean V. Carew, "Individuation and Discrimination in the Classroom," *American Journal of Orthopsychiatry* vol. 46 (July 1976): 401–15.

3. Eleanor Burke Leacock, *Teaching and Learning in City Schools* (New York: Basic Books, 1969), p. 117.

4. Sara Lawrence Lightfoot, "Politics and Reasoning: Through the Eyes of Teachers and Children," *Harvard Educational Review,* vol. 43 (May 1973): 197–244.

5. *Ibid.,* p. 214.

6. This narrative describes a teacher who participated in the research for Lightfoot, "An Ethnographic Study," pp. 171–179.

7. Willard Waller, *Sociology of Teaching* (New York: John Wiley and Sons, 1932), p. 59.

8. Charles A. Valentine, *Culture and Poverty: Critique and Counter Proposals* (Chicago: University of Chicago Press, 1968), p. 80.

9. See, for example, J. McV. Hunt, *Intelligence and Experience* (New York: The Ronald Press Company, 1961); C. Deutch and M. Deutch, "Theory of Early Childhood Environment Programs," in *Early Education: Current Theory, Research, and Action,* ed. R. Hess and R. Bear (Chicago: Aldine Publishing Company, 1968); and R. Hess and V. Shipman, "Early Experience and the Socialization of Cognitive Modes in Children," in *Learning in Social Settings,* ed. Matthew B. Miles and W. W. Charters, Jr. (Boston: Allyn and Bacon, 1970).

10. Marion J. Levy, "Some Hypotheses About the Family," *Journal of Comparative Family Studies,* vol. 1 (1970): 119.

11. Claude Lévi-Strauss, "The Family," in *Man, Culture, and Society,* ed. Harry Shapiro, (New York: Oxford University Press, 1960), p. 267.

12. Margaret Mead, "The Contemporary American Family as an Anthropologist Sees It," in *Social Perspectives on Behavior,* ed. Herman Stein and Richard Cloward (New York: The Free Press, 1958), p. 21.

13. Margaret Mead, *The School in American Culture* (Cambridge, Mass.: Harvard University Press, 1951), p. 7.

14. David Cohen, "Loss as a Theme in Social Policy," *Harvard Educational Review,* vol. 46 (1976): 554.

15. Joseph Featherstone, *What Schools Can Do* (New York: Liveright Publishing Co., 1976), pp. 108–29.

16. R. D. Laing, *The Politics of Experience* (New York: Pantheon Books, 1967), pp. 37, 39–40.

1 / Boundaries and Bridges

1. Robert Dreeben, *On What Is Learned in School* (Reading, Mass.: Addison-Wesley, 1968), pp. 74–84. For another analysis of the functional differences in patterns of relating in families and schools, see Willard Waller, *Sociology of Teaching* (New York: John Wiley and Sons, 1932), pp. 68–79.

2. Gertrude McPherson, *Small Town Teacher* (Cambridge, Mass.: Harvard University Press, 1972), pp. 121–151 and J. W. Getzels, "Socialization and Education: A Note on Discontinuities," *Teachers College Record,* vol. 76 (December 1974), pp. 218–225.

3. Talcott Parsons, "The School Class as a Social System," *Harvard Educational Review,* vol. 29 (1959): 297.

4. Dreeben, *On What Is Learned in School,* p. 35.

5. Parsons, "The School Class as a Social System," p. 301.

6. Dreeben, *On What Is Learned in School,* p. 84.

7. Sara Lawrence Lightfoot and Jean V. Carew, "Individuation and Discrimination in the Classroom" (Washington, D.C.: Office of Child Development, 1974), Research supported by funds from Child Development Associates, Inc.

8. For an insightful discussion of the vacuous symbolism that sustains these public, ritualistic events for parents and teachers, see Richard Warren, "The Classroom as a Sanctuary for Teachers: Discontinuities in Social Control," *American Anthropologist,* vol. 75 (Feb.–June, 1973): pp. 280–291.

9. Lightfoot and Carew, "Individuation and Discrimination."

10. Howard Becker, "Social Class Variations in Teacher-Pupil Relationships," *Journal of Educational Sociology,* vol. 25 (1952): 451–65.

11. McPherson, *Small Town Teacher,* pp. 138–151.

12. For another exploration of the origins and characteristics of teacher authority, see M. Fullan and W. Spady, "The Authority System of the School and Innovativeness: Their Reciprocal Relationships" (Paper presented at the meetings of the Annual Conference of the Canadian Sociology and Anthropology Association, St. John's, Newfoundland, June 1971), pp. 2–7.

13. Samuel Bowles, "Unequal Education and the Social Division of Labor," in *Schooling in a Corporate Society,* ed. Martin Carnoy, (New York: David McKay, 1972), pp. 36–64. For a more comprehensive analysis, see Samuel Bowles and Herbert Gintis, *Schooling in Capitalist America: Educational Reform and the Contradictions of Economic Life* (New York: Basic Books, 1976). I will offer a more in-depth discussion and critique of the various sociohistorical interpretations of the social and economic functions of schools in the concluding chapter herein, "Looking Beyond Fences."

14. Eleanor Burke Leacock, *Teaching and Learning in City Schools* (New York: Basic Books, 1969), pp. 86–113.

15. McPherson, *Small Town Teacher,* pp. 139–40.

16. Sara Lawrence Lightfoot, "Politics and Reasoning: Through the Eyes of Teachers and Children," *Harvard Educational Review,* vol. 43 (1973): 215.

17. *Ibid.*, p. 215.
18. Lightfoot and Carew, "Individuation and Discrimination."
19. The recent studies of urban anthropologists, who describe the enduring and strong informal social networks within working-class communities, provide good analytic frameworks for documenting the dynamic intersections between families and schools. For examples of social network theory and its perspectives on institutional intersection, see Elizabeth Bott, *Family and Social Network: Roles, Norms, and External Relationships in Ordinary Urban Families* (New York: The Free Press, 1971), and Carol Stack, *All Our Kin* (New York: Harper & Row, 1974).
20. Hylan Lewis, "The Changing Negro Family," in *School Children in the Urban Slum,* ed. Joan Roberts (New York: The Free Press, 1967), p. 400.
21. Lightfoot, "Politics and Reasoning," p. 216.
22. For an insightful discussion of intergenerational distance and disassociation, see N. B. Ryder, "The Cohort as a Concept in the Study of Social Change," *American Sociological Review,* vol. 30 (Dec. 1965): 843–61.
23. Philip Slater, "Social Change and the Democratic Family," in *The Temporary Society,* ed. Warren Bennis and Philip Slater (New York: Harper & Row, 1968), p. 40.
24. Conrad Arensberg and Solon Kimball, *Culture and Community* (New York: Harcourt Brace and World, Inc., 1967), p. 377.
25. Willard Waller, *Sociology of Teaching* (New York: John Wiley and Sons, 1932), p. 69.

2 / *The Other Woman: Mothers and Teachers*

1. For examples of research and theory that reflect this focus on maternal neglect and incompetence or familial disorganization and its impact on child development, see J. McV. Hunt, *Intelligence and Experience* (New York: The Ronald Press Company, 1961); C. Deutch and M. Deutch, "Theory of Early Childhood Environment Programs," in *Early Education: Current Theory, Research, and Action,* ed. R. Hess and R. Bear (Chicago: Aldine Publishing Company, 1968); R. Hess, V. Shipman, J. Brophy, and R. Bear, *The Cognitive Environments of Urban Preschool Children* (Chicago: The Graduate School of Education, University of Chicago, 1968); J. Kagan, "His Struggle for Identity," *Saturday Review* 7 December, 1968, pp. 80–82, 87–88; R. Green, "Dialect Sampling and Language Learning," in *Social Dialects and Language Learning,* ed. R. Shuy (Champaign, Illinois: NCTE, 1964).
2. Edward Eggleston, *The Transit of Civilization* (Boston: Beacon Press, 1959), pp. 244–45.
3. *Ibid.*, p. 211.
4. Willard Elsbree, *The American Teacher: Evolution of a Profession in a Democracy* (New York: The American Book Company, 1939), p. 535.
5. *Ibid.*, p. 84.
6. Eggleston, *The Transit of Civilization,* pp. 227–28.
7. Elsbree, *The American Teacher,* pp. 17–31.

8. *Ibid.*, p. 123.

9. *New York State Educational Exhibit* (Chicago, World's Columbian Exposition, 1893), pp. 45–46, quoted in Elsbree, *The American Teacher*, p. 203.

10. *Fourth Annual Report of the Board of Education, Boston* (1841), pp. 45–46, as quoted in Elsbree, *The American Teacher*, p. 201.

11. Jessie Bernard, *Women, Wives, Mothers* (Chicago: Aldine Publishing Company, 1975), p. 21.

12. Elsbree, *The American Teacher*, p. 206.

13. Francis Donovan, *The Schoolma'am* (New York: Frederick A. Stokes Company, 1938), p. 6.

14. *Ibid.*, p. 8.

15. Elsbree, *The American Teacher*, p. 289.

16. *Ibid.*, p. 207.

17. *Ibid.*, p. 537.

18. *Ibid.*

19. Donovan, *The Schoolma'am*, p. 4.

20. Lois Hoffman and Ivan Nye, *Working Mothers* (San Francisco: Jossey-Bass, 1975), chap. 1.

21. Donovan, *The Schoolma'am*, pp. 67–68.

22. Jessie Bernard, *Marriage and Family Among Negroes* (Englewood Cliffs, N.J.: Prentice-Hall, 1966), p. 156, and Sally Wendkos Olds, *The Mother Who Works Outside the Home* (New York: Child Study Press, 1975), p. 2.

23. Bernard, *Marriage and Family Among Negroes*, p. viii.

24. Hoffman and Nye, *Working Mothers*, pp. 45–46.

25. Alva Myrdal and Viola Klein, *Women's Two Roles* (London: Routledge and Kegan Paul Ltd., 1956, revised 1968), p. xvi.

26. I am thankful to Sarah Levine who was primarily responsible for reviewing and synthesizing the literature reported in the historical section of this chapter. She also participated in the writing and presentation of ideas.

27. Jacques Barzun, *Teacher in America* (Boston: Little, Brown, and Company, 1945).

28. Margaret Mead, *The School in American Culture* (Cambridge, Mass.: Harvard University Press, 1951), p. 9.

29. *Ibid.*, p. 10.

30. *Ibid.*

31. Ivan Illich, *Deschooling Society* (New York: Harper & Row, 1970), pp. 45–47.

32. Anna Freud, "The Role of the Teacher," *Harvard Educational Review*, vol. 22 (Fall 1952), p. 231.

33. *Ibid.*, p. 230.

34. Sir Edward Arnold, "Mothers," quoted in Jessie Bernard, *The Future of Motherhood* (New York: Penguin Books, 1974), p. 3.

35. John Abbott, *The Mother at Home; or the Principles of Maternal Duty* (Boston: Crocker and Brewster, 1833), p. 147.

36. Hoffman and Nye, *Working Mothers*, p. 143.

37. Bernard, *The Future of Motherhood*, p. 115.

38. For an extensive discussion and analysis of the sociocultural and

economic factors that contribute to the low status of teachers, see Dan Lortie, *School Teacher* (Chicago: University of Chicago Press, 1975). Also see Gertrude McPherson, *Small Town Teacher* (Cambridge, Mass.: Harvard University Press, 1972) and Myron Brenton, *What's Happened to Teacher?* (New York: Avon Books, 1970).

39. Willard Waller, *Sociology of Teaching* (New York: John Wiley and Sons, 1932), p. 59.

40. Joseph Azzarelli, "Four Viewpoints" in *Struggle for Power in Education,* ed. F. W. Lutz and J. J. Azzarelli (New York: The Center for Applied Research in Education, 1966), chap. 1.

41. Martha Blaxwell and Barbara Reagan, eds., *Women and the Workplace* (Chicago: The University of Chicago Press, 1976), p. 24.

42. Erik Erikson, *Identity, Youth, and Crisis* (New York: W. W. Norton & Company, 1968), p. 265.

43. Jean Curtis, *Working Mother* (New York: The Macmillan Company, 1976), p. 76.

44. *Ibid.,* p. 79.

45. Ruth Kundsin, *Women and Success* (New York: William Morrow and Company, 1974), p. 17.

46. Lotte Bailyn, "Notes on the Role of Choice in the Psychology of Professional Women," in *The Woman in America,* ed. Robert Lifton (Boston: Beacon Press, 1967), p. 242.

47. Kundsin, *Women and Success,* p. 194.

48. Bernard, *The Future of Motherhood,* p. xii.

49. Kundsin, *Women and Success,* p. 92.

50. Hoffman and Nye, *Working Mothers,* pp. 49–50.

51. Bernard, *Women, Wives, and Mothers,* p. 219.

52. Hoffman and Nye, *Working Mothers,* p. 134.

53. *Ibid.*

54. *Ibid.,* p. 139.

55. Bernard, *The Future of Motherhood,* p. 67.

56. *Ibid.,* p. 197.

57. Donovan, *The Schoolma'am,* p. 216.

58. Bernard, *The Future of Motherhood,* p. 202.

59. Jean Baker Miller, *Toward a New Psychology of Women* (Boston: Beacon Press, 1976), p. 11.

60. Sheldon H. White, "Some Goals and Functions of Schools" (Harvard University, 1977), p. 5.

3 / *The Voices of Two Teachers*

1. For sociological analyses of the school as a preparatory, transitional environment, see Talcott Parsons, "The School Class as a Social System: Some of Its Functions in American Society," *Harvard Educational Review,* vol. 29 (Fall 1959), pp. 297–318; Robert Dreeben, *On What is Learned in School* (Reading, Mass.: Addison-Wesley, 1968), and Elizabeth Eddy, *Walk the White Line: A Profile of Urban Education* (New York: Anchor Books, 1967).

2. See Ruth Benedict, "Continuities and Discontinuities in Cultural

Conditioning," *Psychiatry* vol. 1 (May 1938), pp. 161–167, for an excellent anthropological analysis of the differences in the status and power of adults and children in simple and technological societies. Benedict points out that American culture exaggerates those differences and provides little opportunity for children to ritualistically and incrementally learn the patterns of behavior and styles of interaction that they will need in adulthood. For other descriptions of cross-cultural patterns of socialization and child development that underscore the discontinuities between childhood and adulthood in American society, see Erik Erikson, *Childhood and Society* (New York: W. W. Norton and Company, 1950), and Margaret Mead, *Culture and Commitment: A Study of the Generation Gap* (Garden City, N.Y.: Natural History Press, 1970).

3. For an insightful, experiential account of children's perceptions of work and play in the classroom, see Dorothy Cohen, *The Learning Child* (New York: Vintage Books, 1973), pp. 32–33. Cohen observes that children are robbed of very important developmental experiences in this society because there are few opportunities for them to participate in work that is functional to society or meaningful to them. Children recognize the contrived, fabricated quality of most "work" designed by teachers and parents.

4 / *Black Dreams and Closed Doors*

1. Christopher Jencks et al., *Inequality: A Reassessment of the Effect of Family and Schooling in America* (New York: Basic Books, 1972), pp. 253–265.

2. Sara Lawrence Lightfoot, "Politics and Reasoning: Through the Eyes of Teachers and Children," *Harvard Educational Review*, vol. 43 (May 1973): 208.

3. Diane Ravitch, "On the History of Minority Group Education in the United States," *Teachers College Record*, vol. 78 (1976): 213.

4. Christopher Lasch, "The Family and History," *New York Review of Books* (Nov. 1975): 32–33.

5. E. Franklin Frazier, *The Negro Family in the United States* (New York: Holt, Rinehart and Winston, Inc., 1939; rev. ed., 1957), and Stanley Elkins, *Slavery: A Problem in American Institutional and Intellectual Life* (Chicago: University of Chicago Press, 1959).

6. For historical analyses of the black family's existence and stability during this period, see Eugene Genovese, *Roll Jordan Roll: The World the Slaves Made* (New York: Pantheon, 1974); Herbert A. Gutman, *The Black Family in Slavery and Freedom, 1750–1925* (New York: Pantheon, 1976); Robert Abzug, "The Black Family During Reconstruction", in *Key Issues in the Afro-American Experience,* ed. N. Huggins, M. Kilson, and D. Fox (New York: Harcourt Brace Jovanovich, Inc., 1971); and John Blassingame, *The Slave Community* (New York: Oxford University Press, 1972).

7. Joel R. Williamson, "Black Self-Assertion Before and After Reconstruction," in *Key Issues in the Afro-American Experience,* ed. N. Huggins, M. Kilson, and D. Fox (New York: Harcourt Brace Jovanovich, Inc., 1971), p. 232.

8. James E. Blackwell, *The Black Community: Diversity and Unity* (New York: Dodd, Mead, and Company, 1975), p. 36.
9. Frazier, *The Negro Family in the United States,* pp. 87–107.
10. Elkins, *Slavery,* pp. 53–55.
11. *Ibid.,* pp. 81–139.
12. Genovese, *Roll Jordan Roll,* p. 431.
13. See Gutman, *The Black Family in Slavery and Freedom,* pp. 116–117; Genovese, *Roll Jordan Roll,* p. 489; Abzug, "The Black Family During Reconstruction," p. 29; and Blackwell, *The Black Community,* p. 36.
14. Abzug, "The Black Family During Reconstruction," pp. 27–29; and Blassingame, *The Slave Community,* p. 78.
15. Scholars who hold this perspective of the white planters' supportive views of black family life during this period, include R. Fogel and S. Engerman, *Time on the Cross: The Economics of American Negro Slavery* vol. I, pp. 127–130, p. 142. (Boston: Little, Brown, and Co., 1974); and Genovese, *Roll Jordan Roll.* pp. 451–454; pp. 482–484.
16. Blassingame, *The Slave Community,* p. 80.
17. Researchers who underscore the initiating efforts of blacks in maintaining family cohesion include Gutman, *The Black Family in Slavery and Freedom,* pp. 158–165; Blassingame, *The Slave Community,* p. 87; and Abzug, "The Black Family During Reconstruction," pp. 27–28.
18. Newton Edwards and Herman G. Richey, *The School in the American Social Order* (Boston: Houghton Mifflin Co., 1963; 1st ed. 1947), pp. 122–146.
19. Notably Carter G. Woodson, *The Education of the Negro Prior to 1861* (New York: Arno Press and The New York Times, 1968); Henry Bullock, *A History of Negro Education in the South: From 1619 to the Present* (Cambridge, Mass.: Harvard University Press, 1967); and Horace Mann Bond, *The Education of the Negro in the American Social Order* (New York: Octagon Books, 1966; 1st ed., Prentice Hall, 1934).
20. Woodson, *The Education of the Negro Prior to 1861,* p. 2.
21. *Ibid.,* p. 18.
22. Genovese, *Roll Jordan Roll,* p. 432.
23. Allen B. Ballard, *The Education of Black Folk* (New York: Harper & Row, 1973), p. 14.
24. Sing-Nam Fen, "Notes on the Education of Negroes in North Carolina During the Civil War," *Journal of Negro Education,* vol. 36 (1967): 24.
25. Genovese, *Roll Jordan Roll,* p. 562.
26. Blassingame, *The Slave Community,* p. 207.
27. Bullock, *A History of Negro Education in the South,* p. 11.
28. Blassingame, *The Slave Community,* p. 61.
29. Lunsford Lane, *Narrative of Lunsford Lane* (Boston: By author, 1842), p. 21; William Wells Brown, *Narrative of William W. Brown, A Fugitive Slave* (Boston: The Anti-Slavery Office, 1847), pp. 83–84.
30. See R. Fogel and S. Engerman, *Time on the Cross,* vol. I, pp. 149–150, pp. 202–208 and Bullock, *A History of Negro Education in the South,* pp. 3–10.
31. Brown, *Narrative of William Brown,* p. 27.
32. Bullock, *A History of Negro Education in the South,* p. 6.

33. Thomas Pettigrew, *Profile of the American Negro* (New York: D. Van Nostrand, 1964), p. 14.

34. Genovese, *Roll Jordan Roll,* p. 564.

35. Frederick Douglass, *Narrative of the Life of Frederick Douglass* (Boston: Anti-Slavery Office, 1845), pp. 40–41.

36. Blassingame, *The Slave Community,* p. 207.

37. *Ibid.*

38. Bullock, *A History of Negro Education in the South,* p. 5.

39. Thomas H. Jones, *The Experience of Thomas H. Jones, Who Was a Slave for Forty-Three Years* (1871; reprint ed., New York: AMS Press, 1975), p. 19.

40. Lane, *Narrative of Lunsford Lane,* p. 31.

41. Jacob Stroyer, *My Life in the South* (Salem, Mass.: Salem Observer Book and Job Print, 1885), p. 30.

42. Genovese, *Roll Jordan Roll,* p. 565.

43. Douglass, *Narrative of the Life of Frederick Douglass,* pp. 81–82.

44. Blassingame, *The Slave Community,* p. 96.

45. Genovese, *Roll Jordan Roll,* p. 502.

46. Frazier, *The Negro Family in the United States,* p. 309; Jessie Bernard, *Marriage and Family Among Negroes* (Englewood Cliffs, N.J.: Prentice-Hall, 1966), p. 103.

47. Henry Bibb, *Narrative of the Life and Adventures of Henry Bibb, An American Slave* (New York: By Author, 1849), pp. 33–44; Booker T. Washington, *Up From Slavery* (Cambridge, Mass.: 1944).

48. Blassingame, *The Slave Community,* p. 94.

49. Genovese, *Roll Jordan Roll,* p. 508.

50. Blassingame, *The Slave Community,* p. 83.

51. *Ibid.,* p. 99.

52. Ellis O. Knox, "A Historical Sketch of Secondary Education for Negroes," *The Journal of Negro Education,* vol. 9 (1970): 206.

53. Edwards and Richey, *The School in the American Social Order,* p. 279.

54. August Mier and Elliot Rudwick, *From Plantation to Ghetto* (New York: Hill and Wang, 1966), p. 112.

55. *Ibid.*

56. W. Lloyd Warner et al., *Color and Human Nature: Negro Personality Development,* prepared for the American Youth Commission (Washington, D.C.: American Council on Education, 1941).

57. Gutman, *The Black Family in Slavery and Freedom,* pp. 128–129, 139–140, 186–189.

58. Frazier, *The Negro Family in the United States,* p. 311.

59. Horace Mann Bond, *The Education of the Negro in the American Social Order* (New York: Octagon Books, 1966; 1st ed. 1934), pp. 373–74.

60. See Bullock, *A History of Negro Education in the South*; Bond, *The Education of the Negro in the American Social Order*; and Knox, "A Historical Sketch of Secondary Education for Negroes."

61. Mier and Rudwick, *From Plantation to Ghetto,* p. 109.

62. Benjamin Quarles, "Freedom's Black Vanguard," in *Key Issues in the Afro-American Experience,* ed. N. Huggins, M. Kilson, and D. Fox, pp. 176–77.

63. Mier and Rudwick, *From Plantation to Ghetto,* p. 109.
64. *Ibid.*
65. W. E. B. DuBois, "The Negro Common School" (Atlanta University Publications, No. 6, Atlanta, Ga.: Atlanta University Press, 1901), p. 19.
66. Bond, *The Education of the Negro in the American Social Order,* pp. 371–72.
67. Mier and Rudwick, *From Plantation to Ghetto,* p. 114.
68. Horace Mann Bond, "The Extent and Character of Separate Schools in the United States," *Journal of Negro Education,* vol. 4 (1935): 323–24.
69. Bond, *The Education of the Negro in the American Social Order,* p. 377; Elinor Gersman, "The Development of Public Education for Blacks in Nineteenth-Century St. Louis, Missouri," *Journal of Negro Education,* vol. 41 (1972): 35.
70. Simon Marcson, "Ethnic and Class Education," *Journal of Negro Education,* vol. 13 (1944), p. 58.
71. Woodson, *The Education of the Negro Prior to 1861,* pp. 73–76.
72. Mier and Rudwick, *From Plantation to Ghetto,* pp. 114–115.
73. *Ibid.*
74. I am indebted to Marguerite Alejandro-Wright who reviewed the literature on black families during the ante-bellum period with intelligence and care. She also participated in the conceptualization and writing of this historical section.
75. Frances Kellor, *Experimental Sociology* (New York: Macmillan, 1901), p. 300.
76. For further discussion of these and other studies, and on schools' effect on poor and/or black children, see Colin Greer, *The Great School Legend* (New York: Basic Books, 1972).
77. Kenneth Keniston et al., *All Our Children* (New York: Harcourt Brace Jovanovich, 1977), pp. 2–23.
78. Joseph Featherstone, "Youth Deferred," in *What Schools Can Do* (New York: Liveright, 1976), p. 127.
79. For an excellent theoretical and methodological discussion of the ways to study and describe the enduring ecology of family life, see Urie Bronfenbrenner, "The Experimental Ecology of Education," *Teachers College Record,* vol. 78 (Dec. 1976): 157–204.
80. Hope Jensen Leichter, "Some Perspectives on the Family as Educator," *Teachers College Record,* vol. 76 (Dec. 1974): 198.
81. Robert Hill, "Family Strengths: Policy Implications" (Paper presented at the Lilly Endowment Conference on Public Policies Affecting Families and Children: Present Status and Future Directions, Washington, D.C., January 26–28, 1977).
82. Robert Hess and Virginia Shipman, "Early Experience and the Socialization of Cognitive Modes in Children," in *Learning and Social Settings,* ed. Matthew W. Miles and W. W. Charters, Jr. (Boston: Allyn and Bacon, 1970), pp. 178–179.
83. For an excellent critique of the developmental literature on lower-class black children, see Stephen S. Baratz and Joan C. Baratz, "Early Childhood Intervention: The Social Science Base of Institutional Racism," *Harvard Education Review,* vol. 40 (Feb. 1970): 29–50.
84. Ray C. Rist, "Student Social Class and Teacher Expectations: The

Self-Fulfilling Prophecy in Ghetto Education," *Harvard Educational Review,* vol. 40 (August 1970): 411–51.

85. Jane Torrey, "Illiteracy in the Ghetto," *Harvard Educational Review,* vol. 40 (May 1970): 29–50.

86. Kenneth Clark, *Dark Ghetto: Dilemmas of Social Power* (New York: Harper & Row, 1965), pp. 133–148.

87. Charles A. Valentine, *Culture and Poverty: Critique and Counter Proposals* (Chicago: University of Chicago Press, 1968), pp. 78–83.

88. For an in-depth discussion of the deep concern and ultimate value lower-class blacks attach to schooling, see John Scazoni, *The Black Family in Modern Society* (Boston: Allyn and Bacon, Inc., 1971), and Hylan Lewis, "The Changing Negro Family," in *School Children in the Urban Slum,* ed. Joan Roberts (New York: The Free Press, 1967), pp. 397–405.

89. Richard Cloward and James Jones, "Social Class, Educational Attitudes, and Participation," in *Education in Depressed Areas,* ed. A. Harry Passow (New York: Bureau of Publications, Teachers College, Columbia University, 1963), pp. 190–216; Andrew Billingsley, *Black Families in White America* (Englewood Cliffs, N.J.: Prentice-Hall, 1968), pp. 79–83, 181–185.

90. Gutman, "Black Families in America: New Data and Their Implications for Public Policy Revisions" (Paper presented at The Lilly Endowment Conference on Public Policies Affecting Families and Children: Present Status and Future Directions, Washington, D.C., January 26–28, 1977).

91. Office of Policy Planning and Research, U.S. Department of Labor, *The Negro Family: The Case for National Action,* (The Moynihan Report) (Washington, D.C.: U.S. Government Printing Office, 1965).

92. Carol Stack, *All Our Kin* (New York: Harper & Row, 1974).

93. Leichter, "Some Perspectives on the Family as Educator," p. 186.

94. *Ibid.,* pp. 202–203.

95. Sara Lawrence Lightfoot, "A School in Transition: Stories of Struggle and Hope" (Unpublished manuscript, 1976), pp. 9–14.

96. *Ibid.,* pp. 11–12.

97. Herbert Walberg, Robert E. Bole, and Herschel Waxman, "School-Based Family Socialization and Reading Achievement in the Inner City" (Unpublished manuscript, University of Illinois at Chicago Circle, 1977).

98. *Newsweek,* "A New Kind of PTA" (November 15, 1976), p. 105.

99. James P. Comer, "Improving the Quality and Continuity of Relationships in Two Inner-City Schools," *Journal of The American Academy of Child Psychiatry,* vol. 15, no. 3 (Summer 1973), pp. 543–544.

5 / *Looking Beyond Fences*

1. Diane Ravitch, *The Great School Wars: New York City, 1805–1973; The History of the Public Schools as Battlefields of Social Change* (New York: Basic Books, 1974), p. 407.

2. *Ibid.*

3. *Ibid.,* p. 402.

4. Robert Coles, *The South Goes North: Vol. III, Children of Crisis* (Boston: Little, Brown, and Company, 1971), p. 529.
5. David Tyack, *The One Best System: A History of American Education* (Cambridge, Mass.: Harvard University Press, 1974), pp. 5–6.
6. *Ibid.*, p. 28.
7. *Ibid.*, p. 272.
8. *Ibid.*, p. 290.
9. Michael Katz, *The Irony of Early School Reform: Educational Innovation in Mid-Nineteenth Century Massachusetts* (Cambridge, Mass.: Harvard University Press, 1968), p. 159.
10. Michael Katz, *Class, Bureaucracy, and Schools: The Illusions of Educational Change in America* (New York: Praeger Publishers, 1971), pp. 28–55.
11. Samuel Bowles and Herbert Gintis, *Schooling in Capitalist America: Educational Reform and the Contradictions of Economic Life* (New York: Basic Books, 1976), p. 20.
12. David Cohen and Janet Weiss, "Social Science and Social Policy: Schools and Race" *Educational Forum*, vol. 41 (May 1977), p. 395.
13. Erving Goffman, *Asylums: Essays on the Social Situations of Mental Health Patients and Other Inmates* (New York: Anchor Books, 1961), p. 12.
14. Kenneth Boulding, "The Power of Nonconflict," *Journal of Social Issues*, vol. 33 (1977): 26.
15. *Ibid.*, p. 27.
16. *Ibid.*
17. John Seeley et al., *Crestwood Heights: A Study of the Culture of Suburban Life* (Toronto: The University of Toronto Press, 1956), pp. 119–130, 159–164, 224, 234–235, *passim.*
18. Laura Lein, *How to Manage When Both Parents Work* (Cambridge, Mass.: Working Family Project, Center for the Study of Public Policy, 1976).
19. Herbert Gans, *The Urban Villagers: Groups and Class in the Life of Italian-Americans* (New York: The Free Press, 1962), pp. 120–162.
20. Norman Podhoretz, *Making It* (New York: Random House, 1967).
21. James Conant, *Slums and Suburbs: A Commentary on Schools in Metropolitan Areas* (New York: McGraw-Hill, 1961), p. 19.
22. *Ibid.*, p. 18.
23. William Ryan, *Blaming the Victim* (rev. ed.) (New York: Vintage Books, 1976), pp. 3–29.
24. Eliot Liebow, *Tally's Corner: A Study of Negro Street Corner Men* (Boston: Little, Brown, and Co., 1967), p. xii.
25. *Ibid.*, p. 213.
26. Gerald Suttles, *The Social Order of the Slum: Ethnicity and Territory in the Inner City* (Chicago: University of Chicago Press, 1968), p. 234.
27. *Ibid.*, p. 26.
28. Gans, *The Urban Villagers*, p. 265–69.
29. Tyack, *The One Best System*, p. 15.
30. Coles, *The South Goes North*, p. 436.
31. Edward Gondolf offered prose and ideas to the two sections of this

chapter on socio-historical interpretations of communities and schools. I greatly appreciate his insights and his scholarship.

32. Louis Smith and William Geoffrey, *The Complexities of an Urban Classroom* (New York: Holt, Rinehart and Winston, Inc., 1968), p. 52.

33. Sara Lawrence Lightfoot, "A School in Transition: Stories of Struggle and Hope" (Unpublished manuscript, 1976), pp. 10–11.

34. *Ibid.*, pp. 5–7.

35. Jean V. Carew and Sara Lawrence Lightfoot, "First Grade: A Multi-Faceted View of Teachers and Children" (Washington, D.C.: Office of Child Development, 1977).

36. *Ibid.*

37. Robert Dreeben, *On What Is Learned in School* (Reading, Mass.: Addison-Wesley Co., 1968), p. 84.

38. The humanistic approach holds the individual's perception, awareness, and understanding of himself as the only valid measure of personal worth. Contemporary humanism gained impetus from existential philosophers like Kierkegaard, Sartre, and Buber and was translated into interpersonal dynamics by psychologists like Rogers and Maslow. From their writing grew a concern with a reflective, inward search for oneself. Rather than observable behaviors and skills, one's feelings and emotions became the vital indicators of personal growth. For a thorough discussion of the process of self-actualization that is at the center of the humanistic approach, see Carl Rogers, *On Becoming A Person* (Boston: Houghton Mifflin, 1961). George Dennison, *The Lives of Children* (New York: Vintage Books, 1968) is a sensitive translation of humanistic themes into educational philosophy and practice.

39. See Jean Piaget, *The Moral Judgment of the Child* (New York: Harcourt Brace and World, 1932) for a thorough analysis of *the child* as the principal agent in his own education. After years of observing children, Piaget claimed that the child progressively accommodates and assimilates new experiences into his expanding framework or world view. "Teaching means creating situations where structures can be discovered: it does not mean transmitting structures which may be assimilated at nothing other than a verbal level."

40. John Dewey, *Education and Democracy* (New York: The Free Press, 1916), pp. 49–50.

41. Sara Lawrence Lightfoot, *Teacher-Mothers: Conceptions of the Dual Role, A Pilot Study* (Radcliffe Institute, Harvard University, 1976).

42. *Ibid.*

43. Anna Freud, *Psychoanalysis for Teachers and Parents* (New York: Emerson Books, 1935).

44. Lightfoot, *Teacher-Mothers.*

Bibliography

Abbott, John. *The Mother at Home; or the Principles of Maternal Duty.* Boston: Crocker and Brewster, 1833.

Abzug, Robert H. "The Black Family During Reconstruction." In *Key Issues in the Afro-American Experience,* edited by N. Huggins, M. Kilson, and D. Fox. New York: Harcourt Brace Jovanovich, Inc., 1971.

Arensberg, Conrad and Solon Kimball. *Culture and Community.* New York: Harcourt Brace and World, Inc., 1967.

Aries, P. *Centuries of Childhood.* New York: Knopf, 1962.

Ashmore, Harry S. *The Negro and the Schools.* Chapel Hill, N.C.: University of North Carolina Press, 1954.

Azzarelli, Joseph. "Four Viewpoints." In *Struggle for Power in Education,* edited by F. W. Lutz and J. J. Azzarelli. New York: The Center for Applied Research in Education, 1966.

Bailyn, Lotte. "Notes on the Role of Choice in the Psychology of Professional Women." In *The Woman in America,* edited by Ralph J. Lifton. Boston: Beacon Press, 1967.

Ballard, Allen B. *The Education of Black Folk.* New York: Harper & Row, 1973.

Baratz, Stephen S. and Joan C. Baratz. "Early Childhood Intervention: The Social Science Base of Institutional Racism." *Harvard Educational Review* vol. 40, (Feb. 1970), pp. 29–50.

Barzun, Jacques. *Teacher in America.* Boston: Little, Brown, and Co., 1945.

Becker, Howard. "Social Class Variations in Teacher-Pupil Relationships." *Journal of Educational Sociology* 25 (1952): 451–65.

Benedict, Ruth. "Continuities and Discontinuities in Cultural Conditioning." *Psychiatry* vol. 1, (May 1938), pp. 161–167.

Berger, Peter. *Invitation to Sociology: A Humanistic Perspective.* Garden City, New York: Doubleday, 1963.

Berger, Peter and Thomas Luckman. *The Social Construction of Reality: A Treatise on the Sociology of Knowledge.* Garden City, New York: Doubleday, 1966.

Bernard, Jessie. *The Future of Motherhood.* New York: Penguin Books, Inc., 1974.

———. *Marriage and Family Among Negroes.* Englewood Cliffs, N.J.: Prentice-Hall, 1966.

———. *Women, Wives, Mothers.* Chicago: Aldine Publishing Company, 1975.

Bibb, Henry. *Narrative of the Life and Adventures of Henry Bibb, An American Slave.* New York: The Author, 1849.

Billingsley, Andrew. *Black Families in White America.* Englewood Cliffs, N.J.: Prentice-Hall, 1968.

Blackwell, James E. *The Black Community: Diversity and Unity.* New York: Dodd, Mead, and Company, 1975.

Blassingame, John. *The Slave Community*. New York: Oxford University Press, 1972.
Blaxwell, Martha and Barbara Reagen, eds. *Women and the Workplace*. Chicago: University of Chicago Press, 1976.
Bond, Horace Mann. *The Education of the Negro in the American Social Order*. New York: Octagon Books, 1966 (1st ed. Prentice-Hall, 1934).
———. "The Extent and Character of Separate Schools in the United States." *Journal of Negro Education* 4 (1935):321–27.
———. *Negro Education in Alabama: A Study in Cotton & Steel*. Washington, D.C.: The Associated Publisher Inc., 1939.
Bott, Elizabeth. *Family and Social Network: Roles, Norms, and External Relationships in Ordinary Urban Families*. New York: The Free Press, 1971.
Boulding, Kenneth. "The Power of Non-Conflict." *Journal of Social Issues* 33 (1977), pp. 22–33.
Bowles, Samuel. "Unequal Education and the Social Division of Labor." In *Schooling in a Corporate Society*, edited by Martin Carnoy. New York: David McKay, 1972.
Bowles, Samuel and Herbert Gintis. *Schooling in Capitalist America: Educational Reform and the Contradictions of Economic Life*. New York: Basic Books, 1976.
Brenton, Myron. *What's Happened to Teacher?* New York: Avon Books, 1970.
Bronfenbrenner, Urie. "The Experimental Ecology of Education." *Teachers College Record* 78 (Dec. 1976):157–204.
Brown, Henry Box. *Narrative of Henry Box Brown*. Boston: Brown and Stearns, 1849.
Brown, William W. *Narrative of William W. Brown, A Fugitive Slave*. Boston: The Anti-Slavery Office, 1847.
Bullock, Henry A. *A History of Negro Education in the South: From 1619 to the Present*. Cambridge, Mass.: Harvard University Press, 1967.
Carew, Jean V. and Sara Lawrence Lightfoot. "First Grade: A Multi-Faceted View of Teachers and Children." Office of Child Development, Washington, D.C., 1977.
Clark, Kenneth. *Dark Ghetto: Dilemmas of Social Power*. New York: Harper & Row, 1965.
Cloward, Richard and James Jones. "Social Class, Educational Attitudes, and Participation." In *Education in Depressed Areas*, edited by A. Harry Passow. New York: Bureau of Publications, Teachers College, Columbia University, 1963.
Cohen, David. "Loss as a Theme in Social Policy." *Harvard Educational Review* 46 (Nov. 1976), pp. 553–571.
Cohen, David and Janet Weiss. "Social Science and Social Policy: Schools and Race." *Educational Forum*, 41 (May 1977):393–413.
Cohen, Dorothy. *The Learning Child*. New York: Vintage Books, 1973.
Coles, Robert. *The South Goes North: Vol. III Children of Crisis*. Boston: Little, Brown, and Co., 1971.
Comer, James P. *Beyond Black and White*. New York: Quadrangle Books, 1972.

———. "Improving the Quality and Continuity of Relationships in Two Inner-City Schools," *Journal of the American Academy of Child Psychiatry,* vol. 15, No. 3 (Summer 1973), pp. 535–45.

Conant, James. *Slums and Suburbs: A Commentary on Schools in Metropolitan Areas.* New York: McGraw-Hill, 1961.

Cuban, Larry. "Teacher and Community." *Community and the Schools,* Reprint Series No. 3. *Harvard Educational Review* (1969):63–82.

Curtis, Jean. *Working Mother.* New York: The Macmillan Company, 1976.

Davis, Allison. "The Socialization of the American Negro Child and Adolescent. *The Journal of Negro Education* 8 (1939):264–74.

Davis, Allison and John Dollard. *Children of Bondage: The Personality Development of Negro Youth in the Urban South.* Prepared for the American Youth Commission, Washington, D.C.: American Council on Education, 1940.

Davis, Kinsley. "The Sociology of Parent-Youth Conflict." In *The Family: Its Structure and Functions,* edited by R. L. Coser. New York: St. Martins Press, 1964.

Davis, Sheldon. *The Teacher's Relationships.* New York: The Macmillan Company, 1930.

Dennison, George. *The Lives of Children.* New York: Vintage Books, 1969.

Deutch, C. and M. Deutch. "Theory of Early Childhood Environment Programs." In *Early Education: Current Theory, Research, and Action,* edited by R. Hess and R. Bear. Chicago: Aldine Publishing Company, 1968.

Deutsch, Morton. "The Disadvantaged Child and the Learning Process. In *Education in Depressed Areas,* edited by A. Harry Passow. New York: Bureau of Publications, Teachers College, Columbia University, 1963.

Dewey, John. *Education and Democracy.* New York: The Free Press, 1916.

Donovan, Francis. *The Schoolma'am.* New York: Frederick A. Stokes Company, 1938.

Douglass, Frederick. *Narrative of the Life of Frederick Douglass.* Boston: Anti-Slavery Office, 1845.

Dreeben, Robert. *On What Is Learned in School.* Reading, Mass.: Addison-Wesley, 1968.

DuBois, W. E. B. *Black Reconstruction.* New York: Harcourt Brace and Co., 1935.

———. "The Common School and the Negro American." Atlanta University Publications, No. 16. Atlanta: Atlanta University Press, 1911.

———. *Dark Water.* New York: Harcourt Brace and Co., 1920.

———. "Does the Negro Need the Separate Schools?" *Journal of Negro Education* 4 (1935):328–35.

———. "The Negro Common School." Atlanta University Publications, No. 6. Atlanta: Atlanta University Press, 1901.

———. *The Souls of Black Folk.* Chicago: A. C. McClurg and Co., 1903.

Durkheim, Emile. *Education and Society.* New York: The Free Press, 1956.

Ebel, R. L., ed. *Encyclopedia of Educational Research.* 4th ed. New York: The Macmillan Co., 1969.

Eddy, Elizabeth. *Walk the White Line: A Profile of Urban Education.* New York: Anchor Books, 1967.

Edwards, Newton and Herman G. Richey. *The School in the American Social Order*. Boston: Houghton Mifflin Co., 1963 (1st ed. 1947).

Eggleston, Edward. *The Hossier School Master*. New York: Hill and Wang, 1965 (orig. pub. 1871).

———. *The Transit of Civilization*. 1900. Reprint. Boston: Beacon Press, 1959.

Elkins, Stanley. *Slavery: A Problem in American Institutional and Intellectual Life*. Chicago: University of Chicago Press, 1959.

Elsbree, Willard. *The American Teacher: Evolution of a Profession in a Democracy*. New York: The American Book Company, 1939.

Erikson, Erik H. *Childhood and Society*. New York: W. W. Norton and Company, 1950.

———. *Identity, Youth and Crisis*. New York: W. W. Norton and Company, 1968.

Farber, Jerry. *The Student as Nigger*. New York: Pocket Books, Simon and Schuster, 1970.

Featherstone, Joseph. *What Schools Can Do*. New York: Liveright, 1976.

Fen, Sing-Nam. "Notes on the Education of Negroes in North Carolina During the Civil War." *Journal of Negro Education* 36 (1967):24–31.

Flanders, N. A. *Analyzing Teaching Behavior*. Reading, Mass.: Addison-Wesley, 1968.

Fogel, R. and S. Engermen. *Time on the Cross: The Economics of American Negro Slavery*. New York: Little, Brown, and Co., 1974.

Franklin, John Hope. *From Slavery to Freedom*. 2nd ed. New York: Alfred A. Knopf, 1956.

Frazier, E. Franklin. "The Negro Family and Negro Youth." *The Journal of Negro Education* 9 (1940):290–99.

———. *The Negro Family in the United States*. Rev. ed. New York: Holt, Rinehart and Winston, Inc., 1939, 1957.

———. "The Negro in the American Social Order." *The Journal of Negro Education* 4 (1935):293–307.

———. *Negro Youth at the Crossing: Their Personality Development in the Middle*. Prepared for the American Youth Commission, Washington, D.C.: American Council on Education, 1940.

———. "Problems and Needs of Negro Children and Youth Resulting from Family Disorganization." *Journal of Negro Education* 19 (1950): 269–77.

Freud, Anna. *Psychoanalysis for Teachers and Parents*. New York: Emerson Books, 1935.

———. "The Role of the Teacher." *Harvard Educational Review* 22 (Fall 1952):229–35.

Fuchs, Estelle. *Teachers Talk: A View from Within Inner-City Schools*. New York: Anchor Books, 1969.

Fullan, M. and W. Spady. "The Authority System of the School and Innovativeness: Their Reciprocal Relationships." Paper presented at the Annual Conference of the Canadian Sociology and Anthropology Association, St. Johns, Newfoundland, June 1971.

Gans, Herbert. *The Urban Villagers: Groups and Class in the Life of Italian-Americans*. New York: The Free Press, 1962.

Genovese, Eugene. *Roll Jordan Roll: The World the Slaves Made.* New York: Pantheon, 1974.

Gersman, Elinor. "The Development of Public Education for Blacks in Nineteenth-Century St. Louis, Missouri." *Journal of Negro Education* 41 (1972):35–47.

Getzels, J. W. "Socialization and Education: A Note on Discontinuities." *Teachers College Record* 76 (Dec. 1974), pp. 218–225.

Getzels, J. W. and P. W. Jackson, "The Teacher's Personality and Characteristics." In *Handbook of Research on Teaching,* edited by N. L. Gage. Chicago: Rand McNally and Company, 1963.

Goffman, Erving. *Asylums: Essays on the Social Situations of Mental Health Patients and Other Inmates.* New York: Anchor Books, 1961.

Goode, W. J. *World Revolution and Family Patterns.* New York: The Free Press, 1963.

Gordon, Milton. *Assimilation in American Life.* New York: Oxford University Press, 1964.

Grant, Vance and George Lind. *Digest of Educational Statistics* (1975 ed.). Washington, D.C.: U.S. Government Printing Office, 1976.

Green, R. "Dialect Sampling and Language Values." In *Social Dialects and Language Learning,* edited by R. Shuy. Champaign, Ill.: NCTE, 1964.

Green, Thomas. "Schools and Communities: A Look Forward." *Harvard Educational Review* 39 (1969):221–52.

Greer, Colin. *The Great School Legend.* New York: Basic Books, 1972.

Gutman, Herbert A. *The Black Family in Slavery and Freedom, 1750–1925.* New York: Pantheon, 1976.

Harlan, Louis R. *Separate and Unequal.* New York: Atheneum, 1968.

Henry, Jules. *Culture Against Man.* New York: Random House, 1967.

Hess, Robert and Virginia Shipman. "Early Experience and the Socialization of Cognitive Modes in Children." In *Learning and Social Settings,* edited by Matthew B. Miles and W. W. Charters, Jr. Boston: Allyn and Bacon, 1970.

Hess, Robert; Virginia Shipman; J. Brophy; and R. Bear. *The Cognitive Environments of Urban Preschool Children.* Chicago: The Graduate School of Education, University of Chicago, 1968.

Hill, Robert. "Family Strengths: Policy Implications." Paper presented at the Lilly Endowment Conference on Public Policies Affecting Families and Children: Present Status and Future Directions, Washington, D.C., January 26–28, 1977.

Hoffman, Lois and Ivan Nye. *Working Mothers.* San Francisco: Jossey-Bass, 1975.

Holt, John. *Escape from Childhood.* New York: E. P. Dutton, 1974.

Hunt, J. McV. *Intelligence and Experience,* New York: The Ronald Press Company, 1961.

Illich, Ivan. *Deschooling Society.* New York: Harper & Row, 1970.

Jencks, Christopher et. al. *Inequality: A Reassessment of the Effect of Family and Schooling in America.* New York: Basic Books, 1972.

Johnson, Charles S. *Growing Up in the Black Belt: Negro Youth in the Rural South.* Prepared for the American Youth Commission, Washington, D.C.: American Council on Education, 1940.

Jones, Thomas H., *The Experiences of Thomas H. Jones, Who Was a Slave for Forty-Three Years*. 1871. Reprint. New York: AMS Press, 1975.
Kagan, J. "His Struggle for Identity." *Saturday Review* vol. 51, no. 49, 7 December 1968, pp. 80–82, 87–88.
Katz, Michael. *Class, Bureaucracy, and Schools: The Illusions of Educational Change in America*. New York: Praeger Publishers, 1971.
———. *The Irony of Early School Reform: Educational Innovation in Mid-Nineteenth Century Massachusetts*. Cambridge, Mass.: Harvard University Press, 1968.
Kellor, Frances. *Experimental Sociology*. New York: The Macmillan Co., 1901.
Keniston, Kenneth et al. *All Our Children*. New York: Harcourt Brace Jovanovich, 1977.
Knox, Ellis O. "A Historical Sketch of Secondary Education for Negroes." *Journal of Negro Education* 9 (1970):440–53.
Kundsin, Ruth B. *Women and Success*. New York: William Morrow and Company, 1974.
Laing, R. D. *The Politics of Experience*. New York: Pantheon Books, 1967.
Lane, Lunsford. *Narrative of Lunsford Lane*. Boston: By Author, 1842.
Lasch, Christopher. "The Family and History." *New York Review of Books* (Nov. 1975):32–33.
Leacock, Eleanor Burke. *The Culture of Poverty: A Critique*. New York: Simon and Schuster, 1971.
———.*Teaching and Learning in City Schools*. New York: Basic Books, 1969.
Leichter, Hope Jenson. "Some Perspectives on the Family as Educator." *Teachers College Record* 76 (Dec. 1974), pp. 175–217.
Lein, Laura. *How to Manage When Both Parents Work*. Cambridge, Mass.: Working Family Project, Center for the Study of Public Policy, 1976.
Levine, Naomi. *Ocean-Hill Brownsville: A Case History of Schools in Crisis*. New York: Popular Library, 1969.
Lévi-Strauss, Claude. "The Family." In *Man, Culture and Society*, edited by Harry Shapiro. New York: Oxford University Press, 1960.
Levy, Marion J. "Some Hypotheses About the Family." *Journal of Comparative Family Studies* 1 (Autumn 1970): 119–131.
Lewis, Hylan. "The Changing Negro Family." In *School Children in the Urban Slum*, edited by Joan Roberts. New York: The Free Press, 1967.
Liebow, Eliot. *Tally's Corner: A Study of Negro Street Corner Men*. Boston: Little, Brown, and Co., 1967.
Lifton, Robert. *The Woman in America*. Boston: Beacon Press, 1964.
Lightfoot, Sara Lawrence. "An Ethnographic Study of the Status Structure of the Classroom." Doctoral dissertation, Harvard University, Graduate School of Education, June 1972.
———. "Politics and Reasoning: Through the Eyes of Teachers and Children." *Harvard Educational Review* 43 (May 1973), pp. 197–244.
———. "Socialization and Education of Young Black Girls in School." *Teachers College Record* 78 (Dec. 1976), pp. 239–262.
———. "A School in Transition: Stories of Struggle and Hope." (Unpublished manuscript) 1976.

———. *Teacher-Mothers: Conceptions of the Dual Role. A Pilot Study.* Radcliffe Institute, Harvard University, 1976.

Lightfoot, Sara Lawrence and Jean V. Carew. "Individuation and Discrimination in the Classroom." Research supported by funds from Child Development Associates, Inc., Office of Child Development, Washington, D.C., 1974.

———. "Individuation and Discrimination in the Classroom." *American Journal of Orthopsychiatry* 46 (July 1976):401–15.

Lortie, Dan. *School Teacher.* Chicago: University of Chicago Press, 1975.

McPherson, Gertrude. *Small Town Teacher.* Cambridge, Mass.: Harvard University Press, 1972.

Marcson, Simon. "Ethnic and Class Education." *Journal of Negro Education* 13 (1944):57–63.

Marsh, Frank. *The Teacher Outside the School.* New York: World Book Company, 1928.

Mead, Margaret. "An Anthropologist Looks at the Teacher's Role." *Educational Method* 21 (1942):219–23.

———. "The Contemporary American Family as an Anthropologist Sees It." In *Social Perspectives on Behavior,* edited by Herman Stein and Richard Cloward. New York: The Free Press, 1958.

———. *Culture and Commitment: A Study of the Generation Gap.* Garden City, N.Y.: Natural History Press, 1970.

———. *Male and Female.* New York: William Morrow, 1949.

———. *The School in American Culture.* Cambridge, Mass.: Harvard University Press, 1951.

Merton, Robert. *Social Theory and Social Structure* (rev. ed.). Glencoe, Ill.: Free Press, 1957.

Mier, August and Rudwick, Elliot. "Early Boycotts of Segregated Schools: The Alton, Illinois Case, 1897–1908." *Journal of Negro Education* 36 (1967):394–95.

———. *From Plantation to Ghetto.* New York: Hill and Wang, 1966.

Miller, Jean Baker. *Toward a New Psychology of Women.* Boston: Beacon Press, 1976.

Myrdal, Alva and Viola Klein. *Women's Two Roles.* London: Routledge and Kegan Paul Ltd., 1956 (rev. 1968).

Myrdal, Gunnar. *An American Dilemma.* New York: Harper and Brothers, 1944.

National Education Association. *Status of the American Public-School Teacher, 1970–71.* Washington, D.C.: National Education Association, 1972.

Newmann, Fred and Oliver, Donald. "Education and Community." In *Community and the Schools,* Reprint Series No. 3. *Harvard Educational Review,* 1969.

Newsweek. "A New Kind of PTA." November 15, 1976, p. 105.

Northend, Charles. *The Teacher and the Parent.* New York: A. S. Barnes and Company, 1867.

Office of Policy Planning and Research, U.S. Department of Labor. *The Negro Family: The Case for National Action* (The Moynihan Report), Washington, D.C.: U.S. Government Printing Office, 1965.

Ogbu, John. *The Next Generation.* New York: Academic Press, 1974.

Olds, Wendkos Sally. *The Mother Who Works Outside the Home.* New York: Child Study Press, 1975.

Parsons, Talcott. "The School Class as a Social System." *Harvard Educational Review* 29 (Fall 1959), pp. 297–318.

———. *The Social System.* Glencoe, Ill.: Free Press, 1951.

Perry, Arthur. *The Status of the Teacher.* Boston: Houghton Mifflin Company, 1912.

Pettigrew, Thomas. *Profile of the American Negro.* New York: D. Van Nostrand, 1964.

Piaget, Jean. *The Moral Judgment of the Child.* New York: Harcourt Brace and World, 1932.

Podhoretz, Norman. *Making It.* New York: Random House, 1967.

Quarles, Benjamin. "Freedom's Black Vanguard." In *Key Issues in the Afro-American Experience,* edited by N. Huggins, M. Kilson, and D. Fox. New York: Harcourt Brace Jovanovich, Inc., 1971.

Rainwater, Lee. "Crucible of Identity: The Negro Lower-Class Family." *Daedalus* vol. 95 (Winter 1966), pp. 172–216.

Ravitch, Diane. *The Great School Wars: New York City 1805–1973; The History of the Public Schools as Battlefields of Social Change.* New York: Basic Books, 1974.

———. "On the History of Minority Group Education in the United States." *Teachers College Record* 78 (1976):213–28.

Reid, Ira D. "General Characteristics of the Negro Youth Population." *Journal of Negro Education* 9 (1940):278–89.

———. *In a Minor Key: Negro Youth in Story and Fact.* Prepared for the American Youth Commission. Washington, D.C.: American Council on Education, 1940.

Rist, Ray C. "Student Social Class and Teacher Expectations: The Self-Fulfilling Prophecy in Ghetto Education." *Harvard Educational Review* 40 (1970):411–51.

Robinson, James. *A Mother's Letters to a Schoolmaster.* New York: Alfred A. Knopf, 1923.

Rogers, Carl. *On Becoming A Person.* Boston: Houghton Mifflin, 1961.

Rose, Arnold. *The Negro in America.* New York: Harper and Brothers, 1944.

Rothman, David J. *The Discovery of the Asylum: Social Order and Disorder in the New Republic.* Boston: Little, Brown, and Co., 1971.

Ryan, William. *Blaming the Victim* (rev. ed.). New York: Vintage Books, 1976.

Ryder, N. B. "The Cohort as a Concept in the Study of Social Change." *American Sociological Review* 30 (Dec. 1965), pp. 843–861.

Scazoni, John. *The Black Family in Modern Society.* Boston: Allyn and Bacon, 1971.

Seeley, John et al. *Crestwood Heights: A Study of the Culture of Suburban Life.* Toronto: The University of Toronto Press, 1956.

Sennett, Richard and Jonathan Cobb. *The Hidden Injuries of Class.* New York: Random House, 1973.

Silberman, Charles E. *Crisis in Black and White.* New York: Random House, 1964.

Silverman, Leslie (senior advisor). *Selected Statistics on Educational Personnel.* Washington, D.C.: U.S. Government Printing Office, 1970.

Slater, Philip. "Social Change and the Democratic Family." In *The Temporary Society,* edited by Warren Bennis and Philip Slater. New York: Harper & Row, 1968.

Smith, Louis and William Geoffrey. *The Complexities of an Urban Classroom.* New York: Holt, Rinehart, and Winston, Inc., 1968.

Spindler, George. "Education in a Transforming American Culture." *Harvard Educational Review* 25 (1955):145–56.

Stack, Carol. *All Our Kin.* New York: Harper & Row, 1974.

Stroyer, Jacob. *My Life in the South.* Salem, Massachusetts: Salem Observer Book and Job Print, 1885.

Sutherland, Robert L. *Color, Class and Personality.* Prepared for the American Youth Commission, Washington, D.C.: American Council on Education, 1941.

Suttles, Gerald. *The Social Order of the Slum: Ethnicity and Territory in the Inner City.* Chicago: University of Chicago Press, 1968.

Thompson, Daniel C. *Sociology of the Black Experience.* Westport, Conn., London: Greenwood Press, 1974.

Torrey, Jane. "Illiteracy in the Ghetto." *Harvard Educational Review* 40 (1970):29–50.

Tyack, David. *The One Best System: A History of American Urban Education.* Cambridge, Mass.: Harvard University Press, 1974.

Valentine, Charles A. *Culture and Poverty: Critique and Counter Proposals.* Chicago: University of Chicago Press, 1968.

Walberg, Herbert; Robert E. Bole; and Herschel Waxman. "School-Based Family Socialization and Reading Achievement in the Inner City." (Unpublished manuscript) University of Illinois at Chicago Circle, 1977.

Waller, Willard. *Sociology of Teaching.* New York: John Wiley and Sons, 1932.

Warner, W. Lloyd; Buford H. Junkers; and Walter R. Adams. *Color and Human Nature: Negro Personality Development.* Prepared for the American Youth Commission, Washington, D.C.: American Council on Education, 1941.

Warren, Richard. "The Classroom as a Sanctuary for Teachers: Discontinuities in Social Control." *American Anthropologist* 75 (1973): 280–291.

White, Sheldon H. "Some Goals and Functions of Schools." (Unpublished manuscript) Harvard University, 1977.

Williamson, Joel R. "Black Self-Assertion Before and After Reconstruction." In *Key Issues in the Afro-American Experience,* edited by N. Huggins, M. Kilson, and D. Fox. New York: Harcourt Brace Jovanovich, Inc., 1971.

Willie, Charles. *A New Look At Black Families.* New York: General Hall, Inc., 1976.

Woodson, Carter G. *The Education of the Negro Prior to 1861.* New York: Arno Press and The New York Times, 1968.

Zigler, E., and I. L. Child, "Socialization." In *Handbook of Social Psychology,* 2nd ed., vol. III, edited by G. Lindzey and E. Arenson. Reading, Mass.: Addison-Wesley, 1969.

Index